The most important application of just war theory since 9/11. Rochester asks all the difficult questions – an essential book for our time.

John Vasquez, University of Illinois at Urbana-Champaign

Backed by a treasure trove of research, this is an important and up-to-date study of the deterioration of international rules that govern the use of force. It should be read and pondered by international lawyers, international relations theorists, and policymakers who think about how war can be restricted by law.

Michael J. Glennon, Boston University Law School

This important new work suggests that the 'new face of violence' challenges international legal norms as much as it does international peace and security. To his credit, J. Martin Rochester eschews daydreaming of a better world in favor of practical reforms that incentivize compliance and further the United Nations' concern to 'save succeeding generations from the scourge of war.'

Robert P. Barnidge, Jr., Webster University

THE NEW WARFARE

This book looks at the evolving relationship between war and international law, examining the complex practical and legal dilemmas posed by the changing nature of war in the contemporary world, whether the traditional rules governing the onset and conduct of hostilities apply anymore, and how they might be adapted to new realities. War, always messy, has become even messier today, with the blurring of interstate, intrastate, and extrastate violence. How can the United States and other countries be expected to fight honorably and observe the existing norms when they often are up against an adversary who recognizes no such obligations? Indeed, how do we even know whether an "armed conflict" is underway when modern wars tend to lack neat beginnings and endings and seem geographically indeterminate, as well? What is the legality of anticipatory self-defense, humanitarian intervention, targeted killings, drones, detention of captured prisoners without POW status, and other controversial practices? These questions are explored through a review of the United Nations Charter, Geneva Conventions, and other regimes and how they have operated in recent conflicts. Through a series of case studies, including the U.S. war on terror and the wars in Afghanistan, Iraq, Gaza, Kosovo, and Congo, the author illustrates the challenges we face today in the ongoing effort to reduce war and, when it occurs, to make it more humane.

J. Martin Rochester is Curators Distingushed Teaching Professor of Political Science at the University of Missouri-St. Louis and the author of several books on international relations, including *Between Peril and Promise: The Politics of International Law* and *U.S. Foreign Policy in the 21st Century: Gulliver's Travails.*

INTERNATIONAL STUDIES INTENSIVES

Series Editors Mark A. Boyer and Shareen Hertel

International Studies Intensives (ISI) is a book series that springs from the desire to keep students engaged in the world around them. ISI books pack a lot of information into a small space—they are meant to offer an intensive introduction to subjects often left out of the curriculum. ISI books are relatively short, visually attractive, and affordably priced.

Titles in the Series

The Rules of the Game
A primer on International Relations
Mark R. Amstutz

Development Redefined
How the market met its match
Robin Broad and John Cavanagh

**Protecting the
Global Environment**
Gary C. Bryner

A Tale of Two Quagmires
Iraq, Vietnam, and the hard
lessons of war
Kenneth J. Campbell

Celebrity Diplomacy
Andrew F. Cooper

Global Health in the 21st Century
The globalization of disease
and wellness
Debra l. DeLaet and David E. DeLaet

Terminate Terrorism
Framing, gaming, and
negotiating conflicts
Karen A. Feste

Watching Human Rights
The 101 best films
Mark Gibney

The Global Classroom
An essential guide to study abroad
Jeffrey S. Lantis and Jessica DuPlaga

**Democratic Uprisings in the New
Middle East**
Youth, technology, human rights, and
US foreign policy
Mahmood Monshipouri

Sixteen Million One
Understading civil war
Patrick M. Regan

**Violence against Women and
the Law**
David L. Richards and Jillienne Haglund

People Count!
Networked individuals in
global politics
James N. Rosenau

Paradoxes of Power
US foreign policy in a changing world
David Skidmore

**Global Democracy and the World
Social Forums**
Second edition
Jackie Smith and Marina Karides et al.

The New Warfare
Rethinking rules for an unruly world
J. Martin Rochester

**International Relations
as Negotiation**
Brian R. Urlacher

From Jicama to Jackfruit
The global political economy of food
Kimberly Weir

Governing the World?
Addressing "problems
without passports"
Thomas G. Weiss

**Myth and Reality in
International Politics**
Meeting global challenges through
collective action
Jonathan Wilkenfeld

Forthcoming in the Series

A Humbled Superpower
US foreign policy and possibilities
of contrition
Loramy Gerstbauer

Spirits Talking
Conversations on right and wrong in
the affairs of states
Stephen D. Wrage

**American Exceptionalism
Reconsidered**
US foreign policy, human rights, and
world order
*David P. Forsythe and
Patrice C. McMahon*

THE NEW WARFARE

Rethinking rules for an unruly world

J. Martin Rochester

Routledge
Taylor & Francis Group

NEW YORK AND LONDON

First published 2016
by Routledge
711 Third Avenue, New York, NY 10017

and by Routledge
2 Park Square, Milton Park, Abingdon, Oxon OX14 4RN

Routledge is an imprint of the Taylor & Francis Group, an informa business

© 2016 Taylor & Francis

Library of Congress Cataloging in Publication Data
Names: Rochester, J. Martin, author.
    Title: The new warfare : rethinking rules for an unruly world / J. Martin
Rochester.
    Description: New York, NY : Routledge, 2016. | Series: International
studies intensives | Includes bibliographical references.
    Identifiers: LCCN 2015034063| ISBN 9781138191884 (hardback) | ISBN
9781138191891 (pbk.) | ISBN 9781315640242 (ebook)
    Subjects: LCSH: War (International law)
    Classification: LCC KZ6385 .R628 2016 | DDC 341.6–dc23
    LC record available at http://lccn.loc.gov/2015034063

ISBN: 9781138191884 (hbk)
ISBN: 9781138191891 (pbk)
ISBN: 9781315640242 (ebk)

Typeset in Bembo
by Taylor & Francis Books

To Eli, in the hope he and his siblings and cousins live in an ever more peaceful and humane world

CONTENTS

Preface   *xiv*

PART 1
Introduction: Framing the Puzzle   **1**

1   The Changing Nature of War: Do We Need New Rules for
    an Old Problem?   3

    The Context for this Study: The New Warfare 4
    The Purpose of the Book 6
    Trends in War and the Use of Armed Force 7
        Interstate War 10
        Civil War 14
        Terrorism and Extrastate Violence 16
    Challenges to the International Regime Governing the Use of
     Armed Force 19
    The Plan of the Book 22
    Chapter 1 Discussion Questions 22

PART 2
The Laws of War: What Are the Rules?   **29**

2   On Starting a War: The United Nations Charter and Other
    Jus Ad Bellum Rules   31

Historical Efforts to Regulate the Outbreak of War Before 1945 31
   Prior to 1648 31
   The Eighteenth and Nineteenth Centuries 33
   World War I, The Interwar Period, and the League of
   Nations (1914–1939) 34
World War II and the United Nations Charter 36
The Evolution of Jus Ad Bellum *Rules Since 1945: Principle*
and Practice 39
   What Rules Apply to Civil Wars? 44
   What Rules Apply to Humanitarian Intervention? 45
   What Rules Apply to "Self-Defense" Against State and
   Nonstate Actors? 47
Conclusion 50
Chapter 2 Discussion Questions 51

3   On Conducting a War: The Geneva Conventions and Other
    Jus In Bello Rules   54

Historical Efforts to Regulate the Conduct of War Before 1945 55
World War II and Its Aftermath: The 1949 Geneva Conventions
and Other Jus In Bello *Rules 58*
The Evolution of Jus In Bello *Rules Since 1945: Principle and*
Practice 62
   Observing the Rule of "Distinction": Divergence
   between Principle and Practice 62
   What Model Applies: "Warfare" or "Lawfare"? 66
   Regulating Weapons: Drones, WMDs, and Other
   Lethal Tools 68
Conclusion 70
Chapter 3 Discussion Questions 71

4   On Concluding a War: The Absence of *Jus Post Bellum* Rules   75

The Aftermath of War as an Afterthought 75
The Development of Jus Post Bellum *Rules: What Would A Just*
Peace Look Like? 78
Applying Jus Post Bellum *Rules: Easier Said Than Done 81*
Conclusion: Selection of Cases Examining the Laws of War
in Action 82
Chapter 4 Discussion Questions 82

PART 3
The Laws of War: Are They Still Relevant?   **85**

5   Applying *Jus Ad Bellum* Rules to the New Warfare: Cases   89

   The Second Gulf War and Anticipatory Self-Defense 89
   The Osama bin Laden Raid and the War on Terror 95
   Kosovo and the Responsibility to Protect 99
   Conclusion 103
   Chapter 5 Discussion Questions 103

6   Applying *Jus In Bello* Rules to the New Warfare: Cases   108

   The U.S. Drone Campaign: The Legality of Targeted Killings 108
   The Israeli–Palestinian Gaza War of 2008–2009: Engaging in
    Asymmetrical Warfare 114
   The Second Congo War: Rebels, Gangs, and Armies in
    Civil-International Strife 120
   Conclusion 124
   Chapter 6 Discussion Questions 124

7   Applying *Jus Post Bellum* Rules to the New Warfare: Cases   129

   Intervention in Libya 131
   Conclusion 135
   Chapter 7 Discussion Questions 135

PART 4
Conclusion: The Future of War, Peace, and Law   **139**

8   Adapting to the New Face of Violence   141

   What Rules Need Rethinking? 142
     Rethinking Jus Ad Bellum 142
     Rethinking Jus In Bello 147
     Rethinking Jus Post Bellum 150
   Toward a More Advanced Anarchy 150
   Chapter 8 Discussion Questions 152

Index   *154*

PREFACE

This is a book that was percolating for well over a decade. Over the years, in teaching international law, I had always enjoyed the challenge of trying to convince students that international law mattered in an anarchic world of sovereign states. I especially enjoyed engaging students in discussions of the laws of war and explaining to them that what might at first glance seem oxymoronic – making warfare more orderly and civil – was not a fanciful idea but was a very real aspect of the evolution of world affairs. On the skepticism surrounding international law generally and the laws of war in particular, I was always reminded of Hersh Lauterpacht's oft-quoted statement, "If international law is, in some ways, at the vanishing point of law, the law of war is, perhaps even more conspicuously, at the vanishing point of international law." It was actually not hard to make the case that, although historically the rules regulating the resort to war (*jus ad bellum*) and the conduct of war (*jus in bello*) were observed somewhat erratically and imperfectly, they worked better than commonly thought. That is, at least until recently. The problem is that the rules have remained relatively static while the nature of war has changed considerably, creating a disconnect in trying to apply these principles to contemporary conflicts.

This mismatch problem was already evident before September 11, 2001; but the terrorist attack on 9/11, and the events that have followed, have made even plainer the growing inadequacy of the traditional rules given the typical violence that now occurs on the planet. Like most observers, I can still vividly recall the events of 9/11. A month earlier, I had been at the World Trade Center site in New York City checking out the Millennium Hilton hotel for my son's upcoming December wedding; the hotel was barely left standing when the two planes flew into the twin towers, and Manhattan remained dysfunctional for months. The day of the attack, the Pentagon in Washington, D.C. was also targeted; my brother (the Deputy Chief Historian in the Office of the U.S. Secretary of Defense) and others barely escaped injury. The roughly 3,000 souls killed in the WTC attack were not so fortunate. The day after 9/11, I was teaching an international organization course that included several foreign students from the former Yugoslavia, Russia, and Latin America; to my chagrin, almost all said that the United States "deserved" 9/11, since, in their words, "look what you did in Kosovo, where you killed women and children," even though the United States ostensibly was engaged in a "humanitarian intervention" effort to stop ethnic cleansing of Kosovars in Serbia. Here I was a teacher, expected to make sense of all this for my students. Yet it was hard to fit any of this into the lecture notes I had used in my courses. The Iraq, Afghanistan, and other wars subsequent to 9/11 did not fit very neatly either.

So I was already considering writing a book that examined "the new warfare" and called for "rethinking rules for an unruly world" when, in 2013, I was pushed to do so by the publication of journalist Jeremy Scahill's *Dirty Wars*. For me, Scahill pointedly raised the question of whether the United States or any other country could reasonably be expected to observe the existing laws of war when it often found itself up against an adversary that labored under no such compulsion. Scahill believed that nothing had changed, that the United States was still bound by the rules and that failure to comply with the rules meant the United States was fighting "dirty." I was not so sure. Although Scahill raised legitimate criticisms of the manner in which the United States was waging "the war on terror" and other conflicts, he seemed to ignore the fact that the U.S. seemed damned if it did and damned if it did not, inviting opprobrium if it violated international law while inviting possible defeat if it complied. I wanted to explore this dilemma.

I owe a debt of gratitude to Jennifer Knerr, my editor at Routledge, who encouraged me to undertake this project, and to the excellent staff at Routledge who managed the production process, including Ruth Bradley and Jaya Chowdhury. I also owe thanks to my wife, Ruth, who has always been supportive of my writing endeavors. And finally, I dedicate this book to my two sons and daughter-in-laws and eight grandchildren (including the latest, Eli), who, as the new millennium progresses, hopefully will see a more peaceful world where there will be less need for rules regulating violence.

PART I

Introduction

Framing the Puzzle

War, huh good God y'all
What is it good for?
"War," recorded by
Edwin Starr (1970)

War is sometimes justifiable ... and the conduct of war is always subject to moral criticism.

Michael Walzer, *Arguing About War*

War does not determine who is right, only who is left.

Bertrand Russell

We are going to have peace even if we have to fight for it.

Dwight D. Eisenhower

Nothing like D-Day will happen again, not because human nature has improved but because weaponry has. Making war on that grand scale is obsolete.

Herman Wouk, "Never Again," *Washington Post* (June 6, 1994)

Believe it or not ... today we may be living in the most peaceful era in our species' existence.

Steven Pinker, *The Better Angels of Our Nature*

If international law is, in some ways, at the vanishing point of law, the law of war is, perhaps even more conspicuously, at the vanishing point of international law.

Hersh Lauterpacht, *British Yearbook of International Law* (1952)

1

THE CHANGING NATURE OF WAR

Do we need new rules for an old problem?

For almost a half century, between the end of World War II in 1945 and the fall of the Berlin Wall in 1989, the United States and the Soviet Union engaged in an epic struggle known as the Cold War, so named because the two states were virtually never directly involved in actual physical exchange of hostilities against each other, notwithstanding the hostilities experienced by myriad others across the globe who were touched by the conflict and other conflicts. In the wake of the euphoria that attended the end of the Cold War in 1990, President George H.W. Bush proclaimed "a new world order."[1] The latter was short-lived. Euphoria suddenly turned to despair on September 11, 2001, as some 3,000 people – mostly Americans but also foreign nationals from dozens of other countries – perished when the twin towers of the World Trade Center in New York City collapsed after being struck by two airplanes hijacked by al Qaeda terrorists.

9/11 signaled that not only the United States but also other countries were having to confront "a new world disorder," as the familiar features that had defined the international system through much of the post–World War II, Cold War era – a bipolar power and alliance structure built around two superpowers leading two rival ideologically based blocs – had given way to a much more complicated planet characterized by growing diffusion of power and fluidity of alignments, along with an expanding set of actors and agenda of issues, all contributing to a brand new, more uncertain security environment.[2] Epitomized by ISIS and other new players on the international scene, the world today, in the post–Cold War era, strikes some as more unruly than ever.

The Context for this Study: The New Warfare

Among the films nominated for an Academy Award in 2014 for Best Doc-umentary was *Dirty Wars*, based on the book by that name written by journalist Jeremy Scahill.[3] The book and movie examined the top-secret activities of the United States Joint Special Operations Command, CIA Special Activities Division, and other "special ops" divisions of the American national security establishment which were accused of carrying out "targeted killings" and other questionable missions after 9/11 that, it was argued, were violations of international law as well as U.S. domestic law.

The immediate question raised by the very title of the book is whether there has ever been a "non-dirty" war. From the Romans' leveling of Carthage in ancient times, to the use of biological weapons (dead carcasses catapulted over castle parapets) in siege warfare in medieval Europe, to General Sherman's burn-ing of Atlanta and scorched-earth march to the sea during the American Civil War, to the use of chemical weapons during World War I, to the strategic bombing of Dresden and Tokyo and the dropping of the A-bomb over Hir-oshima and Nagasaki in World War II, to the My Lai massacre in Vietnam up to the present day, war has always been, in Sherman's words, "hell," and usually dirty. Granted at times some wars have been fought more in conformity with the "laws of war" than others.

Soldiers always have had to contend with "the fog of war," having to make uncertain, often hair-trigger decisions about the identity and whereabouts of an enemy, along with his intentions and capabilities. The climate for fighting wars arguably is getting foggier. Increasingly, there is also what Michael Glennon has called "the fog of law."[4] Today especially, it would seem harder than ever to fight wars honorably, that is, to observe the rules restricting the resort to armed force (*jus ad bellum*) contained in the United Nations Charter as well as those rules restricting the nature of the force that can be used (*jus in bello*) contained in the Geneva Conventions and other such instruments, further embodied in long-standing customary practice going all the way back to the "just war" tradition of St. Augustine in the fourth century and Cicero and Ancient philosophers before him. "Just war" theorists concede war is horrible, but at times necessary and, depending on how it is waged, a legitimate endeavor. Before criticizing the United States or any other warring country for fighting dirty, one should inquire as to what a "just" war would look like today, not only regarding the circum-stances under which it begins and the way it is conducted but also the manner in which it is concluded (what Michael Walzer has labeled *jus post bellum*).[5] (As a counterpoint to *Dirty Wars*, one might see a movie that appeared at the same time as the Oscar nominee, entitled *Lone Survivor*, based on a true story, in which U.S. Navy Seals in Afghanistan get killed trying to fight cleanly.)

War, always messy, has become an even messier phenomenon. I am referring to the fact that the face of global violence has been changing in terms of its main features. Mary Kaldor and other scholars have described "the new wars."[6] **The new wars** are not altogether new, but they occupy center stage in the drama of world politics in a way they never used to. The use of armed force today increasingly tends to take the form of "force without war," i.e., sporadic, intermittent violence in scattered locales, often involving nonstate actors (including terrorists, militias, guerrillas, and gangs), as opposed to sustained, large-scale armed combat between the uniformed armies of states across well-defined fronts, marked by neat beginnings (formal declarations of war) and neat endings (peace treaties). Interstate war – organized fighting between states, which since the beginning of the state system has been the traditional stuff of the study of world politics, the main scourge of humanity, and the focus of efforts to promote world order – is in decline and relatively infrequent. That is the good news. The bad news is that when it does occur, interstate violence tends to mix with intrastate violence (civil war) and extrastate violence (transnational terrorism) in complex conflagrations, as in recent conflicts in Iraq and Afghanistan, making it difficult to get a handle on the problem conceptually, strategically, and – perhaps most of all – legally.

I am particularly concerned here with how the changing nature of contemporary warfare is playing havoc with both the conventional "rules of engagement" used by armies as well as the laws of war upon which the latter putatively are based (both the rules regulating the outbreak of war and the rules regulating the conduct of war). Terrorism, militias, drone technology, targeted killings, humanitarian intervention, cyberwarfare, and a host of other elements of modern warfare pose special challenges for the UN Charter and other such governance regimes, which were premised on an interstate war paradigm and a post–World War II world that no longer exists. Although there has been some evolution in the body of rules governing the resort to armed force along with what is commonly called "international humanitarian law" (which is supposed to kick in once war is underway), the rules have not kept pace with the changing realities, raising questions about their continued relevance.

Scahill's *Dirty Wars* opens with a quotation from the eighteenth-century philosopher Voltaire: "It is forbidden to kill; therefore, all murderers are punished unless they kill in large numbers and to the sound of trumpets." Voltaire was cynically referring to the fact that humanity had come to accept the proposition that it was okay to kill, as long as it was done in the name of the state and national security, in other words, in interstate war; the taking of a human life might in one context be considered a heinous crime, but done in another context would be considered acceptable, even noble. However, not only is it questionable to call most acts committed in wartime "murder," but, in quoting Voltaire, Scahill is commenting on a largely bygone era, as what wars occur today tend to produce smaller than larger casualties and generally are no longer accompanied by "the sound of trumpets." Scahill himself speaks of "shadow warriors, night raids, secret prisons, drone strikes," and the like. He criticizes the United States after

9/11 for taking the position that "the days of fighting uniformed enemies and national militaries according to the rules of the Geneva Convention were over. 'The world is a battlefield' was the mantra repeated by the ... U.S. national security apparatus ... laying out plans for a borderless global war."[7] It is fair to question whether the United States was abandoning the normal canons of war-fighting, and in the process, opening itself to the charge that it was embarking on a permanent war with no temporal or geographical boundaries and, also, no limits to permissible behavior. However, it is also fair to ask whether the United States was not so much creating a new reality as responding to one that already had emerged, as I have broadly described above.

The Purpose of the Book

I have provided a context for what is to follow. Scahill and others have raised some profound moral and other questions. In evaluating the foreign policy decisions and behaviors of any country, whether the United States or some other state, there are at least three questions one might ask. First, is it *smart*, that is, wise in terms of making practical sense in advancing national security and other national interests? Second, is it *moral*, that is, consistent with basic ethical principles relating to fairness, justice, and humanitarianism? Third, is it *legal*, that is, compatible with international law (and, one might add, a country's own domestic law)? All three are somewhat interrelated, although there can be a tension at times in trying to serve all three desiderata. They are all important, legitimate criteria to apply, although I will be focusing particularly on the legal dimension.

In weighing these considerations, we should keep in mind a good definition of "education" – "learning to cope with ambiguity,"[8] by which is meant not the absence of truth but rather its complexity. The purpose of this book is to engage students, and the larger public as well, in going beyond simplistic black-and-white depictions of good guys/gals and bad guys/gals in world politics, having them struggle with the increasingly murky nature of war and how the latter relates to ongoing efforts to regulate the use of armed force in human affairs.

Among the kinds of questions to be considered are the following: If U.S. soldiers are now, in Scahill's words, "shadow warriors," are they not themselves often up against a shadowy enemy – whether terrorists, guerrillas, rebels, insurgents, warlords, or whatever term one wants to use for an adversary who specializes in "irregular" warfare, what Max Boot has called "invisible armies"?[9] How can states fight and win conflicts against the latter, seemingly weaker foes in "asymmetrical warfare" situations and still comply with international humanitarian law when the enemy tries to level the playing field by observing no rules whatsoever? Was the capture and killing of Osama bin Laden, the mastermind of 9/11, legal; and should we care? Under what circumstances is "anticipatory self-defense" legal in a world of weapons of mass destruction (WMDs)? How does humanitarian intervention in places like Kosovo and Libya square with traditional notions of sovereignty? Are suspected terrorists, housed at Guantanamo Naval Base or some other location, entitled to prisoner of war (POW) protection under the Geneva Conventions? When considering the legality of "targeted killings" ("assassinations"?), should a "lawfare" or "warfare" model apply, that is, should someone like Anwar al-Awlaki (the American radical cleric killed by a U.S. drone strike in Yemen in 2011) be treated as a common criminal entitled to a normal jury trial in a court of law or rather as a combatant who can be killed by executive order? How are drone strikes compatible with international humanitarian law? What is the "battlefield" today – for the United States and other countries experiencing threats from al Qaeda and other such groups, is the war on terror a global conflict, stretching from Boston to Benghazi and beyond, making every area a potential war zone and giving new meaning to "police actions" in international relations? And how does one balance, on the one hand, the need for covert intelligence-gathering and other "dirty" operations in the name of national security (to address existential threats to American and other cities posed by terrorist networks) with, on the other hand, the rule of law and human rights domestically and internationally?

These and many other questions are on the minds of students today – or should be. I hope to contribute in some small way to encouraging citizens to think in a more analytical and sophisticated way about these problems. The rest of this chapter elaborates on the changing nature of war and its implications for, if not ending war, making it more "civilized," oxymoronic as that might sound.

Trends in War and the Use of Armed Force

In his 700-page *The Better Angels of Our Nature*, which traces empirically the decline of violence over the millennia, Steven Pinker concludes, "Believe it or not … today we may be living in the most peaceful era in our species' existence."[10] In a shorter op-ed, he reiterates that "war really is going out of style."[11] Indeed, he goes so far as to argue that violence generally, in almost all its forms – from homicide to war to animal cruelty – is in decline. He is not alone in this assessment, although most commentators limit their observations to war. For example, Gregg Easterbrook: "War has entered a cycle of decline. It is possible that a person's chance of dying because of war has, in the last decade or more, become the lowest in human history." John Mueller has written about "the obsolescence of major war." Joshua Goldstein has written *Winning the War on War: The Decline of Armed Conflict*. Fareed Zakaria reports on a University of Maryland study that found "we are now at the lowest level [of global violence] since the 1950s … . War and organized violence have declined dramatically … . It *feels* like a very dangerous world. But it isn't. Your chances of dying as a consequence of organized violence of any kind are low and getting lower." The Human Security Report Project, conducted by a Canadian research team, has noted "the major decline in the number of conflicts that have taken place since the end of the Cold War, the longer-term decline in international conflict numbers, [and] the reduction in the deadliness of warfare since the 1950s." Micah Zenko and Michael Cohen write: "The world that the United States [and humanity at large] inhabits today is a remarkably safe and secure place. It is a world with fewer violent conflicts ... than at virtually any other point in human history." Nils Petter Gleditsch of the Peace Research Institute in Oslo (PRIO) succinctly states, "Overall, there is a clear decline of war."[12]

Who knew? Certainly it would be hard to infer this from the daily headlines in newspapers, the nightly news reports on television, and the constant stream of messages on the Internet. The average person can be forgiven for thinking these scholars have been imbibing a bit too much or at the very least are indulging in hyperbole. Consider the following sampling of headlines about organized violence in recent times:

- "U.S. Debates Drone Strike on American" (*New York Times*, February 11, 2014), noting the Obama administration was "debating whether to authorize a lethal strike against an American citizen living in Pakistan who some believe is actively plotting terror attacks," which would have been the first such targeted killing of an American citizen abroad since a U.S. drone killed the radical preacher Anwar al-Awlaki in Yemen in 2011.
- "Bomb Syria, Even If It Is Illegal" and "Use Force to Save Starving Syrians" (*New York Times* op-eds of August 27, 2013 and February 11, 2014), arguing that the international community's "responsibility to protect the innocent justifies armed intervention," given over 150,000 civilian casualties inflicted by the Assad regime during the Syrian civil war, including 1,300 killed in a chemical weapons attack, along with almost a million people starving.
- "Civilian Death Toll in Iraq Highest in Years, Fueling Concern of Al Qaeda Resurgence" (*Fox News*, January 2, 2014), noting that "violence in Iraq soared in 2013 to levels not seen in years" (with at least 8,000 civilians killed) in the aftermath of the Second Gulf War, which the United States had initiated against Baghdad in 2003. Upon terminating its involvement in 2011 continued internal sectarian strife and transnational terrorist subversion were left behind. This headline was followed months later with a more ominous news bulletin, "ISIS Seizes Control of Mosul, Iraq's Second Largest City, Forcing 150,000 to Flee" (*International Business Times*, June 10, 2014), reporting on the attempt of a terrorist group (the Islamic State of Iraq and Syria) to establish a jihadist caliphate in Iraq and throughout the Muslim world. ISIS continued to expand its reach in 2015, engaging in beheadings, slaughter of "infidels," and other sordid acts of violence.
- "2,000 Feared Killed in Deadliest Boko Haram Attack in Nigeria" (CNN, January 10, 2015), describing the actions of an Islamic militant group that was specializing in the kidnapping of young girls.
- "Russia Bombing Kills 15 Ahead of Olympics" (*ABC News*, December 29, 2013), noting the attack by suspected Chechen separatists at a Volgograd train

station near Sochi, Russia (the site of the 2014 Winter Olympic Games), which resulted in dozens of people killed or injured.

- "Russia 'Invades' Georgia as South Ossetia Descends Toward War" (*The Telegraph*, August 8, 2008), noting Russia's claim that it was responding to the Georgian government's killing of 1,000 South Ossetian rebels trying to secede from Georgia, with the Georgian president describing the situation as "war." Six years later there was a replay of sorts, with the headline reading "Putin Ready to Invade Ukraine, as Kiev Warns of War" (*Reuters*, March 1, 2014), with Russia this time dispatching 10,000 troops to the Crimean region of Ukraine, eventually annexing the area on the pretext of protecting ethnic Russians threatened by internal strife in that country.
- "The World's Worst War" (*New York Times*, December 16, 2012), noting what was called "Africa's World War" – a massive conflagration triggered by the Rwandan genocide of Tutsis by Hutus in the 1990s that resulted in millions of Rwandan refugees flowing into neighboring Zaire (Congo), eventually drawing Uganda, Zimbabwe, Sudan and other African countries into a protracted conflict that by 2015 had left over 4 million dead and had yet to end (combining elements of interstate war over mineral resources, intrastate ethnopolitical strife, and extrastate violence involving groups such as the Lord's Resistance Army).
- "Terrorists Strike Paris Newspaper, 12 People Killed" (*New York Times*, January 8, 2015), reporting on al Qaeda-affiliated gunmen shooting several journalists at a satirical French newspaper, *Charlie Hebdo*, in retaliation for lampooning Islam.
- "Paris Attacks Kill More Than 100" (*New York Times,* November 13, 2015), announcing several coordinated terrorist attacks by ISIS operatives in the heart of Paris that resulted in several hundred people killed or injured and French President Francois Hollande declaring it "an act of war." This fueled widespread fears that a new chapter had opened in terrorist violence against the West."

Anticipating the findings of Steven Pinker and other contemporary scholars, Ralph Waldo Emerson in 1849 said wistfully, "War is on its last legs; and a universal peace is as sure as is the prevalence of civilization over barbarism. ... The question for us is only how soon?" It would appear we are not there yet, as episodes of violence, of varying scale and with varying degrees of organization, still occur on a fairly regular basis. What is most striking about the above news bulletins, however, is the virtual absence of classic interstate war. In contrast to the "total wars" of the past between entire nations (each mobilizing their people and economy in support of military victory), the few interstate conflicts that occur tend to be characterized – despite the tragic loss of life – as "limited wars" and "low-intensity conflicts" or, more euphemistically, as "overseas contingency operations" and even "peaceful engagement."[13] And, more often than not, the conflicts pit states against nonstate actors. Former U.S. Secretary of Defense Robert Gates alluded to such conflicts when he remarked in 2008, "The Pentagon must concentrate on building a military that can defeat the current enemies:

smaller, terrorist groups and militias waging irregular warfare."[14] Similarly, John Donnelly notes, "U.S. military leaders … now recognize that the nature of warfare itself is changing, from conventional conflicts between nations to 'small wars' – counterinsurgency, counterterrorism, religious, and ethnic strife."[15] These are what are meant by the so-called "new wars."

I have commented that the "new wars" are not altogether new. Certainly, civil wars are nothing novel; as just one example, the T'ai P'ing rebellion in China between 1850 and 1864 cost an estimated 30 million lives, more deaths than were caused in World War I. Terrorism as well is not a recent development; the term itself owes its name to the Reign of Terror in France following the French Revolution in 1789, and by 1900 the problem had become so acute as to occupy a prominent place in the foreign policy deliberations of governments.[16] Indeed, regarding "small wars" generally (what one author calls "teacup wars"),[17] Max Boot reminds us that "low-intensity conflict has been ubiquitous throughout history."[18] Reflecting on the nature of the warfare experienced by American troops in Baghdad during the Second Gulf War, he writes:

> They were undertaking the sort of modest, tedious, mundane intelligence gathering and security operations that have been a cornerstone of counterinsurgency operations since the days of Alexander the Great and Julius Caesar. They were part of a long continuum of soldiers who have struggled to master the rigors of unconventional warfare, just as their enemies were part of an even longer continuum of irregular warriors who have always given conventional armies fits.[19]

Although these sorts of conflicts are not new, it bears repeating that what *is* new is that they have displaced interstate war as the primary focus of security concerns in the state system. Even Boot acknowledges that "insurgency and terrorism have become the dominant forms of conflict – a trend likely to continue into the foreseeable future. Even as conventional interstate clashes dwindle, the number of guerrilla and terrorist groups continues to grow."[20] In order to fully understand the nature of armed conflict in the twenty-first century, we need to go beyond anecdotal accounts and analyze trend data more closely.

Interstate War

Historian Donald Kagan has observed: "Over the past two centuries the only thing more common than predictions about the end of war has been war itself; … statistically, war has been more common than peace, and extended periods of peace have been rare in a world divided into multiple states."[21] Most quantitative analyses of war begin either in 1648 (generally considered the birth of the modern state system, coinciding with the Peace of Westphalia that ended the Thirty Years War) or 1815 (the convening of the Congress of Vienna that ended the Napoleonic Wars). Using a standard operational definition of **international war** that has been employed in the Correlates of War (COW) Project at the University of Michigan (defined as the onset of sustained military hostilities between at least one recognized state and another state or foreign armed force culminating in at least 1,000 battle deaths), one finds that there were 95 international wars between 1816 and 2003; some of these were wars between recognized states, and some were colonial wars fought between a state and a foreign army in pursuit of independent statehood. The COW researchers concluded that "the nineteenth century was significantly less war prone than the twentieth."[22] Another study counts 177 interstate armed conflicts between 1648 and 1989, detecting an overall long-term decline in the incidence of such wars over time.[23]

Even if there has been a modest decline in the *occurrence* of interstate war, the *severity* of wars, as measured by casualties, mounted with the invention of increasingly destructive weapons throughout the twentieth century. Although some wars in prior centuries killed large numbers of people (for example, there were 2 million battle deaths caused by the Thirty Years War), at least twice as many soldiers died in twentieth century wars as in all the wars from 1500 to 1899 combined.[24] These totals do not count those wounded on the battlefield, or the millions of civilian casualties. (World War I was the last major war in which there were more military personnel killed than civilians, as the roughly 10 million combat deaths slightly exceeded the number of civilians killed. World War II saw some 15 million soldiers killed, compared to over 40 million civilians.)

If we take into account the proliferation of nation-states since the end of World War II, which has more than tripled the number of potential candidates for interstate war involvement, then a more impressive case can be made that the post–World War II period up to the present has been relatively free of international wars compared with previous eras of world politics. Although "the number of people killed by armed conflicts since World War II is probably twice that of the entire 1900s and perhaps seven times that of the 1800s," fewer and fewer of these conflicts have been waged between states (as opposed to within states).[25] The decline of interstate war is especially marked since the end of the Cold War. According to one recent study, "since 1990, there have been only five instances of wars between states: the Persian Gulf War (1990–1991) and its aftermath; Eritrea-Ethiopia (1998–2000); India-Pakistan (1997–2003); Iraq versus the U.S. and its allies (2003); and Djibouti-Eritrea (2008).[26] The Uppsala Conflict Data Project (UCDP) reports that between 1989 and 2011, only 6 percent of all armed conflicts worldwide (8 out of a total of 123 wars) were interstate.[27] The Human Security Report Project cites "the dramatic decline in the number and deadliness of international wars since the end of World War II," particularly since the end of the Cold War, as "conflicts between states – especially high-intensity conflicts [resulting in over 1,000 battle-related deaths] – have become very rare since 1989. There has been less than one interstate conflict per year on average since 2000, down from almost 3 in the 1980s."[28]

Traditionally, those who have studied the use of armed force in world politics have been interested most notably in interstate wars fought between *great powers*, especially fought over real estate (with territorial disputes involved in over half of all wars fought since 1648).[29] Much of the history of international politics has seemed to revolve around these sorts of events. Some of these conflicts have been systemic, involving a wide number of states in the international system (such as World War I and World War II), while some have been more confined (such as the Austro-Prussian War of 1866 and the Russo-Japanese War of 1905). One of the most profound changes in world politics has been the gradual movement away from this historical pattern, culminating in a complete break from this habit in the past half-century.

Jack Levy has traced the long-term historical decline in the incidence of great-power war. He found that wars among great powers in the nineteenth and twentieth centuries were underway only one-sixth of the time, compared with an estimated 80 percent of the time in the sixteenth to eighteenth centuries, reflecting the diminishing frequency and duration of such wars. Indeed, perhaps the most salient feature of the Cold War era was the paucity of war involvement by major powers, in particular the complete absence of war (including any exchange of fire) *between major powers themselves* (unless one counts the Korean conflict, in which the United States and China fought against each other). The absence of great-power war since 1945 has been called "**the long peace**." Levy summarizes the significance of the "long peace" as follows:

> The past five centuries of the modern system have witnessed an average of one great power war per decade, but the frequency of great power wars has declined significantly over time. We have experienced only three such wars in the twentieth century and arguably none in the period since the Second World War, and this continues the longest period of great power peace in 500 years. For many centuries war was disproportionately concentrated in the hands of the great powers in Europe, but the twentieth century, and the second half-century in particular, marked a significant shift in warfare from the major powers to the minor powers, from Europe to other regions, and from inter-state warfare to intra-state wars.[30]

The explanation for the decline and disappearance of great-power war is at least threefold. First and foremost, the increasing severity of war over time has made great powers – states having the most to lose in material well-being – less willing to engage each other in hostilities, especially in an age of weapons of mass destruction. Second, growing economic interdependence, not only in trade but also capital and investment, has created further inhibitions on the part of national governments from incurring the costs of the disruptive effects of war. Third, related to the "democratic peace" phenomenon (that is, the fact that democratic states rarely ever fight each other), growing democratization worldwide has lessened the propensity for great powers to war against each other.[31] As suggested above, these factors may be contributing to a decline in interstate war generally, not just great-power war. One study found that between 1945 and 1989, highly developed states (both nuclear and non-nuclear armed) had stopped fighting each other; the author observed that the 48 richest industrial states had had no wars against each other except for the British-Argentine Falklands War in 1982 and the Soviet invasion of Hungary in 1956, leading to hope that, as less developed states become wealthier and also more democratic, wars would be averted.[32]

Although the frequency of interstate war has declined over time, notably among major powers, the distinction between war and peace becomes blurred when one takes into account what has been called "**force without war**." I am not referring here simply to modern-day versions of old-fashioned "gunboat diplomacy" and other displays of military power short of war used by the United States and other countries in the late nineteenth and early twentieth centuries, but rather what has become today a surrogate for war. In the past, interstate armed conflicts of any magnitude were definable in legal terms and had identifiable initiation and termination dates. A "war" usually was said to start when one state issued a formal declaration of war against another state, as in World War II (when the United States declared war on Japan minutes after President Franklin Roosevelt's famous "a date that will live in infamy" speech on December 8, 1941, following the Japanese attack on Pearl Harbor, which in turn was followed by Germany declaring war on the United States). A war normally ended with a formal treaty of peace between the warring parties, as when the Japanese surrendered on board the USS *Missouri* in 1945, bringing World War II to a close. Since World War II, however, for various reasons, states have not issued formal declarations of war prior to initiating hostilities. The hostilities that do occur between two or more states can be isolated one-shot affairs or can go on for days, months, and in some cases years, often interrupted by periods of peace, only rarely concluding with a peace treaty. The Middle East is emblematic of such hostility patterns, in that the several wars fought between Israel and neighbors such as Syria and Lebanon have never fully ended, with intervals of relative quiet alternating with episodic violence.

Abundant cases of force without war (sometimes called "militarized disputes") can be found since 1945. This has included "coercive diplomacy" and "diplomacy of violence," that is, demonstrative *threats* to use force (e.g., U.S. troop mobilizations and naval maneuvers during the 1967 Six Day War between Israel and Arab countries, aimed at convincing the Soviet Union to stay on the sidelines of the conflict rather than intervening), as well as *actual* but low-level use of force (e.g., the U.S. under President Reagan sending a few jets to strafe the headquarters of Libyan leader Muammar Gaddafi in 1986, to dissuade Libya from sponsoring terrorism). Examples of force without war in the post–Cold War era include the border clashes between Peru and Ecuador in 1995 (over a boundary dispute dating back over 50 years); the 1996 missile tests conducted by China in the Taiwan Straits to send a message to Taiwan to refrain from declaring its independence from the mainland, as well as China's stepping up naval patrols and air reconnaissance in the South and East China Sea in the 2000s as a warning to the Philippines and Japan and other states contesting sovereignty over islands claimed by Beijing; and the periodic bombing runs by U.S. planes over Iraq in the 1990s, following the creation of a no-fly zone over northern Iraq aimed at protecting the Kurdish population from Saddam Hussein's military (known as the "whack a mole" policy executed by the Clinton administration, named after an arcade game). Clinton's limited use of force against Iraq included a cruise missile attack against the headquarters of Saddam's intelligence service in Baghdad after the Iraqi leader was discovered plotting to assassinate former president Bush in 1993 during his visit to Kuwait.[33]

We will consider whether the existing rules aimed at regulating "war" are readily applicable as well to "force without war" and armed conflict generally or need some tweaking. Although one can count many instances of states engaging in force without war, the fact remains that such disputes now are less likely to lead to war, as "civil wars continue to be more common than conflicts between two countries."[34] Steven Pinker argues that, in addition to the "long peace" and the decline of interstate war, the world is also witnessing lately an emergent "new peace," as both intrastate and extrastate violence (civil wars and terrorism) are in decline as well.[35] As discussed below, the picture is somewhat more complicated. We will first examine civil wars, and then terrorism.

Civil War

It has been noted that as long as there have been nation-states, there have been conflicts within nation-states that have involved internecine fighting between rival groups. Although **civil war** is not new, it has been an especially visible feature of world politics since 1945 and has come increasingly to preoccupy the international community in the post–Cold War period.[36] The decolonialization process after World War II produced new states in Africa and Asia that, along with fragile economies, often had highly unstable political systems prone to internal unrest, in some cases becoming "failed states" altogether. Civil wars have also taken place in long-established states, in Latin America and elsewhere. K.J. Holsti estimates that "more than two-thirds of all armed conflict in the world since 1945 has taken the form of civil wars."[37] The International Commission on Intervention and State Sovereignty notes, "The most marked security phenomenon since the end of the Cold War has been the proliferation of armed conflicts within states," with the Uppsala Conflict Data Project/PRIO researchers, for example, counting a total of 30 active armed conflicts worldwide in 2010, all of which were categorized as intrastate.[38] As of 2015, some 20 civil wars were ongoing.

As one writer comments, "Today's typical war is civil, started by rebels who want to change their country's constitution, alter the balance of power between races, or secede."[39] Of special consequence for international politics has been the increasing tendency over time for civil wars to become *internationalized* (that is, to involve foreign military forces). One study found that "the percent of civil wars internationalized" rose from 18 percent in the 1919–1939 period to 27 percent in the 1946–1965 period to 36 percent in the 1966–1977 period.[40] During the Cold War, much of the internationalization was driven by the East–West geopolitical competition between the communist and western blocs, with interventions by Washington or Moscow seeking to bolster one of the sides in places such as Vietnam, Afghanistan, Ethiopia, and Nicaragua. The Soviet Union and its proxy states often assisted in "wars of national liberation," in which revolutionary groups trying to overthrow colonial rule (for example, in Angola and Mozambique) resorted to guerrilla warfare insurgency tactics to overcome the stronger conventional military forces of the established authorities, which in turn were trained by the United States or its regional allies in counterinsurgency tactics to resist the guerrillas. These conflicts presaged the aforementioned "small wars" of today.

Clearly, internationalization has continued into the post–Cold War era. Examining the 2010 data cited above, over a quarter of the civil wars involved external actors.[41] However, there is an important difference between the pattern seen during the Cold War and pattern evidenced since. First, civil wars in the post–Cold War era have tended to be rooted far more in ethnic differences than ideological differences, in many cases involving separatist movements seeking to establish their own state, represented by recent ethnopolitical conflicts in Rwanda (between Hutus and Tutsis), Sudan (between blacks and Arabs), and the former Yugoslavia (between Bosnians and Kosovars and their Serb rulers).[42] Second, interventionism in the post–Cold War era has often been multilateral in character, sponsored by regional or global organizations claiming a right of humanitarian intervention in failed or imploding states to relieve mass starvation, stop atrocities, or otherwise provide humanitarian help, as in Somalia (1992), Haiti (1993), Liberia (1993), Libya (2011), and Syria (2014).[43]

Recalling Steven Pinker's optimistic forecast, there is some evidence that there has been a reduction recently in the incidence of civil wars, with one study finding that their frequency peaked in the immediate post–Cold War period in 1992. The *Human Security Report* notes "the dramatic and unexpected decline in the number of civil conflicts that started in the early 1990s after three decades of steady increase."[44] The same researchers, referring to Ted Gurr's Minorities at Risk project, find that Gurr was "correct" in claiming that ethnopolitical conflict as a subset of civil wars had peaked as well in the early 1990s.[45] In addition, it would appear that battle deaths and "high intensity conflict" generally are in steep decline since the end of the Cold War.[46] In other words, even though civil wars remain the dominant form of organized violence on the planet, they may possibly be on a declining trajectory similar to interstate war.

Nonetheless, there is reason to be cautious in assessing these positive findings. First, the potential for internal wars to increase in frequency remains high, given the large number of countries that are candidates for "failed states"; according to one source, "today as many as seventy-three state governments are vulnerable to civil war."[47] Not surprisingly, the regions experiencing the most deadly intrastate conflicts today are Central and South Asia, along with the Middle East and North and sub-Saharan Africa, where one finds the weakest governments. Second, to the extent that internationalization of civil wars remains a problem, such conflicts are "on average twice as deadly as civil wars in which there are no such interventions."[48] Third, the civil wars that do occur tend "to last 20 times as long as international wars"[49]; their average duration is 10 years, with the protracted conflict ending usually through exhaustion of one or both sides rather than through an agreement on power sharing.[50] Finally, related to what Mary Kaldor and others have described as "new wars," these sorts of conflicts (e.g., the Sierra Leone civil war of the 1990s) seem to be morphing into what looks more like gang violence than state-based violence, with civilians increasingly the primary targets. As one author describes this phenomenon:

> Most [of these conflicts], though not all, are more nearly opportunistic predation by packs, often remarkably small ones, of criminals, bandits, and thugs. They engage in armed conflict either as mercenaries hired by desperate governments or as independent or semi-independent warlord or brigand bands. The damage perpetrated by these entrepreneurs of violence ... can be extensive, particularly to the citizens who are their chief prey, but it is scarcely differentiable from crime.[51]

This sort of violence is also often indistinguishable from the kind of nonstate actor violence associated with terrorism.

Terrorism and Extrastate Violence

Indicative of the complexity of armed conflict today is that, coinciding with the "long peace," since 9/11 we have seen what the U.S. Department of Defense has called "the long war" (the Global War on Terror). As noted earlier, Jeremy Scahill and others have complained that the United States has embarked on a permanent war with no temporal or geographical boundaries. In his criticism of U.S. "plans for a borderless global war," Scahill seems to ignore the reality that Robert Barnidge calls attention to, namely that "the contemporary context of warfare has rendered 'outdated' the traditional insistence that armed conflicts can take place only between states or within them."[52] **Terrorism** by its nature tends to involve nonstate actors, often organized in transnational networks of cells, engaging in what amounts to "**extrastate**" violence. As another writer puts it, "transnational terrorism ... [is driving] a rethinking of the battle space and the reconceptualization of the spatial reach of the law of armed conflict."[53] Before considering how modern terrorism has impacted the laws of war, we need first to examine trends relating to terrorism.

One problem in tracking trends on terrorism is that among scholars, lawyers, and policymakers, there is no general agreement on a clear definition of the term. One study notes that the term had at least 109 different definitions between 1936 and 1981, and many others have appeared since.[54] The search for an authoritative definition has been likened to "the Quest for the Holy Grail."[55] It has been said that one person's terrorist is another's freedom fighter. However, if we accept this view, then any act of violence can be excused and legitimized, however barbarous, as long as someone invents a justification.

One simple helpful definition considers terrorism to be "premeditated, politically motivated violence perpetrated against noncombatant targets by subnational groups or clandestine agents, usually intended to influence an audience."[56] This definition suggests that terrorism entails a combination of at least three elements.

First, terrorism ordinarily involves the threat or use of *unconventional violence* – violence that is spectacular, violates accepted social mores, and is designed to shock so as to gain publicity and instill fear in the hope of extorting concessions. Terrorists generally observe no rules of combat whatsoever. Their tactics can include bombings, hijackings, kidnappings, assassinations, and other acts. Among the most high-profile terrorist incidents in recent years, in addition to the 9/11 attacks, were the nerve gas attack in a crowded Tokyo subway in 1995 that killed 12 people and injured 5,500 others (by the Japanese Aum Shinrikyo cult); the bombing of four trains in Madrid, Spain, in 2004, that took the lives of some 200 commuters and wounded 1,400 others (thought to be the work of either Basque separatists or al Qaeda); the 2004 killing of 331 people, including 150 children, in a schoolhouse in Beslan, Russia (by militants supporting Chechen independence); the simultaneous attacks on several luxury hotels in Mumbai, India in 2008, that killed over 150 people and wounded hundreds more, traced to a Pakistani group); and the 2013 shootings at a shopping mall in Nairobi, Kenya, resulting in 72 dead and over 200 wounded (claimed by al-Shabaab, a Somalia-based Islamic jihadist group).

Second, terrorism is characterized by violence that is *politically motivated*. The political context of terrorism distinguishes it from mere criminal behavior such as armed robbery or gangland slayings, which may be every bit as spectacular but are not driven primarily by political motives. One would not ordinarily call the Mafia, for example, a terrorist organization, even though it is heavily involved in international drug trafficking and other criminal activities, at times in league with terrorist groups, prompting references to "narcoterrorism"; the same goes for Mexican and other Latin American drug cartels, granted the distinction between crime and terrorism can be muted at times. Most terrorist groups are more clearly motivated by political goals, ranging from the creation of a national homeland to the elimination of foreign occupation or cultural influence in a region to the total political and economic transformation of society.[57]

The third key distinguishing characteristic of terrorism, following from the first two, is the almost incidental nature of the *targets* against whom the violence is committed. The immediate targets of terrorism – whether people or property, civilian or military – usually have only an indirect relation to the larger aims impelling the terrorist; instead, they are exploited for their shock potential. Sometimes the targets are carefully chosen individuals (prominent business leaders or government officials), while on other occasions they are faceless, nondescript masses (ordinary men, women, and children randomly slaughtered in airports, department stores, and other public places).

There is a fourth ingredient of terrorism we might add, having to do with the identity of the *perpetrators* of such violence. It has been noted that terrorism tends to be the work of nonstate actors, that is, it is mainly the tactic of "outgroups" – the politically weak and frustrated (such as al Qaeda and other radical Islamic fundamentalists throughout the Middle East and South Asia, the Irish Republican Army in Northern Ireland, the Shining Path in Peru, or Basque separatists in Spain) – who see terror as the best tool for contesting the sizable armies and police forces of the governments of nation-states. Although certain excessive forms of violence used by government authorities themselves are sometimes referred to as "state terrorism" – in particular the systematic torture and repression a government inflicts on dissidents within its own society, or assassinations committed by secret state agencies abroad, in addition to indiscriminate attacks on civilian populations – the terrorism label normally does not apply to actions taken by official governmental bodies. Terrorists generally do not wear uniforms, although many in the past have been at least indirectly supported and sponsored by governments.

The definitional problems result in different coding and counting procedures used by the various researchers who try to track terrorism trends, making it hard to compare longitudinal data and determine whether terrorism is on the increase or decrease. Based on statistics reported by the U.S. State Department in its annual *Patterns of Global Terrorism* volumes published over several decades, there was a long-term decline in the incidence of international terrorism between 1980 and 2003. Based on the more recent data furnished by the National Consortium for the Study of Terrorism and Responses to Terrorism (START), the trend is more mixed of late. (START, housed at the University of Maryland, was tasked by the U.S. Department of Homeland Security to compile a Global Terrorism Database as a replacement for the series that the State Department had published. START's definition of terrorism is "the threatened or actual use of illegal force and violence by a nonstate actor to attain a political, economic, religious, or social goal through fear, coercion, or intimidation.")

Using the latter definition, START has reported that global terrorism is on the rise. Its 2013 annual report stated that "while terrorist attacks have in large part moved away from Western Europe and North America to Asia, the Middle East, and Africa, worldwide terrorism is reaching new levels of destructiveness." In 2012, it counted a total of over 8,400 terrorism incidents, killing over 15,000 people, exceeding previous highs. However, it was careful to point out that, of the 85 countries touched by terrorism in 2012, just three (Pakistan, Iraq, and Afghanistan) accounted for more than half of the total attacks (54 percent) and fatalities (58 percent), thus skewing the data in a negative direction.[58] This has led some observers, such as John Mueller and others, to argue that the terrorism threat has been "overblown,"[59] and that "in most places today – and especially in the United States – the chances of dying from a terrorist attack … have fallen almost to zero."[60] Pinker notes that almost every year "more Americans [are] killed by lightning, deer, peanut allergies, [and] bee stings … than by terrorist attacks."[61] On the other side of the debate are scholars such as Bruce Hoffman, who worry over not only potential terrorist attacks on Americans but also the ongoing attacks on civilians in other parts of the world and the growing lethality of those attacks. Whereas in the past it was assumed that "terrorists want a lot of people watching … and not a lot of people dead," their modus operandi seems to have changed, perhaps because of the growing percentage of groups with extreme religious views that animate them.[62]

The fact is that modern industrial society is especially susceptible to nightmarish scenarios given such inviting targets as jumbo jets, giant skyscrapers, nuclear power stations, electronic grids, and computer networks. The existence of modern communications technology enables terrorists to receive instant publicity through the world's mass media and can contribute to an epidemic effect worldwide, in addition to enabling terrorists to coordinate their efforts across regions. Social media have greatly enhanced terrorist recruitment and mobilization capabilities. The "ultimate catastrophe" would be terrorists gaining access to stockpiles of biological, chemical, and nuclear weapons or creating their own weapons of mass destruction (WMDs).[63] Hence, whether terrorism increases or decreases from year to year, it continues to pose a harrowing security challenge for much of humanity.

Challenges to the International Regime Governing the Use of Armed Force

"**International regimes**" have been defined as "sets of governing arrangements" that include "networks of rules, norms, and procedures that regularize behavior and control its effects" in relations among nations.[64] They are an alternative to each country unilaterally pursuing its own foreign policy, and represent an effort to promote a degree of order and cooperation in a decentralized system of sovereign states that is inherently anarchic; that is, they are an attempt at "global governance" in the absence of global government. Regimes exist in various issue-areas. There is a "trade regime," grounded in the World Trade Organization and a number of norms and treaties, governing international economic transactions. There is an "ozone layer" regime, grounded in the Montreal Protocol and related environmental institutions, governing regulation of chemicals that threaten the earth's ozone layer. And so on. The international regime we are interested in studying in this book is arguably the most important of all regimes – the regime governing "armed conflict." As we will discuss, in this issue-area there are really several regimes in one. All show signs of breaking down under stress, as there is some question whether the existing body of norms, rules, and institutions is adequate to cope with the changes in the nature of war that I have described.

Interestingly, when the United Nations Charter was drafted and signed in 1945, the word "war" appeared only once in the entire document – in the Preamble, in the very first line, where it states, "We the Peoples of the United Nations determined to save succeeding generations from the scourge of war, which twice in our lifetime has brought untold sorrow to mankind ... ." In lieu of the term "war," the Charter often refers more generally to "breaches of the peace," seemingly anticipating to some degree the more complex post–World War II world where the problem of regulating the use of armed force would have less to do with preventing World War III but rather with managing an array of "force without war" situations, not only unaccompanied by formal declarations of war but devoid of many of the normal attributes traditionally associated with interstate hostilities.

Even so, although the Charter referred at the beginning to "the Peoples of the United Nations," there is no question that the document was grounded in a *state-centric* view of the world and assumed that the main conflicts to be regulated would be conflicts between *states*. The language of Article 2 (4) is plain: "All Members shall refrain in their international relations from the threat or use of force against the territorial integrity or political independence of any state." Thus, while the Charter took a broad, visionary view of the problem of global violence, it remained one revolving around the traditional actors in world politics and their competition over real estate and other geopolitical objectives. Louis Henkin has argued that the UN Charter has been reasonably effective in addressing these kinds of conflicts that Article 2 aimed to regulate, as "the norm against the unilateral national use of force has survived. Indeed ... the norm has been largely observed ... and the kinds of international wars which it sought to prevent and deter [wars between states] have been infrequent."[65]

However – and this is the rub – the norm against unilateral force has been less effective in the grayish areas discussed earlier in this chapter, such as force without war, and is especially problematic in dealing with the most common forms of planetary violence today, namely intrastate and extrastate hostilities. As Joseph Nye comments, "the doctrine of collective security enshrined in the UN Charter is state-centric, applicable when borders are crossed but not when force is used against peoples within a state."[66] Another commentator similarly notes that the institutional "machinery we have to manage [security] problems is still wired for the sovereign, often state-to-state military confrontations of a bygone era."[67] Anthony Clark

Arend and Robert Beck, among others, have examined "the challenges to the Charter paradigm" and have called for a "post-Charter paradigm."[68]

It is not just the UN Charter and the rules regulating the *outbreak* of armed conflict (what is called *jus ad bellum*) that may be outmoded but also the rules regulating the *conduct* of armed conflict (what is called *jus in bello*, or "international humanitarian law"). William Banks, discussing

> "the state-centric paradigm of international humanitarian law," notes that the latter developed over time from a conception of war based on symmetric conflicts between state armies of roughly equal military strength and of comparable organizational structures... . [It produced] international legal instruments that prescribe rules for the conduct of military operations during armed conflict, including standards for the protection of civilians... . Such universally-agreed upon rules humanize war by setting criteria and limits on such issues as who and what may be targeted, the weapons that may be used, [and] how prisoners of war and other detainees must be treated.[69]

These instruments – the Geneva Conventions and others – have been called into question today not only by "the new wars" but also by larger changes in the very fabric of the state system, including the growth of nonstate actors and the erosion of the state and state boundaries altogether in a world of cyberspace, multinational corporations, and other developments.[70] Some scholars have gone so far as to proclaim "the end of sovereignty" and "the end of geography," stating that "like a mothball, which goes from solid to gas directly, I expect the nation-state to evaporate" and "the era of the nation-state is over."[71]

Mark Twain once said that the report of his death was greatly exaggerated. Similarly, we need to be careful not to exaggerate the reported demise of the nation-state.[72] One need only glance at any world map or globe to see that the nation-state mode of organization continues to define political life on the planet. But if it is premature to consider the nation-state about to be mothballed, less far-fetched is the notion that the body of international law governing armed conflict is at risk.

John Yoo, the Deputy Assistant U.S. Attorney General in the Bush Administration, after the 9/11 attacks seemed to many to be rewriting the rules of war when he defended both the right of the United States to engage in the "preemptive use of armed force" against any enemy that potentially threatened America and the right to use waterboarding (simulated drowning) and other "enhanced interrogation techniques" to extract intelligence that could alert the U.S. to such threats, justifying these actions as follows: "At the end of the cold war, war was still thought of as occurring solely between nation-states. ... The world after September 11, 2001, however, is very different." Yoo contended that in the post-9/11 era, the old rules no longer applied and that "war by other means" would be necessary.[73] In one of his controversial memoranda that seemed to stretch *jus ad bellum* rules, he stated that "the President may deploy military force preemptively against terrorist organizations or the states that harbor or support them, whether or not they can be linked to the specific incidents of September 11." In another memorandum, pertaining to *jus in bello* rules, he stated that "the Geneva Conventions [do not] apply to the detention conditions in Guantanamo Bay, Cuba or to trial by military commission of al Qaeda or Taliban prisoners [housed at Guantanamo]."[74]

Whether or not one agrees with Yoo's interpretation of international law and what rules apply to "the new warfare," there are legitimate questions one can ask about the relevance and effectiveness of the current regime that purports to regulate armed conflict, questions of the sort I raised at the outset for the reader to consider. It may be the case that, "while doubts are always expressed as to the resilience of the law of armed conflict in the face of the changing nature and means of warfare, there is no reason to think that the law cannot adequately respond to contemporary and future wars."[75] The matter of how the existing regime can be adapted to new realities is the subject we are about to explore.

The Plan of the Book

Having introduced the puzzle in Part One, Part Two will examine the main elements of the existing regime – the present corpus of rules pertaining to both *starting* (entering into) an armed conflict (*jus ad bellum*) and *conducting* an armed conflict (*jus in bello*). We will examine in some detail the United Nations Charter, the Geneva Conventions, and other international legal instruments related to war. Part Three will then analyze the challenges posed by "the new warfare," employing several recent, historical case studies to investigate the extent to which there is a mismatch between the traditional rules and contemporary realities. Studying the Second Gulf War in Iraq (2003), the Osama bin Laden raid (2011), the NATO military intervention in Libya (2011), the Israeli–Palestinian Gaza War (2008–09), and other incidents will help flesh out the workings of the laws of war and, in some instances, their unworkability in today's world. We will consider what a "just war" might look like in terms of *jus ad bellum* and *jus in bello*, and also *jus post-bellum* (having to do with how a conflict is concluded). Finally, in Part Four, a concluding chapter will reflect on the future of war and peace and how we might "rethink rules for an unruly world."

Chapter 1 Discussion Questions

1.   In *Dirty Wars*, journalist Jeremy Scahill criticizes the United States for using secret prisons, enhanced interrogation techniques, drone strikes, targeted killings, and other methods in a "borderless, global war" on terror, in violation of international law. Do you agree or disagree with such critics?
2.   Can countries such as the United States be expected to comply with the Geneva Conventions and other rules of international law when they are

often fighting an adversary that ignores the rules completely? Is the United States damned if it does and damned if it does not, on the one hand inviting condemnation if it violates the laws of war and, on the other hand, fighting at a disadvantage and possibly risking defeat if it complies?

3.   What is meant by "asymmetrical warfare," and how does this complicate the observance of the laws of war by the parties to a conflict?

4.   Do you agree with Steven Pinker that "today we may be living in the most peaceful era in our species' existence"? What are the trends in war and the use of armed force – interstate violence, intrastate violence, and extrastate violence? Is global violence increasing or decreasing?

5.   What is meant by "the new wars"?

Notes

1   George H.W. Bush, State of the Union Address, January 29, 1991. Also, see the Summer 1991 issue of *Foreign Policy*.

2   The changes in the international system are described in J. Martin Rochester, *U.S. Foreign Policy in the 21st Century: Gulliver's Travails* (Boulder, CO: Westview, 2008), Chapter 1. As I note, the main features of the Cold War system, particularly the bipolar power and alignment structure, had already started breaking down by the 1970s, long before the Cold War came to an end.

3   Jeremy Scahill, *Dirty Wars: The World Is a Battlefield* (New York: Nation Books, 2013).

4   Michael J. Glennon, *The Fog of Law* (Stanford, CA: Stanford University Press, 2009).

5   Michael Walzer, *Arguing About War* (New Haven, CT: Yale University Press, 2004). On the "just war" doctrine, see Michael Walzer, *Just and Unjust Wars*, 4th edn (New York: Basic Books, 1977).

6   Mary Kaldor, *New and Old Wars*, 2nd edn (Stanford: Stanford University Press, 2007); also, see K.J. Holsti, *The State, War, and the State of War* (Cambridge: Cambridge University Press, 1996), 37.

7   Scahill, *Dirty Wars*, 3–4.

8   This definition was once told to me by a colleague, Bill Brigman.

9   Max Boot, *Invisible Armies* (New York: W.W. Norton, 2013). Also, see Max Boot, "The Evolution of Irregular War: Insurgents and Guerrillas from Akkadia to Afghanistan," *Foreign Affairs*, 92, no. 2 (March/April, 2013): 100–114.

10   Steven Pinker, *The Better Angels of Our Nature: Why Violence Has Declined* (New York: Viking Press, 2011), xxi.

11   Joshua S. Goldstein and Steven Pinker, "War Really is Going Out of Style," *New York Times*, December 18, 2011.

12   Gregg Easterbrook, "The End of War?," *The New Republic* (May 30, 2005); John Mueller, *Retreat from Doomsday: The Obsolescence of Major War* (New York: Basic Books, 1989); Joshua S. Goldstein, *Winning the War on War: The Decline of Armed Conflict Worldwide* (New York: Dutton, 2011); Fareed Zakaria, *The Post-American World*, updated ed (New York: W.W. Norton, 2012), 8–9; Human Security Report Project, *Human Security Report 2009/2010* (Vancouver: Human Security Press, 2010); Micah Zenko and Michael Cohen, "Clear and Present Safety," *Foreign Affairs*, 91, no. 2 (March/April, 2012): 80; and Nils Petter Gledistsch, "The Liberal Moment Fifteen Years On," *International Studies Quarterly*, 52 (2008): 691; in addition, see Gleditsch et al., "Armed Conflict 1946–2001: A New Dataset," *Journal of Peace Research*, 39 (2002): 615–637.

13 "Peaceful engagement" was the term used by the United States to characterize its invasion of Panama in 1989 to remove their leader, Manuel Noriega, from power. "Overseas contingency operations" was the term used by the Obama administration as a substitute for the "war on terror."

14 Robert Gates, quoted in *Philadelphia Inquirer*, May 14, 2008.

15 John Donnelly, "Small Wars, Big Changes," *CQ Weekly*, January 28, 2008: 252.

16 See Walter Laqueur, "Postmodern Terrorism," *Foreign Affairs*, 75, no. 5 (September/October 1996): 24–36.

17 Leslie Gelb, "Quelling the Teacup Wars," *Foreign Affairs*, 73, no. 6 (November/December 1994): 2–6.

18 Boot, *Invisible Armies*, xxvi.

19 Ibid., xx.

20 Ibid.

21 Cited in George Will, "Defense Cuts Reflect Liberals' Blind Optimism in Lasting Peace," *St. Louis Post-Dispatch*, July 17, 1995.

22 "The Inter-State Wars," in Meredith Sarkees and Frank Waylan, *Resort to War, 1816–2007* (Washington, DC: CQ Press, 2010), 188.

23 K.J. Holsti, *Peace and War: Armed Conflicts and International Order, 1648–1989* (Cambridge: Cambridge University Press, 1989).

24 Jack S. Levy and T. Clifton Morgan, "The Frequency and Seriousness of International War: An Inverse Relationship," *Journal of Conflict Resolution* 28 (December 1984): 742.

25 Charles Kegley, Jr., *World Politics: Trend and Transformation*, 12th edn (Belmont, CA: Wadsworth, 2009), 378.

26 Mark A. Boyer, Natalie F. Hudson, and Michael J. Butler, *Global Politics: Engaging A Complex World* (New York: McGraw Hill, 2013), 261.

27 Lotta Themner and Peter Wallensteen, "Armed Conflict, 1946–2010," *Journal of Peace Research*, 48 (2011): 525–536; also, see Lotta Harbom and Peter Wallensteen, "Armed Conflict: 1989–2006," *Journal of Peace Research*, 44 (2007): 623–634.

28 Human Security Report Project, *Human Security Report 2013* (Vancouver: Human Security Press, 2013), 24.

29 Holsti, *Peace*.

30 Jack S. Levy, "War and Peace," in Walter Carlsnaes et al., eds, *Handbook of International Relations* (Thousand Oaks, CA: Sage, 2002), 351. On the long peace, see John L. Gaddis, *The Long Peace* (New York: Oxford University Press, 1987).

31 On these and other war-inhibiting factors, see Bruce Russett and John Oneal, *Triangulating Peace* (New York: W.W. Norton, 2001). Also, *Human Security Report 2013*, 28–33.

32 Mueller, *Retreat from Doomsday*, 78. Also see Max Singer and Aaron Wildavsky, *The Real World Order: Zones of Peace/Zones of Turmoil* (Chatham, NJ: Chatham House, 1993).

33 The term "force without war" is attributed to Barry M. Blechman and Stephen S. Kaplan, *Force Without War: U.S. Armed Forces As A Political Instrument* (Washington, DC: Brookings Institution, 1979). For discussion of "coercive diplomacy," see Alexander George, *Forceful Persuasion: Coercive Diplomacy As An Alternative to War* (Washington, DC: U.S. Institute of Peace, 1991). For discussion of "diplomacy of violence," see Thomas C. Schelling, *Arms and Influence* (New Haven, CT: Yale University Press, 2008). On "militarized disputes," see Faren Ghosn, Glenn Palmer, and Stuart Bremer, "The MID3 Data Set, 1993–2001: Procedures, Coding Rules, and Description," *Conflict Management and Peace Science*, 21 (2004): 133–154.

34 *Human Security Report 2013*, 12.

35 Pinker, *The Better Angels of Our Nature*, Chapter 6.

36 On civil wars, see Donald M. Snow, *Uncivil Wars* (Boulder, CO: Lynne Rienner, 1996); and Sarkees and Wayland, *Resort to War*, Chapter 5.

37 K.J. Holsti, "War, Peace, and the State of the State," *International Political Science Review*, 16 (October 1995): 320.

38 International Commission on Intervention and State Sovereignty, *The Responsibility to Protect* (Ottawa: International Development Research Centre, 2001), 4; and Themner and Wallensteen, "Armed Conflict, 1946–2010." The latter study counted all conflicts in which at least 25 battle-related deaths occurred; only four of the conflicts resulted in at least 1,000 battle related deaths.

39 "The World's Wars," *Economist*, March 12, 1988: 19–20.

40 Melvin Small and J. David Singer, "Conflict in the International System, 1816–1977," in Charles W. Kegley and Patrick J. McGowan, eds, *Challenges to America: United States Foreign Policy in the 1980s* (Beverly Hills, CA: Sage, 1979), 100.

41 *Human Security Report 2013*, 12, notes that "internationalized intrastate conflict has become more common in recent years."

42 On ethnopolitical conflict, see Ted Robert Gurr and Barbara Harff, *Ethnopolitical Conflict in World Politics* (Boulder, CO: Westview Press, 1994).

43 See Tonya Langford, "Things Fall Apart, State Failure, and the Politics of Intervention," *International Studies Review*, 1 (Spring 1999): 59–79.

44 *Human Security Report 2009/2010*, 5.

45 *Human Security Report 2013*, 17.

46 Bethany Lacina, Nils Petter Gleditsch, and Bruce Russett, "The Declining Risk of Death in Battle," *International Studies Quarterly*, 5 (2006): 673–680. Also, see *Human Security Report 2013*, 89.

47 Charles W. Kegley and Shannon Blanton, *World Politics: Trend and Transformation* (Boston, MA: Wadsworth, 2012–2013), 219. See the annual Failed State Index provided by the journal *Foreign Policy*.

48 Human Security Report Project, *Human Security Report 2012* (Vancouver: Human Security Press, 2012), 12. On how external intervention in civil wars complicates war termination, see David Cunningham, "Blocking Resolution: How External States Can Prolong Civil Wars," *Journal of Peace Research*, 47 (March 2010): 115–127.

49 Graham Bowley, "The Fights That Do Not Want to End," *New York Times*, May 24, 1990.

50 James D. Fearon, "Iraq's Civil War," *Foreign Affairs*, 86 (March/April 2007): 4. On the duration of civil wars, and how multi-party conflicts are harder to end, see David Cunningham, *Barriers to Peace in Civil War* (Cambridge: Cambridge University Press, 2011).

51 John Mueller, *The Remnants of War* (Ithaca, NY: Cornell University Press, 2007), 1.

52 Robert P. Barnidge, "A Qualified Defense of American Drone Attacks in Northwest Pakistan Under International Humanitarian Law," *Boston University International Law Journal*, 30 (2012): 436.

53 Louise Arimatsu, "Spatial Conceptions of the Law of Armed Conflict," in Robert P. Barnidge, ed., *The Liberal Way of War* (Burlington, VT: Ashgate, 2013), 167.

54 Based on a study by Alex Schmid, cited in Anthony Clark Arend and Robert J. Beck, *International Law and the Use of Force* (New York: Routledge, 1993), 140. On December 9, 1985, the UN General Assembly adopted a resolution that attempted to define terrorism as any acts that "endanger or take innocent human lives, jeopardize fundamental freedoms, and seriously impair the dignity of human beings." The 2004 Report of the Secretary-General's High-Level Panel on Threats, Challenges, and Change defined terrorism as "any action … that is intended to cause death or serious bodily harm to civilians or combatants, when the purpose of such an act … is to intimidate a population, or to compel a government or an international organization to do or abstain from doing an act."

55 Schmid, quoted in Arend and Beck, *International Law and Use of Force*, 140. On the "ambiguity" of the term and doubts that any consensus can be reached, see Anna Oehmichen, "Force Qua Terrorism," in Sanford R. Silverburg, ed., *International Law:*

Contemporary Issues and Future Developments (Boulder, CO: Westview Press, 2011), 448–450.

56 *Patterns of Global Terrorism 2001* (Washington, DC: U.S. Department of State, 2002), xvi.

57 Robert Pape, in *Dying to Win* (New York: Random House, 2005), argues that most terrorist groups, particularly those with grievances about foreign occupation of their homeland, are rational actors with specific goals and a calculus aimed at achieving those goals.

58 The 2012 START "Global Terrorism Database" report, accessed March 9, 2014 at www.start.umd.edu/news/despite-fewer-attacks-western-world-global-terrorism. The Memorial Institute for the Prevention of Terrorism and other research centers also report trend data along these lines.

59 John Mueller, *Overblown* (New York: Free Press, 2006). Also see his "Is There Still A Terrorist Threat: The Myth of the Omnipresent Enemy," *Foreign Affairs*, 85, no. 5 (September/October 2006): 2–8; and Marc Sageman, *Leaderless Jihad: Terror Networks in the 21st Century* (Philadelphia: University of Pennsylvania Press, 2008).

60 Zenko and Cohen, "Clear and Present Safety," 83.

61 Pinker, *The Better Angels of Our Nature*, 345. Also, see Paul Campos, "Undressing the Terrorist Threat," *Wall Street Journal*, January 9, 2010.

62 The "watching vs. dead" statement is attributed to Brian Jenkins of the RAND Corporation, cited by Bruce Hoffman, *Inside Terrorism* (New York: Columbia University Press, 1998), 198. Also, see Hoffman, "The Myth of Grass-Roots Terrorism," *Foreign Affairs*, 87, no. 3 (May/June 2008), which criticizes Marc Sageman's view that al Qaeda has been decimated and no longer is a global threat.

63 See Graham Allison, *Nuclear Terrorism* (New York: Times Books, 2004).

64 Robert O. Keohane and Joseph S. Nye, *Power and Interdependence* (Boston, MA: Little, Brown, 1977), 19. Also see Stephen D. Krasner, "Structural Causes and Regime Consequences: Regimes As Intervening Variables," in Stephen D. Krasner, ed., *International Regimes* (Ithaca, NY: Cornell University Press, 1983).

65 Louis Henkin, *How Nations Behave*, 2nd edn (New York: Columbia University Press, 1979), 146. John F. Murphy, "Force and Arms," in Christopher C. Joyner, ed., *The United Nations and International Law* (Cambridge: Cambridge University Press, 1997), 102, supports Henkin.

66 Joseph S. Nye, "What New World Order?" *Foreign Affairs*, 71, no. 2 (Spring 1992): 90.

67 Maryann K. Cusimano, ed., *Beyond Sovereignty*, 4th edn (New York: St. Martin's Press, 2011), 4.

68 Arend and Beck, *International Law and the Use of Force*, 5 and 69.

69 William C. Banks, *New Battlefields/Old Laws: Critical Debates on Asymmetric Warfare* (New York: Columbia University Press, 2011), 4–5.

70 In addition to ibid., see Arimatsu, "Spatial Conceptions"; and David Wippman and Matthew Evangelista, eds, *New Wars, New Laws?: Applying Laws of War in 21st Century Conflicts* (Ardsley, NY: Transnational, 2005).

71 Joseph A. Camilleri and Jim Falk, *The End of Sovereignty?* (London: Edwin Elgar, 1992); Richard O'Brien, *Global Financial Integration: The End of Geography* (London: Pinter, 1992). The "mothball" quote is from Nicholas Negroponte, cited in Keith Shimko, *International Relations: Perspectives and Controversies*, 2nd edn (Boston, MA: Houghton Mifflin, 2007), 215; the "nation-state era is over" quote is from Anthony Giddens, cited in Shimko, *International Relations*, 216.

72 For a counterpoint to the writings in Note 71, see Paul Kennedy, "The Future of the Nation-State," in his *Preparing for the Twenty-First Century* (New York: Vintage, 1993); and Stephen D. Krasner, "Sovereignty," *Foreign Policy* 122 (January/February 2001): 68–74.

73 Quoted in "An Interview With John Yoo," accessed January 10, 2014 at www.press. uchicago.edu/Misc/Chicago/960315.html. See Yoo's *War By Other Means* (New York: Atlantic Monthly Press, 2006).
74 Cited in Michiko Kakutani, "What Torture Is and Isn't: A Hard-Liner's Argument," *New York Times*, October 31, 2006.
75 Arimatsu, "Spatial Conceptions," 186.

PART 2

The Laws of War

What Are the Rules?

On *jus ad bellum*:

> When the UN Charter was written, it established an organization that was given a host of specific tasks, the most important of which was the maintenance of peace and security... . It set forth specific rules intended to regulate the behavior of states, especially with respect to the use of force. ... Article 2(4) establishes a general *proscription* on both the actual use of force and the threat to use such force. It outlaws not only recourse to "war" ... but any use of force that is against the territorial integrity or political independence of another state.
>
> Anthony Clark Arend and Robert Beck, *International Law and the Use of Force*

> Building on our evolved understanding of sovereignty, R2P [the "responsibility to protect"] asserts that when states cannot or will not protect their populations from the worst crimes, other states, acting through the UN, should do so... . We must be ready to use all means ... to protect populations from genocide, ethnic cleansing, war crimes and crimes against humanity. It also means that, as a last resort, the international community will be prepared to take collective action, including military force, through the Security Council.
>
> Kofi Annan, former UN Secretary-General, in a speech in April 2012

On *jus in bello*:

They can try to kill me, and I can try to kill them. But it is wrong to cut the throats of their wounded or to shoot them down when they are trying to surrender. These judgments are clear enough, I think, and they suggest that war is still, somehow, a rule-governed activity, a world of permissions and prohibitions – a moral world, therefore, in the midst of hell.

Michael Walzer, *Just and Unjust Wars*

Although some of the [international humanitarian] law is immensely detailed, its foundational principles are simple: the wounded and sick, POWS and civilians are to be protected, military targets must be attacked in such a manner as to keep civilian casualties and damage to a minimum; ... and the use of certain weapons ... is prohibited, as also are other means and methods of warfare that cause unnecessary suffering.

Adam Roberts, "Counter-Terrorism, Armed Force
and the Laws of War," *Survival*, 44

On *jus post bellum*:

[Endgames] have received far less attention than other phases of war. A few books look at the ends of individual wars, and there is a small academic literature on what political scientists call war termination. But in general, endgames have been as neglected by scholars as they have been by policymakers.

Gideon Rose, *How Wars End: Why We
Always Fight the Last Battle*

2

ON STARTING A WAR

The United Nations Charter and Other *Jus Ad Bellum* Rules

This chapter examines the historical development and current status of international law aimed at restricting the resort to the use of armed force in relations between nations *(jus ad bellum)*. The next chapter will examine the historical development and present state of international law pertaining to the kinds of actions that are allowed once an armed conflict is underway, regardless of how it commenced *(jus in bello)*. If the rules limiting the onset of war were fully effective, there would be little need for rules governing what one can or cannot do during wartime.

Historical Efforts to Regulate the Outbreak of War Before 1945

Prior to 1648

Throughout history there have been attempts to regulate the outbreak of war, going at least as far back as the "**just war**" position advanced by St. Augustine at the turn of the fifth century and the teachings of the Catholic Church in medieval Europe. Relying on "natural law," Christian theologians drew no distinction between morality and legality. This view held that the use of armed force was legitimate and legal as long as the purpose was not self-aggrandizement or petty revenge but rather correction of a major wrongdoing (and as long as the means employed were proportionate to the provocation).[1] St. Augustine wrote: "Just wars are usually defined as those which avenge injuries, when the [actor] ... against which warlike action is to be directed has neglected either to punish wrongs committed by its own citizens or to restore what has been unjustly taken by it."[2] The thirteenth century theologian St. Thomas Aquinas, in *Summa Theologica*, added that, in order for a war to be just, it not only had to have a just cause but also had to be initiated by a "proper authority"; private individuals could not start a war.

Hugo Grotius, the Dutch jurist often referred to as "the father of international law," wrote his *De Jure Belli ac Pacis* (*On the Laws of War and Peace*) in 1625, borrowing the ideas of just cause and lawful authority from the Catholic Church but grounding them in secular principles rather than faith. He died in 1645, three years before the **Peace of Westphalia** ended the Thirty Years War and gave birth to the modern state system. Prior to Westphalia, the main mode of political organization in Europe was feudalism, a crazy-quilt pattern of duchies, walled cities, kingdoms, and assorted other entities tied together in a complex web of overlapping hierarchies of authority and multiple loyalties, with the Holy Roman Emperor on much of the continent having nominal dominion over secular matters and the Pope over all religious matters. The so-called *Westphalian state system* that replaced the feudal order in Europe and eventually spread out across the globe was what we now take for granted as the natural order of things – a collection of clearly identifiable political units ("nation-states"), each with a relatively well-defined set of territorial boundaries and population over which a central government exercises sovereign rule through executive, legislative, and judicial institutions based in its national capital. By "**sovereignty**" is meant the existence of a single supreme authority that can claim the exclusive right to rule over that patch of real estate and people and that recognizes no higher authority outside those borders (whether it be the Pope or any other body).

Although there is some debate among scholars whether 1648 was the pivotal moment in the development of the state system, there is general agreement that Westphalia helped to usher in "a new diplomatic arrangement – an order created by states, for states."[3] Leo Gross, in an oft-quoted statement, went so far as to argue that the "the Peace of Westphalia, for better or worse, marks the end of an epoch and the opening of another. It represents the majestic portal which leads from the old world into the new world."[4] Although Grotius did not live to see the Peace of Westphalia, his treatise *On the Laws of War and Peace* did lay the foundation for the ongoing project of addressing the core challenge of the Westphalian system, that is, how one manages to create a degree of order (peace and security) in a decentralized system of sovereign states, what some have called the problem of "cooperation under anarchy." Grotius not only envisioned the need for a body of rules to regulate the recourse to war in the state system, but he even anticipated future debates in the twenty-first century, for example whether there is any right of "*anticipatory* self-defense." Long before the Bush Doctrine and the U.S. claiming the right to engage in the preemptive use of armed force (to be discussed later), Grotius had this to say about initiating an attack based on forestalling a supposedly imminent act of aggression by one's adversary:

> Fear with respect to a neighboring power is not a sufficient cause. For … self-defense to be lawful it must be necessary; and it is not necessary unless

we are certain, not only regarding the power of our neighbor, but also regarding his intention … . That the possibility of being attacked confers the right to attack is abhorrent to every principle of equity. Human life exists under such conditions that complete security is never guaranteed to us.[5]

Before we examine what contemporary international law has to say about self-defense and other such matters, we need to trace further the history of *jus ad bellum* between 1648 and 1945.

The Eighteenth and Nineteenth Centuries

In the eighteenth and nineteenth centuries, legal efforts were devoted more to making war a more civilized affair than to actually banishing or restricting its occurrence. (We will discuss the development of such *jus in bello* rules in the next chapter.) War became accepted as a fact of life, not a pathology to be prevented. In fact, the rise of nationalism, with mercenary armies replaced by conscript armies of citizen-soldiers expected to defend and die for their country, tended to romanticize and glorify war, making it an almost chivalrous enterprise. Under the doctrine of "**Reason of State**," grounded in the concept of sovereignty, it was the prerogative of states and their leaders to make war anytime they chose if they felt inclined to do so. There were no higher principles, derived from natural law, that rulers were bound by. Instead the "positive" law that replaced natural law at this time as the basis for legal systems owed to consent, to the will of the sovereign. The distinction between just and unjust wars became moot. As one commentator put it in 1880, "[I]nternational law has consequently no alternative but to accept war, independently of the justice of its origin, as a relation which the parties to it may set up if they choose."[6] This coincided with the view of the nineteenth-century Prussian military strategist Carl von Clausewitz, who cavalierly said that "war is policy by other means," meaning that it was merely an extension of foreign policy, just another tool in the policymaker's toolbox that could be used to further national interests, and that a leader should always keep the ultimate political objectives in mind. The only nicety that had to be followed in the event of starting a war was that the aggressor had to formally declare it so that all might know when the wartime clock started ticking, which set in motion the rupture of diplomatic relations between the parties and other legal fallout. It was still possible to have instances of "force without war," but hostilities of any sizeable nature were expected to trigger a formal declaration signifying a "state of belligerency."

In some respects, despite the matter-of-fact acceptance of war as part of the human condition, the nineteenth century was somewhat peaceful, at least in the hundred years following the Napoleonic Wars and, also, if one ignored the European conquest of much of Africa and Asia. The period between the end of the Napoleonic Wars in 1815 and the beginning of World War I in 1914 has been called by some "the century of peace," referring to the fact that there was no large, systemic war akin to the two interstate conflicts that bookended the period; there were only smaller wars, such as the Crimean War, the Franco-Prussian and Austro-Prussian Wars, and some others. The **Concert of Europe**, created at the Congress of Vienna peace conference in 1815, met periodically whenever tensions arose; it was credited with facilitating a "concert of powers" approach to world order through which the European great powers often were able to peaceably resolve their disputes over territory and other issues, partly through carving up colonies abroad, although this became harder to do as their imperialist competition heated up and World War I neared.

To the extent that laws of war applied in this period, whether *jus ad bellum* or *jus in bello*, they were considered applicable only to the nation-states that comprised "the community of nations," which generally excluded most of the peoples of Africa and other colonial areas. The latter were not seen as enjoying any sovereignty, much less entitled to the formality of a declaration of war before being seized. There were simply no rules whatsoever governing "**non-international armed conflict**," whether colonial wars or civil wars and other conflicts that did not fit neatly into the Westphalian order. This "state-centric" focus of international law would continue into the twentieth century, even after World War I, although the Great War did change some thinking about *jus ad bellum* norms, especially whether, with the advent of "total war," humanity could afford to remain so blasé about the resort to force.

World War I, The Interwar Period, and the League of Nations (1914–1939)

Inis Claude has written that "the twentieth century [saw] the establishment of the prescription that multilateral agencies are essential to the conduct of international affairs."[7] He primarily attributes the growth of international organization in the twentieth century, particularly the creation of broad multipurpose intergovernmental organizations such as the League of Nations and the United Nations, to the scourge of war: "The organizing movement of the twentieth century can be interpreted as a reaction to the increasingly terrible consequences of armed conflict."[8] Likewise, David Kennedy, in discussing "the move to institutions" in the twentieth century, notes that the Great War (the name first given to WWI), "was a 'catalyst,' a 'crucible,' a 'sudden storm sweeping away the old order.'"[9]

The First World War lasted four years. It started in August 1914, following the assassination of Archduke Ferdinand, the heir to the Austro-Hungarian throne, by a Serbian dissident, which led to the cycle of troop mobilizations and war declarations by Austria, Germany, and Turkey on one side, pitted against Britain, France, and Russia on the other, with dozens of other countries eventually joining the fray. Even though Kaiser Wilhelm, the German leader, promised that it would be a short, relatively costless war and that "the boys would be home before the leaves fell," it was not until the autumn of 1918 that the war ended. The conflict introduced the new technologies of poisoned gas, aerial bombardment, submarine warfare, rapid-fire weapons (rifles that could fire up to 20 bullets per minute and machine guns that could fire 200 to 400 rounds per minute), and other instruments capable of producing unprecedented carnage. According to one account, "among French men who were 19 to 22 at the outbreak of the war, more than 35 percent were buried by its end."[10] "The war caused the political, economic, and human ruin of Europe. The flower of its youth died in the trenches: one million British, 1.3 million French, two million Germans, two million Russians, and hundreds of thousands of Italians, Turks, Romanians, Bulgarians, Americans and others."[11] As noted earlier, this did not count civilian fatalities, nor those who were wounded.

Although World War I did not sweep away the old order – it failed to prevent another world war from beginning within one generation later – the scale of destruction did at least cause leaders to make the first explicit attempt to *outlaw* war and, in the process, to revive the "just war" tradition, however modest the effort and however unsuccessful it proved to be. The **League of Nations Covenant**, produced by the Paris Peace Conference in 1919, was eventually ratified by 73 countries, representing most of the international system at the time. A notable exception was the United States, which despite pleadings by President Woodrow Wilson, who had been among the leading champions of the League, refused to become a party due to the preference of the American public and the U.S. Senate to "return to normalcy" (to the traditional isolationism and unilateralism that had characterized much of American foreign policy since the founding of the country).

The Covenant contained a modest prohibition against war, stating (in Article 12) that the only obligation of member states to refrain from the recourse to armed force was that (1) they at least submit all disputes "likely to lead to a rupture" to "arbitration or judicial settlement or to enquiry by the [League] Council" and (2) they exhaust all such peaceful settlement procedures and "in no case resort to war until three months after the award by the arbitrators or the judicial decision or the report of the Council." In effect, even though the Covenant (in Article 10) provided that "the Members of the League undertake to respect and preserve as against external aggression the territorial integrity and existing political independence of all Members of the League," all that was mandated was a cooling-off period. Member states that did not observe this requirement were to be subject to collective sanctions by the League, a threat that failed to deter or punish acts of aggression in the interwar period, such as Italy's attack on Ethiopia in 1935, which was met with only half-hearted economic penalties ("a brief boycott of Italian-made shoes").[12] The Covenant only referred to "war" and did not address situations short of war.

In addition to the League Covenant, another attempt in the Interwar Period to restrict the recourse to war was the 1928 General Treaty for the Renunciation of

War (also known as the **Kellogg-Briand Pact**), also ratified by almost every nation at the time, including the United States. (Technically, it is still in force today, with almost 70 parties.) It contained a more ambitious denunciation of war than the Covenant, but one with even less teeth. It proclaimed that "the parties solemnly declare ... that they condemn recourse to war ... and renounce it as an instrument of national policy" and that "the settlement of all disputes ... shall never be sought except by pacific means." The Pact was silent as to whether the use of force in "self-defense" or in the service of the League was permissible or not. Such a blanket proscription against the use of armed force proved to be a wholly naïve, hollow, pious statement. Nonetheless, the treaty was used as a basis for charging Germany and other Axis Powers with violations of international law during World War II.

World War II and the United Nations Charter

As devastating as World War I was, it paled by comparison with World War II, in which some 60 million people (soldiers and civilians) perished, three times as many as in the First World War, amounting to roughly 3 percent of the world population at the time. Although the Axis Powers (Germany under Adolph Hitler, Italy under Benito Mussolini, and Japan under Emperor Hirohito) had been engaged in aggressive behavior throughout the Interwar Period, World War II did not begin until Germany's invasion of Poland in September 1939, which caused Britain and France to declare war on Germany. The Soviet Union, which under Josef Stalin had signed a Non-Aggression Pact with Germany, did not enter the war until Hitler ignored the agreement and German forces invaded the USSR in June 1941. The United States entered the war following the Japanese attack on Pearl Harbor in December 1941, resulting in the United States declaring war on Japan, followed by Germany and Italy declaring war on the United States. All told, over 60 countries – virtually the entire state system – participated in the war, which lasted until Japan's formal surrender on the *USS Missouri* on September 2, 1945, shortly after the dropping of two atomic bombs on Hiroshima and Nagasaki.

The Allied Powers, led by the United States and Great Britain, called themselves the "United Nations," with the name suggested by President Franklin Roosevelt and first mentioned in the United Nations Declaration signed by the Allies in 1942. The U.S. State Department had produced a full first draft of the **UN Charter** by 1943, while the war was still raging and the ultimate victory was far from secured.[13] Even as the war was still going on in both Europe and Asia, delegates from 50 nations met in San Francisco on April 25 to negotiate a final draft of the Charter, which was signed on June 26. By October 24, the document had been ratified by a majority of the signatory states, thus officially bringing the Charter into force and the **United Nations** into existence. Over the next several decades, the membership of the United Nations would almost quadruple, reaching 193 states by 2014.

It was understood that signing and ratifying a treaty such as the UN Charter created legal obligations for member states. What exactly did the Charter commit the UN membership to?[14]

Building on the League of Nations and seeking to learn from its failure, the founders of the United Nations sought in the Charter to specify more clearly the proscription against the use of armed force in international relations and to provide stronger enforcement machinery should the norm be violated. Chapter 1, in Article 1 (1), plainly notes that the primary purpose of the organization is "to maintain peace and security" and "to take effective collective measures" toward that end. As noted earlier, under Article 2 (4), all members are obligated to "refrain ... from the threat or use of force against the territorial integrity or political independence of any state." Here the Charter borrowed language from the League Covenant. However, where the Charter differed is that *any first use of armed force* by one state against another state – no matter how limited or whenever undertaken for whatever purpose – constitutes aggression and is illegal. Indeed, the Charter broadened the general proscription to include even the *threat* to use force. The prohibition of aggression is now considered a "peremptory norm" (*jus cogens*) that no state can opt out of.

In lieu of armed force, Chapter VI, Article 33 of the Charter urges "pacific settlement of disputes" through such mechanisms as mediation, arbitration, and adjudication, including the International Court of Justice (World Court) which was established as a new judicial body by the ICJ Statute attached to the Charter. Force may be used legally only under the following two conditions: (1) in *self-defense* by an individual state or alliance of states (such as NATO) in response to an armed attack by another state; or (2) in the service of the United Nations as part of a *collective security* operation or other operations approved by the UN Security Council. (There is a third possibility – in the service of a regional security organization [such as the Arab League or Organization of American States] as long as it is approved by the Security Council – but this generally is subsumed under the second condition.)

Regarding the first condition above, Chapter VII, Article 51 states: "Nothing in the present Charter shall impair the inherent right of individual or collective self-defense if an armed attack occurs against a Member of the United Nations." In other words, if you are attacked, you have a legal right to use force to defend yourself. Regarding the second condition above, even if you are not attacked but another member of the UN is attacked, you may use armed force as part of a UN-authorized coalition against the aggressor. Chapter VII gives expression to the "collective security" concept that was pioneered by the League of Nations, but it contains more elaborate language and more detailed implementation procedures. Article 39 empowers the Security Council to "determine the existence of any threat to the peace, breach of the peace, or act of aggression" and then to "decide what measures" should be taken to address the situation. What constitutes "aggression" was left vague, a "breach of the peace" vaguer, and a "threat to the peace" even more so.

Articles 41 and 42 refer to the possible use of economic as well as military sanctions against violators of the Charter and are followed by further articles providing for a Military Staff Committee and other machinery. Articles 42 and 43 state that "should the Security Council consider that [economic and non-military sanctions] ... would be inadequate ... , it may take such action by air, sea, or land forces as may be necessary" and that "All Members of the United Nations ... undertake to make available to the Security Council ... armed forces." Decisions taken by the Security Council under Chapter VII are binding on the entire membership. It remained to be seen how military forces would be organized, commanded, and paid for.

There was much fanfare and euphoria surrounding the creation of the United Nations. Understandably, out of the ashes of a global war, world leaders thought, or at least hoped, they were creating a new world order. President Harry Truman, who assumed the American presidency after Roosevelt's death two weeks before the San Francisco Conference convened, opened the conference with the bold prediction that the delegates were about to construct "machinery which will make future peace not only possible, but certain."[15] Former U.S. Secretary of State Cordell Hull proclaimed, "There will no longer be need for spheres of influence, for alliances, for balances of power, or any other of the special arrangements through which, in the unhappy past, the nations strove to safeguard their security or to promote their interests."[16]

Alas, idealism mixed with realism, in particular the self-serving assumption on the part of the United States and the other major winners of World War II who designed the organization that collective security would be implemented primarily through the leadership of a handful of great powers. Only five countries – the United States, Russia, China, Britain, and France – are given permanent seats, with veto power, on the **UN Security Council**, the body charged with the main responsibility for peace and security, including authorizing collective security under Chapter VII. (The Council has 15 member states, the "Perm Five" along with 10 other states serving two-year terms on a rotating basis. The Chinese seat originally held by Taiwan has been occupied by the People's Republic of China since 1971.) Whereas Security Council resolutions under Chapter VII are binding on all UN members, most resolutions passed by the General Assembly – the plenary body in which each state has one vote and decisions are taken by majority rule – are nonbinding. Like the weather, the General Assembly could talk about war and peace issues, but couldn't do much about them.

From the start, collective security suffered from several questionable premises: (1) that, although the veto privilege (i.e., the need for Perm Five unanimity) invited gridlock, great power unity would enable the Security Council to avoid paralysis and act when necessary; (2) that alignments would remain sufficiently flexible and alliance commitments unencumbered to permit the mobilization of grand coalitions against aggressors; (3) that it would be relatively simple to define aggression and assign culpability; and (4) that a grand coalition could be formed that would invariably be superior to any aggressors' forces, thus successfully deterring the illegal use of force – what potential aggressor would dare risk taking on the entire world? – or punishing it when it occurred. The Cold War shattered any hopes of great power unity. The other premises met with their own contradictions. The most fundamental problem was that veto power meant that not only could any one of the Perm Five block the ability of the Security Council to enforce the collective security provisions of Chapter VII against other states, but Chapter VII in effect could never be invoked against any of The Five themselves. If the Perm Five were the self-appointed policemen and guardians of world order, who would police the policemen?

However unfair the governing arrangements may seem, they have been agreed to by much of the international community. The Charter contains rules that continue to operate and represent legal obligations, however unjust they are. The *jus ad bellum* rules themselves, in banning the first use of armed force for any reason, in essence gave preference to the preservation of *peace* more than the attainment of *justice*. The "just war" doctrine of earlier eras had allowed the use of force to right a wrong – to resort to force if there was a "just cause." But after World War II, the craving for peace (and the desire of the victorious powers to maintain the status quo) overrode any claims about justice, as the use of force was forbidden even if aimed at promoting "human rights" or "self-determination," or as a reprisal to punish the perpetrator of some harm, or whatever struck one as morally justified. The only exceptions permitted were self-defense and collective security, in response to "a threat to the peace, a breach of the peace, or an act of aggression."

Having provided a description of the formal rules governing *jus ad bellum* embodied in the United Nations Charter, we now turn to an examination of how these rules have functioned in practice and have evolved over time, including the extent to which they have or have not been complied with. We will want to see especially how the changing nature of warfare has posed challenges to the "Charter paradigm."

The Evolution of *Jus Ad Bellum* Rules Since 1945: Principle and Practice

There have been very few amendments to the UN Charter since its inception, so there has been virtually no change in the formal rules we just reviewed. Even if the world has changed a great deal since 1945, the Charter has not. However, international law evolves over time, not only through treaty law but also **customary** **law** – state *practice*. Customary law is considered a source of international law no less than treaties. Customary rules of international law are those practices that have been widely accepted as legally binding by states over a period of time as evidenced by repeated usage. They are not written down, unless codified in treaty form; but they nonetheless are understood to constitute rules that prescribe conduct and regulate behavior. There is some disagreement over what percentage of states in the international system must support a customary practice before it can be said to constitute a rule of international law, although it is assumed that the practice must be nearly universal. There is also some debate over whether, if a practice is nearly universal, it is thus binding on all states or whether the few holdouts (as sovereign states) can continue to reject the rule.

Admittedly, as vague as treaty language can be at times, custom tends to suffer from even more ambiguity in terms of both the content of the law and how many states have consented to observe the rule. The challenge is to determine what *evidence* exists – in the form of what governments say (in their official statements) and, more importantly, what they *do* (in their actual behavior) – to support the rule in question and demonstrate it has in fact become "law." An example commonly cited to illustrate the workings of customary law is the state practice that developed in the immediate aftermath of the first satellite being put into orbit around Earth on October 4, 1957, the Sputnik spacecraft launched by the Soviet Union. The fact that no state protested this as a violation of its air space, and hence there was general acquiescence to the claim by the USSR that they had the right to place satellites over the territory of other states, effectively created customary law on this subject. Of course, there was no treaty law in existence that applied to outer space at the time, so there was no tension between the new customary rule and already existing rules.

In contrast, we have seen how in the peace and security area the UN Charter established a substantial set of rules presumed to be binding as treaty law. What happens when, due to new developments, states start engaging in practices that may be at odds with the treaty or at least create tensions with the treaty requirements? A time-honored principle in international law is *pacta sunt servanda* – treaties are to be obeyed, once a state becomes a party. In other words, if state practice increasingly conflicts with the treaty, we do not conclude that customary law trumps treaty law but rather that international law is being violated often and is in need of strengthening. What has been the record of compliance with the UN Charter?

Since 1945, the United Nations has evidenced a very mixed record in terms of compliance with the provisions relating to the use of armed force. Between 1945 and 1990, in only a few cases did the promise of collective security come close to being fulfilled, most notably in the Korean War in 1950 (when the United Nations responded to North Korean aggression against South Korea) and the First Gulf War in 1990 (when the United Nations responded to Iraq's aggression against Kuwait). These cases were unusual, however – made possible in the first instance by the Soviet Union's absence from Council proceedings (due to Moscow's protesting the seating of the Nationalist Chinese in place of the Communist Chinese, rendering the USSR unable to cast a veto against UN action) and in the second instance by Iraq's extraordinarily brazen, unprecedented attempt to eliminate another UN member, coupled with the momentary unity of the Perm Five in the immediate post–Cold War era (with China agreeing to abstain rather than veto authorization of force). Even these two cases did not represent collective security in the full sense. In the Korean case, the Council (through Resolutions 83 and 84) technically only recommended that members provide military assistance in a united command, which was permitted to use the UN flag and whose commander was to be selected by the United States. In the Kuwait case, the Council (through Resolution 678) merely authorized member states to "use all necessary means" to "restore international peace and security in the area," contracting out to the United States and any other willing partners the job of repelling Iraqi aggression, with no clear instruction as to how much direction would occur through the UN itself. In addition to these two cases, mandatory economic sanctions were authorized under Chapter VII on two occasions during the Cold War – against Rhodesia in 1966 and against South Africa in 1977 – both involving white minority apartheid regimes thought to pose a "threat to the peace."

During the Cold War, between 1946 and 1989, over 250 vetoes were cast on the UN Security Council, often frustrating the capacity of the organization to act. For the first 20 years, the Soviet Union was responsible for 90 percent of the vetoes; in the 1970s and the 1980s, it was the United States that most frequently resorted to the veto, as it often was in disagreement with the Third World bloc of countries that had gained numerical influence in the UN following decolonialization. However, with the end of the Cold War, the Security Council became somewhat more functional. Between 1990 and 2000, only about a dozen or so vetoes were cast, while over 600 resolutions were passed (an average of 64 a year), compared with an average of 14 a year over the entire previous history of the organization. There were more frequent meetings as well, some years numbering as many as 200–300 sessions. While there had been only a couple dozen resolutions specifically taken under Chapter VII before 1990, there have been over 150 such resolutions since.[17] Since 1990, in over two dozen instances a variety of military and economic sanctions have been authorized. Partial trade bans (e.g., on technology transfers) and travel bans (e.g., overseas aviation) have been implemented against such states as Libya, Haiti, Iraq, the former Yugoslavia, Somalia, North Korea, and Iran, and even nonstate actors such as rebel groups in Sierra Leone and other African countries. Military force as well has been authorized in Bosnia, East Timor, Libya, Haiti, and other hotspots.

Still, the success of the UN role in collective security must not be exaggerated, given both the questionable effectiveness of the sanctions in some cases (e.g., as punishment for North Korea's and Iran's development of nuclear weapons in violation of the Nuclear Nonproliferation Treaty) and their total absence in other cases (e.g., UN inability to punish U.S. aggression against Iraq in 2003 and Russia's invasion of Georgia in 2008 and the Ukraine in 2014). Despite some positive trends in the post–Cold War era, the Security Council continues to fall short of the hopes of its architects, most recently experiencing divisiveness over a number of issues, including whether to authorize action to address the civil war in Syria;

as one newspaper headline put it in 2011, "With Rare Double UN Veto on Syria, Russia and China Try to Shield Friend."[18]

It was precisely the failure of Chapter VII that resulted in a creative alternative that came to be known as "peacekeeping." **Peacekeeping** is an innovation that was never mentioned in the UN Charter, i.e., it is a practice that has no legal basis in the Charter, falling somewhere between the peaceful settlement procedures provided for in Chapter VI and the collective security role envisioned in Chapter VII. Often labeled the "Chapter VI ½" action, peacekeeping goes far beyond a mediating role yet falls far short of collective security. Peacekeepers – the so-called "blue helmets," who are usually unarmed – are typically sent by the UN Security Council into conflict zones to support and monitor cease-fire lines and facilitate conflict termination, intended to provide a neutral military presence and buffer between belligerents rather than punish an aggressor. They cannot be dispatched to the soil of the conflicting parties without their consent and can be ordered out at any time the host countries desire.

Peacekeeping missions have ranged from the 224 observers sent to the Sinai to supervise the uneasy truce following the first Arab–Israeli war in 1948 (UNTSO) and the 40 observers placed on the India–Pakistan border during the conflict over Kashmir in 1949 (UNMOGIP), to the 6,000 soldiers sent to the Middle East during the Suez crisis of 1956 (UNEF, which was the first major deployment of UN peacekeeping troops) and the 2,000 soldiers sent to maintain the cease-fire in the Cyprus civil war in 1964 (UNFYCIP), to the 22,000 troops sent to the former Yugoslavia during the Bosnian conflict in 1992 (UNPROFOR) and the 26,000 authorized to go to Sudan in 2008 to deter further bloodshed in Darfur (UNAMID, jointly mounted with the African Union and constituting the largest peacekeeping operation in UN history). The end of the Cold War saw an explosion of peacekeeping operations, as there were more peacekeeping missions authorized between 1988 and 1992 than in the entire previous history of the UN, with peacekeepers in Afghanistan, Angola, Namibia, Nicaragua, El Salvador, Cambodia, and elsewhere. Peacekeeping has remained an important UN function. As of 2015, the UN had 16 different peacekeeping operations worldwide, totaling over 100,000 troops, police, and civilian personnel drawn from over 100 countries, with a budget of more than $8 billion.[19]

As the post–Cold War era has worn on, peacekeeping has taken on a more expansive meaning, morphing frequently into "peace enforcement" and "peacebuilding." As with peacekeeping, these terms are not mentioned in the UN Charter. **Peace enforcement** has been labeled by some as "Chapter VI ¾," because it refers to the use of armed force by UN military personnel who, as in Somalia in 1992, may have arrived on the scene as neutral peacekeepers but, being fired on by governmental or rebel forces and prevented from carrying out their mission, are then cast into what amounts to a collective security role of punishing violators of the UN Charter. **Peacebuilding** refers to helping to create, following the conclusion of a conflict, the conditions necessary for a long-term, durable peace, such as rebuilding bridges and infrastructure, removing land mines, managing refugee repatriation, as well as developing police and judicial institutions and conducting democratic elections, often in societies that have never experienced democracy and that in some instances are failed states teetering on anarchy.[20]

Where does this leave us in evaluating the extent to which the *jus ad bellum* rules contained in the UN Charter have been working, or whether they are at variance with state practice? I have noted that the UN record in the war and peace area since 1945 has been mixed. The fact that there has been such an apparent need for peacekeeping, peace enforcement, peacebuilding, and the like might suggest how deficient the Charter proscription against the use of armed force has been. However, some scholars have offered empirical evidence indicating that the UN's performance may be better than generally thought, especially in the recent past and if one takes a broad view of effectiveness. A Rand Corporation study of "major UN-led nation-building operations from 1945 to the present" concludes that the UN was successful in two-thirds of the cases studied; successes included Namibia (1989–1990), El Salvador (1991–1996), Cambodia (1991–1993), Mozambique (1992–1994), Sierra Leone (1999), and East Timor (1999); failures included, most notably, the Congo (1960–1964).[21] As another study, *Human Security Report*, noted (in keeping with the trend data on warfare cited in the first chapter), "the number of armed conflicts around the world declined by more than 40 percent" after 1990, at least partly because "with the Security Council no longer paralyzed by Cold War politics, the UN spearheaded a veritable explosion of conflict prevention, peacemaking, [peacekeeping], and post-conflict peace-building activities."[22]

Regarding interstate war in particular, recall Louis Henkin's contention that the United Nations has been "reasonably effective in addressing [the] kinds of conflicts that Article 2 [of the Charter] aimed to regulate."[23] Commenting on the growing respect for "the territorial integrity norm" since 1945, Mark Zacher has noted that, while territorial conquest has been a commonplace occurrence throughout much of the history of the Westphalian state system, the last successful use of armed force for purposes of territorial annexation was Morocco's seizure of the Spanish Sahara in 1976.[24] One could argue that what made it possible for U.S. President George H. W. Bush to use the United Nations to mobilize a near-universal collective security coalition against Iraq when it attacked Kuwait in the First Gulf War in 1990 was Saddam Hussein's defiance of what had become an almost sacred norm since 1945, the principle that it is unacceptable to eliminate another UN member; perhaps if Saddam had been willing to settle for a sliver of Kuwait or for installing a puppet, satellite government there, he might have had more success. (As of this writing, it is unclear how Russia's takeover of the Crimea in the Ukraine will play out, although one reason it attracted such international attention in 2014 was the rarity of such behavior in recent times, reflected in U.S. Secretary of State John Kerry's angry response that "you just don't in the 21st century behave in 19th-century fashion." It seemed the exception that proved the rule.)

A contrary view is expressed by Michael Glennon, who argues that state practice – in effect, customary law – has superseded the UN Charter, that states may mouth support for Article 2 (4) but in fact regularly ignore it in their actual conduct, and that the proscription against the first use of armed force has "collapsed" as "the rules of the Charter do not today constitute binding restraints on intervention by states."[25] He bases his conclusion on a few empirical studies showing numerous military interventions since 1945, including a study by Herbert Tillema that counted 690 "overt foreign military interventions" between 1945 and 1996.[26] Glennon relies heavily on the legal concept of *desuetude* – the notion that "laws may be abrogated ... by passive agreement through custom."[27] How can expert observers such as Henkin and Glennon be so divergent in their assessment of the status of the current "rules on the books" that regulate the resort to armed force? The explanation is that they seem to be comparing apples and oranges, with Henkin referencing pure interstate wars and Glennon, in contrast, focusing much of his attention on external intervention in civil wars. Not surprisingly, given the state-centric character of the Charter, the application of the Charter's *jus ad bellum* rules has proven much more problematic in the latter category of disputes, in civil wars, especially when intrastate violence intermingles with interstate violence (and at times extrastate violence). As Glennon himself states, "Law cannot regulate acts that it is unable to place in categories ... . If use of force is to be made subject to law, we must be able to sort it into categories."[28]

If Glennon overstates the "collapse" of the Charter in failing to acknowledge its continued relevance in regulating traditional interstate armed conflict, he is much closer to the truth in calling attention to the Charter's inadequacy in identifying and regulating other categories of conflict, the kinds that we have noted have become more prevalent and that pose "challenges to the Charter paradigm."

What Rules Apply to Civil Wars?

Traditionally, international law has been primarily concerned with "international armed conflict," not "non-international armed conflict." Civil wars have fallen into the latter category and have been on the periphery of international law. After World War II, "**wars of national liberation**," in which rebels seeking self-determination fought wars of independence against Britain, France, and other colonial powers, did not fit neatly into either category; the rebels insisted these conflicts were "international" in character, while the colonial powers did not want to legitimize these struggles by agreeing they were covered under international law. With the decolonialization process having run its course, "wars of national liberation" for the most part have lost their relevance. Still, the distinction between "international" and "non-international" armed conflict remains fuzzy and has become increasingly so as interstate and instrastate violence have blended together.

The contemporary rules governing the outbreak of hostilities have been inadequate to cope with internal wars and mixed internal–external conflicts (involving outside intervention).[29] During the Cold War, to the extent that the United Nations became involved in such conflicts, the organization usually relied on the vague "threat to the peace" phrase in Article 39 as legal justification for taking action. It was always hard, and still is difficult, to sort out the obligations that international actors have in situations of civil strife, partly because what international law exists in this area is based mostly on customary law open to varying interpretations and partly because of the inherent complexities of these situations. The general, traditional norm has been nonintervention in the affairs of other countries, reflected in the UN General Assembly's adopting the Declaration on the Inadmissibility of Intervention in the Domestic Affairs of States and the Protection of their Individual Sovereignty; adopted in 1966, as a nonbinding resolution, the Declaration, at best, is what is called "soft law."

In these sorts of conflicts, it is often the case that, rather than one state engaging in an armed attack on another state, there is a government seeking foreign support to quell a rebellion or a rebel group seeking foreign support to overthrow a government. The rules governing the right of a state to intervene militarily in an internal conflict in another state are fairly straightforward: the former can intervene as long as it has the permission of the latter's government but, otherwise, cannot. The intrusion of foreign troops or clandestine agents in a domestic conflict on the side of the rebels to subvert an established government constitutes aggression and is a violation of the UN Charter. However, foreign military assistance cannot be provided to a government on the brink of collapse either, because a government has a legal right to invite such assistance only if it can claim to exercise effective control and authority over its population. The problem, of course, is that this is the very condition that is often in dispute during a civil war. The rules failed to regulate the insurgency–counterinsurgency dance of the United States and the Soviet Union during the Cold War. They continue to be plagued by difficulties in the post–Cold War era, made all the more vexing with the emergent norm of "humanitarian intervention."

What Rules Apply to Humanitarian Intervention?

It has been noted that foreign involvement in civil wars in the post–Cold War era frequently has taken the form of "**humanitarian intervention**." Has humanitarian intervention been added to the list of conditions under which a state can resort to armed force?

The so-called Clinton Doctrine stated that "if somebody comes after innocent civilians and tries to kill them *en masse* because of their race, ethnic background, or religion, and it's within our power to stop it, we will stop it."[30] Although couched more in terms of legal authority than power, UN Secretary-General Kofi Annan appeared to endorse this same principle when he said that the protection of human rights must "take precedence over concerns of state sovereignty," that sovereignty cannot provide "excuses for the inexcusable," and that the UN Charter "was issued in the name of 'the peoples,' not the governments of the United Nations."[31] The traditional view is that international law grants "no right unilaterally to charge into another country to save its people from their own leaders."[32] But what about *multilateral* intervention, an action taken by the international community at large, triggered by either ethnic cleansing or other atrocities committed by a dictatorial regime (as in the case of the 1992 UN-authorized intervention to protect Bosnians in the former Yugoslavia) or the collapse of civil order and the spread of starvation and suffering in failed states (as in the case of the UN-authorized intervention in Somalia that same year)? If the international community waits for an invitation before acting in these situations, a humanitarian response may be impossible because no repressive regime would welcome external oversight in the first case, and there would be no functioning regime able to issue the invitation in the second case.

Although nowhere does the UN Charter mention "humanitarian intervention," Kofi Annan argued that the international community not only had a right to act in such situations but had a **"responsibility to protect,"** what quickly became known as the **"R2P"** doctrine. Annan was giving voice to the principle first articulated by the Canadian-sponsored International Commission on Intervention and State Sovereignty in 2001, and endorsed by a majority of UN members in a General Assembly vote in 2005. There is a widely held view that "humanitarian military intervention now must be multilateral to be legitimate,"[33] and presumably must be authorized by the Security Council; yet international law is not entirely clear on this point. As William Slomanson notes, "The permissible contours of humanitarian intervention have not been defined in a way that represents a meaningful State consensus. An essential reason is that ... neither word has been precisely defined."[34] What remains debatable, for example, is when humanitarian intervention can go beyond protecting civilians from harm and, in addition, can force regime change – removing the government in power, as happened with Libyan dictator Muammar Gaddafi during the Libya civil war in 2011; not all parties on the Security Council that voted for the resolution authorizing military intervention to stop the slaughter intended for the mandate to include regime change and were upset when it occurred.

Indeed, many critics of R2P have raised concerns that humanitarian intervention threatens Westphalian ordering arrangements insofar as it represents a frontal assault on sovereignty. In particular, critics argue that it is at odds with the UN Charter, in that it contradicts Article 2 (7), which stipulates that "nothing contained in the Charter shall authorize the United Nations to interfere in matters which are essentially within the domestic jurisdiction of any state." Although Article 2 (7) adds that "this principle shall not prejudice the application of enforcement measures under Chapter VII," many UN members have expressed fears that such language is an invitation for Security Council members to meddle in the domestic affairs of smaller, weaker states.[35] Of greatest concern is a state or group of states using the R2P norm as a pretext to bring about regime change without any UN approval, as happened with the NATO bombing of Serbia in 1999 that ended the ethnic cleansing of Kosovo along with the reign of Serb leader Slobodan Milosevic. The 114 members of the Non-Aligned Movement, representing the developing nations, have condemned such intervention, declaring it has "no legal basis under the Charter."[36]

We will examine the Kosovo case later in some detail. Humanitarian intervention became a heated issue during the Syrian civil war that began in 2011, with some commentators arguing that the atrocities inflicted by the Assad regime were so massive – over 150,000 civilian casualties, including 1,300 people killed by chemical weapons, and over a million displaced persons – that the United States or any other state, even without Security Council approval, would have a moral right, if not legal right, to intervene militarily.[37] (Recall the news headlines in Chapter 1, "Bomb Syria, Even If It Is Illegal" and "Use Force to Save Starving Syrians.") The theory and practice of humanitarian intervention remains mired in controversy.

What Rules Apply to "Self-Defense" Against State and Nonstate Actors?

"Self-defense" is not defined in the UN Charter any more than is "aggression." The UN General Assembly attempted to define "aggression" in a 1974 resolution, but to little effect. The closest there is to a definitive statement of the rules governing these matters is the 1986 World Court case *Concerning Military and Paramilitary Activities In and Against Nicaragua (Nicaragua v. United States)*. The United States under the Reagan administration argued that the Marxist government that had come to power in Nicaragua in 1979 was trying to export communist revolution in the hemisphere, supporting leftist insurgents in El Salvador, Honduras, and other neighboring states in an effort to topple the pro-Western governments there. In response, the United States, invoking the right of collective self-defense under Article 51 of the UN Charter on behalf of El Salvador and Honduras, claimed it had the right not only to support rebels (the "contras") seeking to overthrow the government of Nicaragua but also mine and blow up Nicaraguan ports and harbors. Nicaragua before the World Court charged the United States with committing aggression in violation of the UN Charter. The ICJ ruled in favor of Nicaragua, finding that, although there was evidence Nicaragua had been providing some support to rebel groups in neighboring countries, the level of military support provided did not reach the level necessary as to constitute an "armed attack" on those countries sufficient to trigger the "self-defense" justification by the United States in attacking Nicaragua. "The Court emphasized that any armed attack giving rise to a right of self-defense or collective self-defense must be a significant attack. Mere border incidents could not give rise to the right of self-defense ... and the right to use force on the territory of another state."[38]

Nonetheless, "self-defense" remains a contentious term. Take, for example, Israel's frequent claims that it has a right to attack alleged Hamas terrorists in Gaza and the West Bank in response to rocket attacks on Israeli villages from the Palestinian territories, or to attack Hezbollah terrorists in Lebanon who are also accused of firing missiles at Israeli civilians; Israeli targets have included terrorist headquarters, recruitment centers, weapons convoys, munitions stockpiles, and other targets. Israel also has sent warplanes to bomb targets in Syria thought to be connected to terrorist activities, and has intercepted Turkish and Iranian cargo ships suspected of transporting weapons to militants.

Aside from the inevitable collateral damage and killing of innocent civilians that almost always accompanies Israeli raids, an issue we will take up later under *jus in bello* rules, there are several thorny *jus ad bellum* issues here. First, while Israel might characterize many of its actions as reprisals aimed both at punishing past attacks by terrorists as well as discouraging future attacks, neither reprisals nor deterrence constitute self-defense measures that are allowable under the UN Charter. Second, neither Hamas nor Hezbollah are states. (Hamas partially governs the Palestinian territories, controlling Gaza, while another Palestinian faction, Fatah, governs the West Bank. Hezbollah has been called a "substate," insofar as it exercises control over parts of Lebanon.)[39] Since the Charter mainly speaks to armed attacks by one state against another state, it is unclear what rules apply to nonstate actors, such as Hamas and Hezbollah; when Israel claims it is not attacking Lebanon or Syria but rather terrorist groups within those borders, to many it seems a distinction without a difference. Third, we have noted that there is no universally accepted definition of "terrorism" that can provide a legal basis for targeting groups thought to be engaging in acts of terrorism.

Fourth, perhaps the thorniest issue is whether there is any right of "**anticipatory self-defense**," i.e., the right to engage in the *preemptive* use of military force, in anticipation of an imminent threat. During the Six-Day War in June 1967, Israel claimed it was acting in self-defense when, faced with three Arab armies having mobilized on its border and Egypt having closed the Straits of Tiran (an international waterway) to Israeli shipping, the Israeli air force struck first, quickly defeating the Arab forces. Israel made a similar claim when, in 1981, it destroyed an Iranian nuclear reactor near Baghdad in Operation Opera, aimed at preventing the completion of what Tel Aviv insisted was an Iraqi nuclear weapons facility that could have seriously threatened Israeli security. Many observers labeled Israel the aggressor in both instances, especially in the latter case, where the threat seemed less certain or imminent.[40]

The United States has been at the center of similar controversy in recent years. The United States was clearly attacked on September 11, 2001, when airplanes struck the World Trade Center in New York City and the Pentagon in Washington, D.C. However, the attack was perpetrated not by another state but by a nonstate actor, al Qaeda. Since al Qaeda had been based in Afghanistan, whose Taliban government had harbored Osama bin Laden and his Islamic fundamentalist followers, the United States within two weeks of 9/11 launched an invasion of Afghanistan and overthrew the Taliban regime. Many international lawyers questioned whether the terrorist attacks of 9/11 qualified as an "armed attack" under Article 51, and, even if it did, whether the United States had the right to attack Afghanistan when the state itself was only indirectly involved in the attack.[41]

What rules of international law apply here? In 1985, for the first time, the United Nations formally went on record condemning terrorism; the UN General Assembly unanimously approved Resolution 40/61, which unequivocally "condemns, as criminal, all acts ... of terrorism wherever and by whoever committed" and "calls upon states to fulfill their obligations under international law to refrain from organizing, instigating, assisting, or participating in terrorist acts in other States, or acquiescing in activities within their territory directed toward the commission of such acts." The resolution attempted to define terrorism as any acts that "endanger or take innocent human lives, jeopardize fundamental freedoms, and seriously impair the dignity of human beings." However, neither the latter nor any other terminology contained in over a dozen multilateral treaties dealing with terrorism (e.g., several "anti-skyjacking" conventions as well as conventions on "suppression of terrorist bombings" and "suppression of financing of terrorism") offer an authoritative definition of terrorism.

None of the latter conventions address the question: To what extent can State A (say, the United States) enter the territory of State B (say, Afghanistan) to apprehend or kill actors (such as Osama bin Laden and his associates) thought to have been responsible for a terrorist attack on State A? Generally speaking, international law does not condone a state trespassing into another state to abduct alleged criminals or terrorists or to utilize force on that state's territory against third parties, since that would be a violation of the latter's sovereignty. One exception, however, is if the host state is unable or unwilling to exercise its "state responsibility" to prevent criminals or terrorists within its borders from harming the nationals of other states. Although state practice has been inconsistent, the general rule is that, if State B is not clearly sponsoring or harboring the terrorists but merely finds itself used as a refuge, State A cannot intrude on State B's sovereignty by engaging in military activity on its soil without its permission. On the other hand, if State B can be shown to be an active sponsor or close collaborator giving succor to the terrorists and has not taken adequate steps to prevent terrorism, then State A is on stronger legal footing in taking military action.[42]

As many legal issues as were raised by the United States attack on Afghanistan after 9/11, Washington found itself on far more questionable legal footing when it invaded Iraq in 2003. The most interesting legal argument advanced by

Washington to justify the attack was the right of "anticipatory" (*preemptive*) self-defense. Seemingly in violation of the UN Charter's ban on the first use of armed force, such a justification had been relied on by Israel in the aforementioned instances in 1967 and 1981. The "just war" tradition provides some support for this position, but clearly Grotius and other just war thinkers put the onus on the attacker to demonstrate that the resort to force was necessary. To the extent that there exists a customary right of anticipatory self-defense, the **Caroline case** is often cited for guidance. In 1837, the *Caroline*, a ship owned by U.S. nationals and docked on the American side of the Niagara River, was attacked by the British navy and sent over Niagara Falls because the British feared that the vessel would be used to support an insurrection by Canadian rebels; U.S. Secretary of State Daniel Webster, in protesting the action, stated that, for such action to be legal, it would have to be demonstrated that "the necessity of that self-defense is instant, overwhelming, and leaving no choice of means, and no moment of deliberation."[43]

In justifying its invasion of Iraq, the Bush administration claimed that there was reason to believe that Iraq under Saddam Hussein had chemical weapons and other WMDs, that it was a state sponsor of terror, and that it posed a threat to U.S. security that could not be ignored in the post-9/11 era. Bush went so far as to articulate the so-called **Bush Doctrine**, which gave the United States the right to engage in the preemptive use of armed force against any country thought to possibly pose a threat to U.S. security.[44] However, critics argued it did not meet the *Caroline* test, that it appeared to be a preventive war rather than a preemptive war, a war Washington wanted to fight rather than one it needed to fight. They pointed out that no attack by Iraq was imminent, there was no clear evidence it still possessed WMDs, and there was no clear connection between Iraq and the 9/11 terrorists. Moreover, critics worried that the Bush Doctrine was a dangerous deviation from the UN Charter that could invite and legitimize all kinds of first strikes, including, hypothetically, an attack by Pakistan against nuclear-armed India or India against nuclear-armed Pakistan.

The existential question looming over all this is whether, in an age of WMDs, a state, say the United States, must wait and absorb the first shot – which could be a radioactive bomb or anthrax or nerve gas attack on New York City or Washington – before it can legally respond in self-defense. This question and other such questions complicate the application of *jus ad bellum* rules today.

Conclusion

We will return to these questions and examine them more closely in Chapter 5, when we focus on three case studies that illustrate the problematical nature of applying *jus ad bellum* rules today (the 2003 U.S. invasion of Iraq in the Second Gulf War, the 2011 U.S. Osama bin Laden raid in Pakistan and the War on Terror, and the 1999 NATO humanitarian intervention in Kosovo). However, we first need to shift our attention from *jus ad bellum* rules to *jus in bello* rules, a subject taken up in the next chapter.

Chapter 2 Discussion Questions

1. What is meant by *jus ad bellum*?
2. Discuss the historical evolution of rules governing the resort to the use of armed force in "international armed conflict" and "non-international armed conflict," including just war theory, the League of Nations Covenant, and the United Nations Charter.
3. Today, under the United Nations Charter, what are the circumstances under which a state legally can use armed force against another state?
4. To what extent does the UN Charter permit either "anticipatory (pre-emptive) self-defense" or "humanitarian intervention" as a basis for the resort to armed force, and how have these norms complicated the workings of international law?
5. To what extent can State A enter the territory of State B to apprehend or kill actors thought to have been responsible for a terrorist attack on State A?

Notes

1 See Michael Walzer, *Just and Unjust Wars* (New York: Basic Books, 1977); and William V. O'Brien, *The Conduct of Just and Limited War* (New York: Praeger, 1981).
2 Cited in Anthony Clark Arend and Robert J. Beck, *International Law and the Use of Force* (New York: Routledge, 1993), 14. The authors draw on the work of John Norton Moore in their historical treatment of the "development of the legal norms relating to the recourse to force."
3 K.J. Holsti, *Peace and War: Armed Conflicts and International Order, 1648–1989* (Cambridge: Cambridge University Press, 1991), 25.
4 Leo Gross, "The Peace of Westphalia, 1648–1948," *American Journal of International Law*, 42 (January 1948): 28.
5 Hugo Grotius, *On the Laws of War and Peace*, Book II, Trans. by A. C. Campbell (Kitchener, Ontario: Batoche Books, 2001), Chapter 1, XVII and Chapter 22, V.
6 Cited in Arend and Beck, *International Law and the Use of Force*, 17.
7 Inis L. Claude, "The Record of International Organizations in the Twentieth Century," Tamkang Chair Lecture Series 64, Tamkang University, Taiwan, January 1986, 25 (mimeo).
8 Ibid., 2.
9 David Kennedy, "The Move to Institutions," *Cardozo Law Review*, 8 (April 1987): 852.
10 Michael Gerson, *Washington Post*, March 4, 2011.
11 David W. Ziegler, *War, Peace, and International Politics*, 4th edn (Boston, MA: Little, Brown, 1987), 20.
12 William R. Slomanson, *Fundamental Perspectives on International Law*, 3rd edn (Belmont, CA: Wadsworth, 2000), 119.
13 Stephen C. Schlesinger, *Act of Creation: The Founding of the United Nations* (Boulder, CO: Westview, 2003), 38–40.
14 On the rules governing the resort to armed force under the UN Charter, see Arend and Beck, *International Law and the Use of Force*; John F. Murphy, "Force and Arms," in

Christopher C. Joyner, ed., *The United Nations and International Law* (Cambridge: Cambridge University Press, 1997), 97–130; Gerhard von Glahn and James Taulbee, *Law Among Nations*, 8th edn (New York: Longman, 2007), Chapter 20; Oscar Schachter, "The Right of States to Use Armed Force," *Michigan Law Review*, 82 (1984): 1620–1646; Mary Ellen O'Connell, *International Law and the Use of Force* (New York: Foundation Press, 2004); and Christine Gray, *International Law and the Use of Force*, 3rd edn (New York: Oxford University Press, 2012).

15 *U.S. Department of State Bulletin*, April 29, 1945, 789.

16 Cited in Abba Eban, "The UN Idea Revisited," *Foreign Affairs*, 74, no. 5 (September/October 1995): 39–40.

17 Trend data on Security Council usage, including vetoes, resolutions, meetings, and other aspects, are reported in Peter Wallensteen and Patrik Johansson, "Security Council Decisions in Perspective," in David M. Malone, ed., *The UN Security Council: From the Cold War to the 21st Century* (Boulder, CO: Lynn Rienner, 2004), 17–33; Susan C. Hulton, "Council Working Methods and Procedures," in Malone, *The UN Security Council*, 237–251; and Linda Fasulo, *An Insider's Guide to the UN* (New Haven, CT: Yale University Press, 2004), Chapter 5.

18 *New York Times*, October 6, 2011.

19 For UN peacekeeping statistics, see the "Peacekeeping Fact Sheet" provided by the United Nations Peacekeeping homepage accessed February 5, 2014 at www.un.org/en/peacekeeping/resources/statistics/factsheet.shtml. On the positive contribution UN peacekeeping has made to conflict resolution, see Virginia Page Fortna, *Does Peacekeeping Work? Shaping Belligerents' Choices After Civil War* (Princeton, NJ: Princeton University Press, 2008).

20 In his 1992 *Agenda for Peace* report to the Security Council, UN Secretary-General Boutros Boutros-Ghali discussed a spectrum of conflict management roles the United Nations might play before hostilities, during hostilities, and post-hostilities that included peacekeeping, peace enforcement, peacebuilding, collective security, and other functions. UN Doc. S/24111, June 17, 1992.

21 James Dobbins et al., *The UN's Role in Nation-Building: From the Congo to Iraq* (Santa Monica, CA: Rand Corporation, 2005).

22 Human Security Center, *Human Security Report* (New York: Oxford University Press, 2005), 8.

23 See Note 65 in Chapter 1.

24 Mark W. Zacher, "The Territorial Integrity Norm: International Boundaries and the Use of Armed Force," *International Organization*, 55 (Spring 2001): 215–250.

25 Michael J. Glennon, *Limits of Law, Prerogatives of Power: Intervention After Kosovo* (New York: Palgrave, 2001), 84.

26 Ibid., Chapter 3 surveys empirical research on the use of armed force since 1945. The Tillema study is cited on page 69.

27 Ibid., 60.

28 Ibid., 70.

29 See Arend and Beck, *International Law and the Use of Force*, Chapter 6; Glennon, *Limits of Law*, Chapter 4; and Lori Fisler Damrosch, ed., *Enforcing Restraint: Collective Intervention in Internal Conflicts* (New York: Council on Foreign Relations, 1993).

30 Quoted in Walter McDougall, "America and the World at the Dawn of A New Century," *WIRE* 7 (December 1999).

31 Quoted in Judith Miller, "Sovereignty Isn't So Sacred Anymore," *New York Times*, April 18, 1999.

32 David J. Scheffer, "Use of Force after the Cold War," in Louis Henkin et al., eds *Right v. Might* (New York: Council on Foreign Relations Press, 1991), 144.

33 Martha Finnemore, "Constructing Norms of Humanitarian Intervention," in Peter J. Katzenstein, ed., *The Culture of National Security: Norms and Identity in World Politics* (New York: Columbia University Press, 1996), 170.

34 Slomanson, *Fundamental Perspectives on International Law*, 463.

35 On the Article 2 (7) controversy and other aspects of R2P, see Sean D. Murphy, *Humanitarian Intervention: The United Nations in An Evolving World Order* (Philadelphia: University of Pennsylvania Press, 1996); J. L. Holzgrefe and Robert O. Keohane, eds, *Humanitarian Intervention: Ethical, Legal, and Political Dilemmas* (Cambridge: Cambridge University Press, 2005); and Arend and Beck, *International Law and the Use of Force*, Chapter 8.

36 Cited in Glennon, *Limits of Law*, 158. Glennon furnishes quotations representing the official positions of many different states objecting to unilateral humanitarian intervention (159–160).

37 On the morality vs. legality of humanitarian intervention in Syria, see Michael N. Schmitt, "Legitimacy versus Legality Redux: Arming the Syrian Rebels," *Journal of National Security Law and Policy*, 7 (2014): 139–159. For a comparison of the Libya and Syria cases, see J. Craig Barker, "The Responsibility to Protect: Lessons from Libya and Syria," in Robert P. Barnidge, ed., *The Liberal Way of War* (London: Ashgate, 2013), 63–85.

38 Mary Ellen O'Connell, "The *Nicaragua* Case: Preserving World Peace and the World Court," in John E. Noyes et al., eds, *International Law Stories* (New York: Foundation Press, 2007), 340–370.

39 On "substate actors," see Michael Crawford and Jami Miscik, "The Rise of the Mezzanine Rulers," *Foreign Affairs*, 89, no. 6 (November/December 2010): 123–132.

40 In the 1967 case, John Quigley questions the Israeli legal claim of self-defense in *The Six-Day War and Israeli Self-Defense* (Cambridge: Cambridge University Press, 2012). The 1981 attack on the Iraqi nuclear reactor was condemned by the UN Security Council as a violation of the Charter.

41 See Anna Oehmichen, "Force Que Terrorism: International Law in the Wake of 9/11," in Sanford R. Silverburg, ed., *International Law: Contemporary Issues and Future Developments* (Boulder, CO: Westview Press, 2011), 448–459.

42 For a discussion of international law pertaining to terrorism, see Arend and Beck, *International Law and the Use of Force*, Chapter 9; and Zdzislaw Galicki, "International Law and Terrorism," *American Behavioral Scientist*, 48 (February 2005): 743–757.

43 On anticipatory self-defense, see Arend and Beck, *International Law and the Use of Force*, Chapter 5.

44 George W. Bush, "The National Security Strategy of the United States of America," annual report to the U.S. Congress, Washington, DC, September 2002.

3

ON CONDUCTING A WAR

The Geneva Conventions and Other *Jus In Bello* Rules

Over the centuries, humanity, having failed to ban war altogether, has attempted to make it at least more humane by regulating its conduct through agreed upon rules of engagement. Some of the efforts to inject a dose of civility into warfare have seemed paradoxical and slightly comical, such as the prohibition (embodied in the Hague Convention of 1899) against the use of "dum-dum" expanding bullets and the use of "deceit" in the form of misrepresenting a flag of truce or wearing Red Cross uniforms as a disguise – especially at a time when using poisonous gas and other horrendous weapons was legally permissible. The entire notion of humanizing war does seem oxymoronic. As General George S. Patton remarked during World War II, "[w]ar is a bloody, killing business. You've got to spill their blood, or they will spill yours."[1] However, as absurd as they might appear and as erratic as their observance has been, the laws governing the conduct of war (*jus in bello*) have often succeeded in limiting the brutal nature of war to some extent.[2]

Jus in bello rules are known as "**international humanitarian law**" as well as "the law of war" or "the law of armed conflict." The International Committee of the Red Cross has defined international humanitarian law (IHL) as the "set of rules which seek ... to limit the effects of armed conflict. It protects persons who are not or are no longer participating in the hostilities and restricts the means and methods of warfare."[3] Although IHL has had some success in civilizing warfare, it faces growing challenges today, given "the new warfare." As two writers put it in an essay entitled "Jousting at Windmills," "For almost a century, the international community has attempted to codify ... international humanitarian law. The cornerstone of this attempt to govern action on and off the battlefield was achieved in the course of the late nineteenth and twentieth centuries in the Hague and Geneva Conventions. The question today remains whether modern international humanitarian law is viable in light of changing threats posed by terrorists [and other actors]."[4] This ongoing quest to make war a less barbaric affair − it goes back well before the nineteenth and twentieth centuries − may strike some as comparable to Don Quixote's "impossible dream." Before we can take up the latest challenges to this *jus in bello* project, we need to trace the history.

Historical Efforts to Regulate the Conduct of War Before 1945

Among the first principles of IHL is the **principle of distinction** − distinguishing between *combatants*, who are fair game as targets during a conflict, and *noncombatants*, who are generally accorded special protections. Even prior to the "just war" tradition rooted in the Catholic Church teachings of St. Augustine in the fourth century and St. Thomas Aquinas in the thirteenth century and the natural law writings of Grotius in medieval Europe, "a number of ancient and widely embraced codes already required that belligerents exercise care not to kill civilians. Although each civilization expressed this requirement slightly differently, the motivation remained the same: to spare civilians from the brutality of warfare."[5] As Geoffrey Best observes, "From as far back as there is written evidence of the laws of peoples and the decrees of kings come examples of injunctions to distinguish in combat between warriors and the rest."[6] In the Old Testament (Deuteronomy) and other ancient texts, women and children were singled out as deserving of preferential treatment.

Aquinas and other Catholic theologians during the Middle Ages converted the principle of distinction from a moral obligation into a legal obligation and extended protection to peasants, merchants, and "anyone not bearing arms." It was Grotius, and later the eighteenth-century philosopher Jean-Jacques Rousseau, who developed the norm that not only noncombatants but even combatants themselves − no matter what side of a just or unjust war they were on − were entitled to compassion and decent treatment, once they were captured or laid down their arms. Most of these rules were in the form of customary law. The famous **Lieber Code**, drafted in 1863 by Union Army legal advisor Francis Lieber during the American Civil War in order to regulate treatment of prisoners and other issues, was among the first efforts to codify the laws of war; regarding the matter of distinction, it read: "All enemies in regular war are divided into two general classes … into combatants and noncombatants, or unarmed citizens of the hostile government."

As noted earlier, the nineteenth century and early twentieth century saw numerous efforts to regulate the conduct, if not the outbreak, of war. The first major multilateral treaty that attempted to regulate modern warfare was the **Declaration of Paris in 1856**, which placed restrictions on sea warfare, prohibiting privateering, circumscribing contraband goods subject to seizure, and delimiting the conditions for implementing a naval blockade against enemy coastlines. Other treaties followed, including the **Geneva Convention of 1864** for the Amelioration of the Condition of Soldiers Wounded in Armies in the Field, revised in 1906; the Hague Conventions with Respect to the Laws and Customs of War, produced by the 1899 Hague Peace Conference, covering a wide range of concerns relating to both land and sea warfare; and the landmark **1907 Hague Conventions** produced by a follow-up conference. The latter revised the 1899 rules and contained annexed Regulations which – modeled largely on the Lieber Code – were to be the basis for the laws of war during World War I and World War II, including rules governing treatment of prisoners of war (POWs). These treaties were ratified by most countries.

Although a body of rules that had been developed during the American Civil War became the foundation for much of international humanitarian law, IHL itself was presumed to apply almost exclusively to international armed conflict between the armies of sovereign states, in keeping with the state-centric assumptions of the Westphalian world order. For example, "irregular" fighters were not treated as combatants entitled to POW status but could be shot as spies, saboteurs, or other "unprivileged belligerents." The **Martens Clause** in the 1899 Hague Convention II attempted to address the issue. Corri Zoli describes the nature of the debate that occurred at the time:

> Leading military powers (Russia, Germany) sought to treat so-called *francs-tireurs* (literally free shooters) as unprivileged belligerents subject to execution upon capture, whereas less powerful states (e.g., Belgium) viewed them as lawful combatants rightfully resisting or throwing off colonial occupation …
> . [One defender of *francs-tireurs* said] 'A *franc-tireur* is emphatically not a person whose warfare is bound to disgust any soldier,' … and certainly 'not a perfidious or barbarous or fantastically fiendish foe.' Instead, 'a *franc-tireur* is a free man, who fights to defend his own farm or family against foreign aggressors, but who does not happen to possess certain badges and articles of clothing catalogued by Prussia in 1870'.[7]

The Martens Clause was an attempted compromise between the competing viewpoints that tried to clarify the situation of irregular fighters, but it was so vague as to be useless. The ingrained state-centric view prevailed. Under the Regulations of Hague Convention IV of 1907, in order to be given proper care as a **POW**, soldiers had to meet four conditions: (1) they had to be under the command of a responsible authority (i.e., part of a chain of command); (2) they had to wear a fixed distinctive emblem (i.e., had to wear a uniform with proper insignia); (3) they had to carry their arms openly (i.e., they could not give the appearance of being civilians); and (4) they had to comply with the laws and customs of war (i.e., they had to abide by the rules created by states for states). If the question of how to treat different categories of combatants was an issue before 1945, it would become a "more vexing phenomenon" after 1945, with "the proliferation of new types of irregular forces whose nature did not correspond to the traditional requirements of the law of war governing lawful combatants."[8]

Aside from the problem of distinguishing between regular and irregular forces and which rules should apply to whom, there was the growing problem of honoring the distinction between combatants and civilians. By the twentieth century, as military technology and strategy evolved – with ever more lethal weaponry and with whole societies and economies involved in war efforts and considered legitimate targets – it became harder to maintain that distinction. World War I witnessed submarine and air warfare along with economic warfare, resulting often in indiscriminate targeting of the civilian population. The civilian death toll in World War I almost equaled the military death toll.

Despite setbacks, efforts continued after World War I to strengthen the laws of war, including placing restrictions on certain types of weapons that could be used in combat. One such effort was the attempt to limit the use of chemical weapons, an area in which there had been a long history of "arms control." One author notes that "the Manu laws of [ancient] India forbade the use of poison weapons; so, a millennium later, did the warfare regulations which the Saracens drew from the Koran."[9] The ancient Romans and Greeks supposedly also observed a proscription against the use of poisoned weapons. In 1675, shortly after the Peace of Westphalia, Germany (Prussia) and France signed the Treaty of Strassbourg banning poisoned bullets. The 1899 Hague Convention that banned dum-dum bullets also banned the use of projectiles filled with poison gases. Nonetheless, mustard gas, hydrogen cyanide, and other chemical agents were used extensively on the battlefield in World War I, causing horrible effects; on April 22, 1915, at Ypres, Belgium, some 6,000 British and French troops were killed in a chemical attack by the Germans. The response of the international community was the **Geneva Protocol of 1925**, which banned the first use of chemical weapons by any state but was interpreted to permit the production, stockpiling, and use of chemical weapons in retaliation for another state's prior use. Although thousands of tons of chemical weapons were manufactured by Germany, the United States, and other countries before and during World War II, they were not used in combat; whether due to the mutual fears of the warring parties associated with unpredictable chemical arsenals or growing moral sensibilities against chemical warfare, the norm held throughout World War II.[10] No such norm had yet developed covering the use of an emerging new technology – the atomic bomb. Later in the chapter we will discuss more recent efforts to regulate not only chemical weapons but biological and nuclear weapons as well as various kinds of conventional weapons.

In the Interwar Period, there was some attempt to codify rules governing aerial warfare. Unlike existing treaties regulating war on land and at sea, there was no such treaty governing the military use of airspace, only customary law with its vague principles calling for minimizing harm to civilians. This was not surprising, since the airplane was a new innovation, having just been invented in 1903. As

Captain Elbridge Colby said in 1925, "There is no vast body of aerial law to which we can resort for guiding rules."[11] There was an effort to develop a treaty, the Hague Convention of 1923, which sought to ban aerial targeting of population centers and civilian property; but it was never ratified by enough states to come into force. Hence, as World War II approached, there was no clear, explicit legal restriction on aerial bombardment. If the "total war" that interstate war had become by 1939 complicated the application of the "distinction" principle, the growth of intrastate and extrastate violence (associated with "limited war") after 1945 would complicate the problem further.

World War II and Its Aftermath: The 1949 Geneva Conventions and Other *Jus In Bello* Rules

Both the Germans and the Allied Powers engaged in aerial bombardment of major population centers during World War II. The Nazis used V-1 and V-2 rockets to destroy large swaths of London and other cities, while the Allies engaged in "strategic bombing" campaigns over German cities such as Dresden and Japanese cities such as Tokyo, followed by the dropping of the atomic bomb on Hiroshima and Nagasaki. Strategic bombing, done toward the latter part of the war, was not limited to the destruction of military targets such as munitions factories, or even more broadly to vital communications and transportation infrastructure, but was also aimed at reducing the enemy's morale and will to fight; it was this psychological warfare that later led critics to draw comparisons between Allied behavior and "terrorism." Almost as many people (roughly 100,000) died in some conventional air raids, such as over Tokyo, as died in the atomic bomb attacks. Clearly, World War II saw the virtual collapse of the principle of "distinction."

World War II also saw various "war crimes," including mistreatment of captured soldiers. The 1929 Geneva Convention on Treatment of Prisoners of War had sought to add protections to POWs beyond those in the Hague Regulations, but failed to prevent abuse of captured soldiers by the armed forces of several countries, such as the massacre of thousands of Polish officers at Katyn in 1940 by the Soviet Army and the Bataan Death March (the forced 60-mile march of American and Filipino prisoners) by the Japanese. Nazi leaders were held responsible for similar "war crimes" at the postwar Nuremberg Trials, as well as being charged with "crimes against humanity" in the form of not only genocide against Jews during the Holocaust but also atrocities committed against large numbers of civilians.

In 1949, four **Geneva Conventions** were drafted to address the problems experienced during World War II, notably the indiscriminate violence committed against innocent civilians and the mistreatment of prisoners of war. Eventually achieving universal acceptance, the Geneva Conventions have become the core body of written rules comprising international humanitarian law. The Conventions themselves are founded on the three essential principles that had defined *jus in bello* obligations since the beginning of the "just war" tradition – not only *distinction*, but also *necessity* and *proportionality*.[12] All three principles represent customary law aimed at minimizing suffering caused by armed conflict, now codified in the four Geneva treaties.

We have already discussed the principle of *distinction*, which requires combatants to make every effort to distinguish between those engaged in hostilities and those who are not and to do everything possible to minimize harm to the latter, including never intentionally firing on civilians and civilian property and, where collateral damage is unavoidable, to keep it as low as can be. The other two principles are closely related and follow from the first principle. The **principle of necessity** requires combatants to use armed force only when necessary, as a last resort when a military objective is at stake and cannot be achieved through other means. For example, if one can achieve an objective without firing into a heavily populated area, one is obligated to pursue that approach. The **principle of proportionality** requires combatants to refrain from excessive use of armed force and to use only that amount of force that is commensurate with what military advantage is to be gained. For example, it would be a violation of this principle if one killed hundreds of people in a parade merely to destroy one tank that might be part of the parade, since the benefit would be small relative to the cost. It needs to be emphasized that the unintentional killing or injuring of civilians and destruction of their property is permissible under IHL as long as the conditions of distinction, necessity, and proportionality are satisfied.[13] Although the 1949 Geneva Conventions were not in place during World War II, the Allied strategic bombing campaign over enemy cities arguably violated customary law insofar as subsequent studies showed that the huge loss of life and devastation caused by the aerial attacks failed to achieve the objective of sapping German or Japanese morale or other military objectives as effectively as planners had assumed; undertaken late in the war, when victory was almost assured, it was not clear what purpose was served by such use of force.

The 1949 Geneva Conventions sought not only to strengthen the principle of distinction as regards who can be targeted in wartime but also who is considered a combatant as opposed to a noncombatant and what treatment applies to each. In some ways, the conventions built on the earlier Hague and Geneva treaties, while in other respects they codified rules that had never been formally expressed before. The **First Geneva Convention**, for the Amelioration of the Condition of the Wounded and Sick in Armed Forces in the Field, provides protection for sick and wounded soldiers on land during war. It also offers special protection for medical personnel (and transports) and clergy, in recognition of the services they perform for troops. The **Second Geneva Convention**, for the Amelioration of the Condition of the Wounded and Sick and Shipwrecked Members of Armed Forces at Sea, provides similar protections for sailors engaged in maritime warfare, including protection of hospital ships. The **Third Geneva Convention**,

Relative to Treatment of Prisoners of War, affords POWs protections in terms of judicial proceedings as well as the labor performed and other conditions of incarceration, and requires that they be released immediately upon cessation of hostilities. The **Fourth Geneva Convention**, Relative to the Protection of Civilian Persons in Time of War, specifically offers protection for civilians, including forbidding deliberate or indiscriminate attacks on civilian populations.

As with the UN Charter, the Geneva Conventions are state-centric in the sense they were meant to apply mainly to interstate war. As William Banks comments, "Under Geneva, there are two kinds of wars: interstate (or international) armed conflicts and intrastate (or internal) armed conflicts. The former invoke the full panoply of the laws of war … ; the latter do not trigger all the regulations for the conduct of war but provide limited humanitarian protection for civilians and those captured or detained."[14] In other words, nonstate actors involved in "non-international" armed conflicts are given relatively few protections. For example, the Third Geneva Convention (Article 4), borrowing from the 1907 Hague Convention, stipulates a fourfold set of criteria that a combatant must meet in order to be considered a "lawful combatant" entitled to POW treatment if captured: the individual (1) must be part of a regular chain of command; (2) must wear a fixed insignia recognizable at a distance; (3) must carry arms openly; and (4) must conduct operations in accordance with the laws of war. As Banks notes, "It is virtually impossible for nonstate actors to meet these criteria and thus to become lawful combatants under humanitarian law."[15]

However, in an effort to provide at least minimal humanitarian safeguards for all actors in all armed conflicts, including irregular forces (rebels and guerrillas) and others involved in a *non-international* armed conflict, the four Geneva Conventions contain what is called "**Common Article 3**": "Persons taking no active part in the hostilities, including members of armed forces who have laid down their arms [surrendered] and those placed *hors de combat* by sickness, wounds, detention, or any other cause, shall in all circumstances be treated humanely." Such persons, who are no longer actively participating in hostilities, whether due to voluntary or forced withdrawal, are generally to be considered "noncombatants" along with civilians. Common Article 3 prohibits "cruel treatment and torture" and "outrages upon personal dignity, in particular humiliating and degrading treatment." Common Article 3 also states that if such persons are detained and tried, sentences must be "pronounced by a regularly constituted court affording all judicial guarantees."

The problem is states have often failed to observe Common Article 3, given their ambivalence in applying international humanitarian law in non-international armed conflicts for fear of rewarding and legitimizing rebel groups who seemed unlikely to reciprocate humanitarian behavior. For example, although the United States and the South Vietnamese generally, albeit reluctantly, treated the Viet Cong insurgents as POWs during the Vietnam War in the 1960s, the Viet Cong and their North Vietnamese sponsors did not give captured American and South

Vietnamese prisoners the same level of respect.[16] In addition to Common Article 3, Article 5 of the Third Geneva Convention Relating to Treatment of Prisoners of War provides that, if there is doubt as to the status of a detainee (whether the latter should be considered a POW or "unlawful combatant"), the status should be determined by a "competent tribunal." (The term "unlawful combatant" does not explicitly appear in the Geneva Convention or any other treaty, but the concept is implied.) This begged the question of not only what rules should apply to unlawful combatants but also what constitutes a "competent tribunal."

Precisely because the Geneva Conventions gave scant attention to the application of IHL in non-international armed conflicts, an attempt was made in the 1970s to add two protocols to the 1949 treaties aimed at clarifying the status and protections of irregular fighters and others involved in such conflicts. **Additional Protocol I**, on The Protection of Victims of International Armed Conflicts, essentially reiterated the rules in the 1949 conventions but included "wars of national liberation" in the category of international armed conflicts, thus bringing rebels fighting against colonial rule or foreign occupation more closely under the expanded protections of the Third Geneva Convention on Prisoners of War. Equating wars of national liberation with international wars and relaxing the fourfold test for lawful combatant status (e.g., eliminating the requirement of a fixed insignia), something urged by Third World countries, proved controversial; although over 170 states are parties to the protocol, many are not, including the United States, which disapproved of according insurgents a level of respectful treatment normally reserved for POWs of state armies. **Additional Protocol II**, on The Protection of Victims of Non-International Armed Conflicts, aimed to supplement Common Article 3 in providing stronger protections for actors engaged in non-international armed conflicts. This was even more controversial, as it was unclear how to draw the line between rioting ("mere disturbances and tensions") and civil unrest on the one hand and full-scale civil war on the other, and also how far to extend protections to not just guerrillas but terrorists. Here, too, ratification was uneven, with some 160 countries supporting the protocol; and others, such as the United States, refusing. Although the Protocols are viewed by many as embodying current customary law, the lack of universal participation along with somewhat vague language in some sections has continued to plague those agreements.

The 1949 Geneva Conventions and the 1977 Protocols remain the main operant *jus in bello* rules today. As Robert Barnidge notes, "the Four Geneva Conventions were hardly without their own shortcomings even before 11 September. As Sir Hersch Lauterpacht put it in 1952, 'beneficent as they are, [they] abound in gaps, compromises, obscurities, and somewhat nominal provisions.' ... Less than thirty years after the adoption of the Four Geneva Conventions, two additional protocols were adopted. ... Liberals and others have engaged in passionate debate about the adequacy and applicability of this treaty framework to the post-11 September context."[17]

How have these rules functioned in practice, especially of late, given the "new warfare"? In the next section, we will discuss the many challenges presented by the war on terror and other increasingly complex types of conflicts.

The Evolution of *Jus In Bello* Rules Since 1945: Principle and Practice

There is general acknowledgment that "international humanitarian law accepts that there is no such thing as a perfectly 'clean' war."[18] The changing nature of conflict invites ever "dirtier" wars that IHL seeks to manage.

Jus in bello rules are activated once war is underway. But how does one even know when war is underway, or has ended, when not only do wars now go undeclared but many are of the sporadic, low-intensity variety without clear definition? It was hard enough in the 1986 *Nicaragua vs. United States* World Court case to define what constitutes an "armed conflict"; it is all the more difficult to ascertain whether a "state of war" exists in the case of a "war on terror," which tends to lack temporal or geographical boundaries altogether. Likewise, even if an armed conflict clearly exists, how does one categorize it as "international" or "non-international," when many conflicts combine elements of interstate, intrastate, and extrastate violence? Although the 1977 Geneva Protocols I and II sought to clarify these terms and provide guidance on what rules to apply, they only seemed to muddle the issues further.

In Barnidge's view, **asymmetrical warfare**, where a weaker party is incentivized to level the playing field against a stronger foe by ignoring the accepted rules of engagement, while the superior party observes the rules only at its own peril at risk of defeat, "poses perhaps the greatest challenge to international humanitarian law since the establishment of the United Nations at the end of World War II and the adoption of the Geneva Conventions in 1949."[19] Barnidge is not alone. William Banks, in *New Battlefields/Old Laws*, notes that "existing laws are not well-suited to take into account these asymmetries ... . Because the Hague and Geneva Conventions and Protocols do not account adequately for non-state groups waging transnational attacks or prolonged campaigns of terrorism, ... today's new battlefields may be left unregulated so that parties in the conflict are without guidelines."[20] He adds: "New circumstances require a fresh look at established core humanitarian law principles of distinction, proportionality, military necessity, and prevention of unnecessary suffering."[21]

Observing the Rule of "Distinction": Divergence between Principle and Practice

We noted that the principle of "distinction" broke down during both World War I and World War II, leading to the Fourth Geneva Convention in 1949 and other instruments aimed at strengthening the principle. Sadly, where "at the beginning of the twentieth century, 85 to 90 per cent of casualties in war were military," "by the late 1990s, the proportions of a hundred years ago [had] been almost reversed, so that nowadays approximately 80 per cent of all casualties in war are civilian."[22] The record of compliance with the norm of "distinction" in recent years has been decidedly mixed.

On the one hand, Colin Kahl has argued that since the Vietnam War there have been growing efforts by the U.S. military to sensitize its troops to IHL requirements, as the Department of Defense has adopted directives "requiring that enlisted troops and officers alike receive instruction in the laws of war during basic training or in academies" and "once deployed, when being trained in the rules of engagement (ROE)."[23] During the First Gulf War in 1991, when U.S.-led Operation Desert Storm forces expelled Iraqi forces from Kuwait, American soldiers were issued a pocket card that read as follows:

(A)   Do not engage anyone who has surrendered, is out of battle due to sickness or wounds, is shipwrecked, or is an aircrew member descending by parachute from a disabled aircraft.

(B)   Avoid harming civilians unless necessary to save U.S. lives. Do not fire into civilian populated areas or buildings which are not defended or being used for military purposes.

(C)   Hospitals, churches, shrines, schools, museums, national monuments, and other historical or cultural sites will not be engaged except in self-defense.

(D)   Treat all civilians and their property with respect and dignity.

(E)   Treat all prisoners humanely and with respect and dignity.

The card added a boldfaced reminder:

1.   FIGHT ONLY COMBATANTS.
2.   ATTACK ONLY MILITARY TARGETS.
3.   SPARE CIVILIAN PERSONS AND OBJECTS.
4.   RESTRICT DESTRUCTION TO WHAT YOUR MISSION REQUIRES.[24]

As inconsistent as U.S. behavior in following these rules may have been during the First Gulf War, it was considerably better than Iraq's. As David Scheffer comments, "the Gulf War was the most significant test of the laws of war since World War II.... . The record of Iraqi compliance was dismal. Examples of Iraq's conduct include the following: the detention of foreign hostages in Iraq as 'human shields' ... the placement of military targets within civilian areas ... the torture of Kuwaiti citizens ... [and] the mistreatment of prisoners of war from the coalition forces, including televised interrogations," all violations of the Geneva Conventions.[25] Even in the case of the U.S. "shock and awe" aerial bombing campaign over Baghdad that opened the Second Gulf War in 2003, the *New York*

Times reported that the American commanders took "extraordinary steps to limit collateral damage. The Army's Third Infantry Division [had] a team of lawyers to advise on whether targets are legitimate under international conventions – and a vast database of some 10,000 targets to be avoided, such as hospitals, mosques, and cultural or archaeological treasures."[26] Similarly, even as the United States inflicted hundreds of drone strikes on suspected al Qaeda sanctuaries in remote areas on the Pakistan–Afghanistan border in recent years, aimed at eliminating terrorist cells and bringing the Taliban to the bargaining table (in the process possibly infringing on Pakistan's sovereignty), American commanders took special precautions to try to limit civilian casualties in urban areas even at the risk of exposing U.S. soldiers to enemy fire.[27]

Notwithstanding efforts by the United States and others to honor the "distinction" principle, the fact remains that the nature of contemporary warfare creates added pressures working against this principle. Countries such as the United States, due to domestic political pressure to avoid ground combat operations that could result in heavy military casualties, are inclined to rely instead, as in Kosovo and Iraq, on "shock and awe" air campaigns or, in the case of Afghanistan, pilotless drone strikes, which, however surgically aimed at targets of military necessity, inevitably result in substantial collateral damage to civilian lives and property. Meanwhile, intrastate and extrastate conflicts exacerbate these problems because rival factions in civil wars often sack towns and villages, brutalizing the sympathizers of the other side, and terrorists tend to designate randomly selected noncombatants as their prime targets. While some state actors may use "human shields" and target civilians during war (recall Iraq's behavior cited above), non-state actors do more so. In the case of both guerrillas and terrorists, especially the latter, combatants often consciously hide behind civilians while also considering them valuable as strategic targets. Eric Jensen succinctly describes the calculus that leads "those who engage in hostilities against organized armed forces" to exploit the laws of war:

> These fighters purposely blend in with the civilian population during military operations in order to increase their effectiveness and survivability due to their opponent's desire to protect civilians. They rely on the respect for law by military forces who, in an effort not to harm innocent civilians, refrain from attacking fighters who operate within the civilian population.[28]

Max Boot is more blunt: "Guerrilla and terrorist tactics always have been the resort of the weak against the strong. That is why insurgents wage war from the shadows; if they fought in the open, like a regular army, they would be annihilated."[29]

How can one side be expected to follow the prescribed ROE when the other side is playing by different rules? To put it simply, "what if opposing troops set up a mortar emplacement next to, or even in, a school yard or hospital car park? What if opposing troops hide in densely packed civilian residential areas? What if those engaged in an armed attack do not distinguish themselves from the civilian population by wearing uniforms, or consciously disguise themselves as civilians? These are not mere legal conundrums. They are practical problems facing members of the armed forces."[30] There is a tendency to hold organized armies to a higher standard of conduct than unorganized armies. Indeed, some scholars even argue that, since terrorism in asymmetrical warfare is "the weapon of the weak," terrorists should be cut some slack in the way they use force. Obviously, such thinking does not help enforce IHL.

Jus in bello rules traditionally have tried to protect civilians through defining combatants as those forces marked by the wearing of proper uniforms or at least distinctive insignia. Although it is understood that combatants may be targeted, IHL creates incentives for them to stand out from civilians by according such actors POW status if captured and thus entitled to the protection of the Third Geneva Convention. One question that arises here is whether, in trying increasingly to treat all parties in a conflict humanely (through Common Article 3 of the Geneva Conventions and the 1977 Additional Protocols that somewhat relaxed the fourfold criteria for lawful combatants and extended minimum safeguards to all actors), the international community undermined the incentives for irregular fighters to observe the distinction principle. If even the worst offenders, who not only fail to wear insignia but observe no rules whatsoever and commit the most heinous offenses imaginable against innocents, can be assured of decent treatment when captured, are we rewarding rather than deterring such behavior?[31]

Another question that arises is how to define "persons taking no active part in the hostilities," a category referred to in Common Article 3 of the Geneva Conventions as enjoying "immunity" from attack. Take, for example, "the case of private military contractors, tens of thousands of whom [have supported] U.S. forces in Iraq, Afghanistan, and elsewhere. ... Contractors perform activities ranging from preparing food and building bases to delivering armaments and fuel, ... gathering intelligence, providing personal security ... and training soldiers in the use of military hardware. ... [Military contractors] are in practice more akin to combatants than they are to civilians. Yet the Geneva Conventions generally regard them as civilians because they do not meet the formal requirements of combatant status. ... Most contractors do wear company hats or polo shirts with the company logo, but is this sufficient to be recognizable 'at a distance' as required by Article 4 [of the Third Geneva Convention]?"[32] What about terrorists, "who often 'rejoin' the civilian population immediately after engaging in hostile acts by simply putting down a weapon and walking home"? It can be difficult "to identify terrorists-to-be before attacks are actually carried out."[33] And if caught during the daytime, what is the exact legal status of such persons if they are "part-timers" – "a farmer by day and a fighter at night"?[34]

The United States, on capturing al Qaeda fighters in Afghanistan after 9/11, branded most of them "**unlawful combatants**" (or "**enemy combatants**") not entitled to POW protection, jailing over 500 of them at the U.S. naval base at

Guantanamo Bay, Cuba (Gitmo). Although the United States could claim it acted legally in denying al Qaeda members POW status, given the latter's failure to meet Geneva POW criteria, the United States was accused of violating international law in other respects. In particular, it was not clear that the "unlawful combatant" designation was determined by a "competent tribunal" as required by the Third Geneva Convention, or if the prisoners should have been treated as mere criminals deserving jury trials and due process under U.S. Constitutional law, or possibly considered "noncombatants" if some were only involved indirectly in a support role (say, as a cook or chauffeur). There was also the issue of indefinite detention; even if they had been accorded POW status, requiring their release upon conclusion of hostilities, who could say when the "war on terrorism" might be over? In addition, in some instances the Guantanamo prisoners were subjected to "enhanced interrogation methods," such as prolonged sleep deprivation and waterboarding, that bordered on torture, in violation of Common Article 3 of the Geneva Conventions. There was some disagreement over how far such methods could go to extract vital information from prisoners.[35] If you could save thousands of lives from a catastrophic terrorist attack on a large city through slightly "enhanced" interrogation techniques used with one terrorist, would it not be moral as well as wise even if not strictly legal? Others questioned, though, whether such methods were effective in intelligence-gathering and worth the risk of staining one's reputation, encouraging the enemy to treat American prisoners similarly, and possibly breeding more terrorists.[36]

What Model Applies: "Warfare" or "Lawfare"?

Many critics of U.S. treatment of al Qaeda prisoners at Gitmo complained that the prisoners were given neither POW protections nor the right of due process and jury trial normally accorded criminals charged with crimes, instead being caught in legal limbo as "unlawful combatants." The larger question raised here is whether terrorism should be considered by its nature a military security matter subject to the rules associated with "armed conflict" or rather a law enforcement matter subject to the rules associated with policing and the criminal justice system – in other words, should we apply a **"warfare" or "lawfare" model** in addressing such concerns?[37] Geoffrey Corn notes that although the United States maintains that since 9/11 it has been fighting a "war on terrorism," "many experts in international law insist that such operations are not armed conflicts at all, but 'extraterritorial law enforcement' operations."[38] United Nations officials who have tried to develop guidelines for dealing with terrorism have contended that "the norm should be that terrorists should be dealt with as criminals, through legal processes of arrest, trial, and judicially decided punishment."[39] If this is the case, then it is not so much the rules of "international humanitarian law" (the laws of war) that apply but "human rights law" and municipal (domestic) laws.

Alberto Gonzalez, White House Counsel to President George W. Bush, in defending the administration's labeling of Gitmo prisoners as "unlawful combatants," stated that "the war against terrorism is a new kind of war" that "renders obsolete Geneva's strict limitations on questioning of enemy prisoners and renders quaint some of its provisions."[40] But were the provisions of the U.S. Constitution guaranteeing "due process" and a "speedy, public trial" to defendants also quaint, or did they not apply to apprehension and incarceration of terrorists? The problem is that, even if it was understandable that the United States did not want to grant the prisoners POW status (since they did not meet the Geneva criteria) and did not want to entitle them to regular jury trials in domestic courts (since they were accused of committing not crimes but acts of war, and allowing them to confront witnesses and mount a public defense might compromise U.S. intelligence sources), they were at least entitled to minimal protections under Common Article 3, as long as the "war on terrorism" could be considered a "non-international armed conflict." This leads us back to the "warfare vs. lawfare" question as to whether the prisoners were seized on a traditionally defined "battlefield," something that Jeremy Scahill (the *Dirty Wars* author) and others have rejected.

The "lawfare vs. warfare" question has been at the center of the debate over "**targeted killings**," defined as "the intentional, premeditated and deliberate use of lethal force ... against an individual."[41] The United States has been criticized not only for its treatment of captured prisoners but, even more so, for its increasing tendency not to bother with capture at all and instead, through drone strikes and other means, to engage in *targeted killings* of suspected terrorists in Pakistan, Afghanistan, Yemen, and other locales (characterized by critics as "assassinations" or "arbitrary executions"). As one author frames the issue, "The question that arises in the context of targeted killings is whether terrorists can be killed as illegal fighters or if they need to be tried before a court. The answer to this question depends on the context. In peacetime, they will have to be afforded the usual fair trial rights; in an armed conflict, however, they may be treated as illegal fighters."[42] Again, the United States considers itself at "war" with terrorists and, thus, entitled to kill the latter as "unlawful combatants." The Obama administration has claimed that the targets are carefully selected as posing an imminent threat after determining capture is not feasible, and are approved by a Foreign Intelligence Surveillance Court backed by other legal safeguards; in addition, the targeting is said to meet the IHL requirements of necessity, distinction, and proportionality.[43]

There is some support for the U.S. view among international lawyers, although considerable opposition as well, with critics questioning whether an armed conflict as such exists, and even if it does, whether the targets are accurately identified based on solid intelligence with adequate judicial oversight.[44] UN Special Rapporteur Philip Alston, arguing in favor of the "lawfare" paradigm, has expressed concern that "in the legitimate struggle against terrorism, too many criminal acts have been re-characterized so as to justify addressing them within the framework of the law of armed conflict."[45] Alston reminds that human rights treaties generally presume one is innocent and cannot be "executed" until proven guilty through a fair judicial procedure. How realistic, though, is it to expect the United States or any other state to treat suspected terrorists the way one might treat a bank robber – through capture (i.e., arrest), reading the alleged criminal his "Miranda rights" (the right to remain silent, the right to an attorney, etc.), and arranging proper arraignment and trial, especially when there is reason to believe that the person may be plotting a major terrorist attack. Not only are military personnel not trained in policing techniques, but undue delay in trying to apprehend suspects may prove catastrophic.

Regulating Weapons: Drones, WMDs, and Other Lethal Tools

Earlier in the chapter, it was noted that *jus in bello* rules include what weaponry may or may not be used in war. This often takes the form of "arms control" regimes. For example, in 1980, the international community produced a treaty called the Convention on Prohibitions on Use of Certain Conventional Weapons Which May Be Deemed to Be Excessively Injurious and to Have Indiscriminate Effects, which banned such devices as booby traps, exploding toys, and napalm. In 1998, the **Ottawa Landmine Treaty** outlawed the use of anti-personnel landmines, which have been called "the Saturday night special" of civil wars and had resulted in countries such as Kampuchea being called "a nation of amputees" due to all the mines left over from conflict in the 1980s.[46] As of 2015, over 100 countries were parties to the former treaty, and over 160 had joined the latter agreement. No treaty covers IEDs (improvised explosive devices), a favorite weapon of roadside bombers used in asymmetrical warfare.

As injurious and indiscriminate as booby traps and landmines may be, other categories of weaponry are far more so. Among the most important arms control treaties restricting the weapons of war are ones that limit the production and use of **weapons of mass destruction (WMDs),** namely the "ABC" weapons – atomic or nuclear, biological, and chemical weapons. We discussed the 1925 Geneva Protocol that banned the first use of lethal chemical weapons; it was generally observed until Iraq under Saddam Hussein used deadly chemical agents against Iran as well as his own Kurdish population in the 1980s. As a follow-up, the 1993 **Chemical Weapons Convention (CWC)** created a total ban on the development and use of such weapons. Although 190 states are parties, there are a few holdouts, such as Israel, Egypt and North Korea. The counterpart to the CWC is the 1972 **Biological Weapons Convention (BWC),** which likewise bans the development and use of biological agents such as anthrax, smallpox virus, and various toxins. Ratified by 170 countries, it has been largely observed, although the Soviet Union is rumored to have used germ warfare in Afghanistan in the 1980s.

As for nuclear weapons, the 1970 **Nuclear Nonproliferation Treaty (NPT)** obligated already existing members of the "nuclear club" who possessed nuclear weapons not to transfer them to non-nuclear states and obligated the latter not to develop or acquire them. As of 2015, every country was a party to the NPT except for Israel, India, and Pakistan, although signatories North Korea and Iran were thought to have violated the treaty by pursuing a nuclear weapons program. Atomic or nuclear weapons have not been used since Hiroshima and Nagasaki. Interestingly, unlike in the case of chemical and biological weapons, there is no explicit rule banning the use of nuclear weapons in warfare. If one country were to initiate a conventional attack against another country, the right of self-defense that the UN Charter permits the second country includes the right to retaliate with nuclear strikes if that country is one of the nuclear "haves." At least that is the position the United States took throughout the Cold War, when Washington was concerned that, without the threatened nuclear deterrent, the Soviet Union might be tempted to take advantage of its superiority in tanks and conventional forces in Eastern Europe to invade Western Europe. A 1961 UN General Assembly resolution outlawing the use of nuclear weapons had no legal effect. In 1994, the General Assembly voted to ask the World Court in The Hague for an advisory opinion on the question: "Is the threat or use of nuclear weapons in any circumstances permitted under international law?" The General Assembly request followed a similar request made earlier by the World Health Organization. The World Court ended up equivocating on this issue, although many commentators have argued that nuclear weapons are covered under the body of customary and treaty law prohibiting the use of weapons that inflict indiscriminate harm on civilians.

In addition to ABC weapons regulation, the "D" weapon – the use of **drones** – has attracted considerable attention and controversy of late. Unmanned drones have been the weapon of choice for the United States in its "targeted killings" in the war on terrorism, since they can accurately identify and eliminate enemy fighters while minimizing American military casualties. Unlike weapons of mass destruction, drones are surgically precise weapons. Indeed, they are considered so accurate that some have argued that not only is it permissible for the United States and other states to engage in drone warfare but that they are morally and legally obligated to use these weapons rather than conventional air power or other conventional forces due to their potential to cause less collateral damage.[47] However, the same arguments made against targeted killings generally have been made against drones in particular, that they wrongly presume a warfare paradigm rather than lawfare paradigm, they excessively expand the "battlefield," they violate the sovereignty of targeted countries, and they amount to arbitrary execution. In addition, critics contend that, because they do not entail risk of casualties for the user (as operators are based thousands of miles away from the battlefield), drones encourage more use of force than might otherwise occur and may lead to a "Playstation mentality to killing."[48] They also are seen as a "dishonorable" form of fighting that only breeds further resentment and thus further terrorists; in this regard, Walzer posits as a moral principle that "you can't kill unless you are prepared to die."[49] Moreover, since the U.S. drone program is mostly managed by the CIA and implemented by non-uniformed joystick operators at CIA headquarters, this makes for excessive secrecy, with inadequate transparency in terms of the procedures used to target militants as well as reporting the amount of collateral damage.

Reliable data on casualties caused by U.S. drone strikes are hard to come by. A 2012 Stanford University Law School report based on statistics gathered by the Bureau of Investigative Journalism in London found that, despite their supposed precision, "drone strikes kill, maim, and traumatize too many civilians." The study found that between 2004 and 2012, drone strikes killed over 2,500 people in Pakistan, roughly 500 of whom (20 percent) were civilians; only 2 percent of all casualties were "high level targets."[50] Another study, by the New America Foundation, reported that civilians constituted only 10% of all casualties, while yet another study found the figure as low as 4 percent.[51] Commenting on the difficulty of ascertaining accurate measures of the ratio of civilian to combatant fatalities, UN Secretary-General Kofi Annan once said: "The truth is that no one really knows ... . The victims of today's atrocious conflicts are not merely anonymous, but literally countless."[52] Any civilian death is tragic. The key legal question is whether the United States can claim to have done everything possible to keep collateral damage to a minimum.

The UN Special Rapporteur's analysis of targeted killings concluded that "there is broad agreement that drones themselves are not illegal weapons... . There is, however, a notable lack of consensus on how to apply the rules of international law that regulate the use of force to drones."[53] As another writer states, "Drone strikes ... constitute a serious, sustained, and visible assault on the generally accepted meaning of certain core legal concepts, including 'self-defense,' 'armed attack,' 'imminence,' 'necessity,' 'proportionality,' 'combatant,' 'civilian,' and 'armed conflict.'"[54] Although the UN Rapporteur insisted that "the central norms of international law need not, and should not, be abandoned to meet the new challenges posed by terrorism,"[55] international lawyers as well as foreign policy practitioners continue to struggle with adapting *jus in bello* as well as *jus ad bellum* rules to "the new warfare."[56]

Conclusion

We will return to *jus in bello* questions and examine them more closely in Chapter 6, when we focus on three case studies that illustrate the difficulty of applying international humanitarian law and related norms to contemporary conflicts (the U.S. drone campaign in Pakistan and Yemen, the Israeli–Palestinian Gaza War of 2008–2009, and the Second Congo War). In the next chapter, we look briefly at what Michael Walzer and others have called *jus post bellum* concerns – how to bring a conflict to a just and hopefully durable peace.

Chapter 3 Discussion Questions

1. What is meant by *jus in bello*? "International humanitarian law"?
2. Discuss the historical evolution of rules governing the conduct of war, including the Hague and Geneva Conventions.
3. Discuss the key principles (distinction, necessity, and proportionality) that form the core of international humanitarian law.
4. How does contemporary international law attempt to distinguish between "regular" and "irregular" forces as well as between "combatants" and "noncombatants"? What do the four Geneva Conventions of 1949 have to say about the rules that apply to these different categories of actors?
5. One observer notes, "The question today remains whether modern international humanitarian law is viable in light of changing threats posed by terrorists [and other actors]." Discuss the challenges posed by "the new warfare."

Notes

1   "Patton's Speech to the Third Army: 'Americans Play to Win All the Time,'" June 8, 1944, accessed March 7, 2014 at www.national review.com/weekend/history/history-patton-print111001.html.
2   On *jus in bello* and efforts to regulate the conduct of war, see Gerhard von Glahn and James Larry Taulbee, *Law Among Nations*, 8th edn (New York: Pearson, 2007), Chapter 21; and Stefan Kirchner, "Modern International Humanitarian Law," in Sanford R. Silverburg, ed., *International Law: Contemporary Issues and Future Developments* (Boulder, CO: Westview Press, 2011), 231–256.
3   Quoted in Von Glahn and Taulbee, *Law Among Nations*, 628.
4   David M. Crane and Daniel Reisner, "Jousting at Windmills," in William C. Banks, ed., *New Battlefields/Old Laws: Critical Debates on Asymmetric Warfare* (New York: Columbia University Press, 2011), 67. The Banks book is an excellent collection of essays on how "asymmetrical warfare" is posing many challenges for the traditional *jus in bello* rules.
5   Daphne Richemond-Barak, "Nonstate Actors in Armed Conflict: Issues of Distinction and Reciprocity," in Banks, *New Battlefields/Old Laws*, 111. On early efforts to restrain war in Ancient Greece, see Josiah Ober, "Classical Greek Times," in Michael Howard et al., eds, *The Laws of War: Constraints on Warfare in the Western World* (New Haven, CT: Yale University Press, 1994), 12–26. In early medieval Europe, see Geoffrey Parker, "Early Modern Europe," in Howard et al., *The Laws of War*, 40–58.
6   Geoffrey Best, *War and Law Since 1945* (Oxford: Clarendon Press, 1994), 24.
7   Corri Zoli, "Humanizing Irregular Warfare," in Banks, *New Battlefields/Old Laws*, 200–202.
8   Boleslaw A. Boczek, *International Law: A Dictionary* (Lanham, MD: Scarecrow Press, 2005), 434. See Chapter IX on "International Humanitarian Law."
9   J.P. Perry Robinson, "Origins of the Chemical Weapons Convention," in Benoit Morel and Kyle Olson eds, *Shadows and Substance: The Chemical Weapons Convention* (Boulder, CO: Westview, 1993), 40.
10 There is some evidence that chemical weapons might have been used in a limited fashion by Italy against Ethiopia in the 1930s and by Japan against China during World War II, but the historical record generally supports the view that the Geneva Protocol was abided by for decades following World War I. For evidence, see ibid.

11 Cited in Peter R. Faber, "The Development of US Strategic Bombing Doctrine in the Interwar Years: Moral and Legal?," *Journal of Legal Studies* (1996/1997); accessed March 9, 2014 at www.usafa.af.mil/dfl/journal/volume7/faber.html.

12 The International Committee of the Red Cross has drafted an informal text that summarizes the humanitarian rules that apply to armed conflict, entitled *Fundamental Rules of International Humanitarian Law Applicable to Armed Conflict* (1979). For an overview of IHL, see Curtiss F.J. Doebbler, *Introduction to International Humanitarian Law* (Washington, DC: CD Publishing, 2005).

13 On collateral damage, see Doebbler, *Introduction to International Humanitarian Law*, 47; and T. McCormack and A. McDonald, *Yearbook of International Law* (Cambridge: Cambridge University Press, 2004), 41–42. On proportionality, see Robert P. Barnidge, "The Principle of Proportionality Under International Humanitarian Law and Operation Cast Lead," in Banks, *New Battlefields/Old Laws*, 171–189.

14 Banks, *New Battlefields/Old Laws*, 6.

15 Ibid.

16 On the poor treatment of American POWS in Vietnamese camps, see Stuart I Rochester and Frederick Kiley, *Honor Bound: The History of American Prisoners of War in Southeast Asia, 1961–1973* (Los Angeles, CA: University Press of the Pacific, 2005).

17 Robert P. Barnidge, "Introduction," in Barnidge, ed., *The Liberal Way of War* (London: Ashgate, 2013), 5.

18 Kirchner, "Modern International Humanitarian Law," 237.

19 Barnidge, "The Principle of Proportionality," 188.

20 Banks, *New Battlefields/Old Laws*, 2–3.

21 Ibid., 2. On the challenges to IHL today, see also Judith Gail Gardam, *Necessity, Proportionality, and the Use of Force by States* (Cambridge: Cambridge University Press, 2004); and M. Cherif Bassiouni, "The New Wars and the Crisis of Compliance with the Law of Armed Conflict by Non-State Actors," *The Journal of Criminal Law and Criminology*, 98 (2007–2008): 711–810.

22 Mary Kaldor, *New and Old Wars*, 2nd edn (Stanford, CA: Stanford University Press, 2007), 107. Some observers put the civilian casualty rate as high as 90 percent. Steven Pinker, in *The Better Angels of Our Nature: Why Violence Has Declined* (New York: Viking Press, 2011), 317, argues that the 80–90 percent casualty rate figure for civilians is exaggerated and is "bogus," given the difficulty of accurately counting bodies in contemporary wars.

23 Colin Kahl, "How We Fight," *Foreign Affairs*, 85, no. 6 (November/December 2006): 85.

24 Cited in Vaughan Lowe, *International Law* (New York: Oxford University Press, 2007), 283–284. Michael Walzer argues that U.S. intentions were better than actual behavior during the First Gulf War; although "taken overall, the targeting was far more limited and selective than it had been, for example, in Korea or Vietnam," the air campaign resulted in destruction of water treatment plants and other vital Iraqi infrastructure. See Walzer, *Arguing About War* (New Haven, CT: Yale University Press, 2004), 10–11 and 94–96.

25 David J. Scheffer, "Use of Force After the Cold War," in Louis Henkin et al., eds, *Right vs. Might* (New York: Council on Foreign Relations Press, 1991), 141–142.

26 "How Precise Is Our Bombing?," editorial, *New York Times*, March 31, 2003. The *Times* added that "the allies deserve credit for conducting the most surgically precise bombing effort in the history of warfare." See also Kahl, "How We Fight," 89.

27 See Lara Dadkhah, "Empty Skies Over Afghanistan," *New York Times*, February 18, 2010. The U.S. policy, developed by General Stanley McChrystal, was driven not only by legal and moral considerations but at least as much by strategic considerations, namely the aim of employing a "counterinsurgency" strategy designed to "win hearts and minds" of the Afghan people.

28 Eric Jensen, "Direct Participation in Hostilities," in Banks, *New Battlefields/Old Laws*, 85.

29 Max Boot, *Invisible Armies* (New York: W.W. Norton, 2013), xxiv.

30 Lowe, *International Law*, 285. On how terrorists are advantaged by the laws of war, see Kenneth Anderson, "Who Owns the Rules of War?," *New York Times Magazine*, April 13, 2003.

31 Even if the 1949 Geneva Conventions and the 1977 Protocols do not extend "combatant" status to guerrillas and terrorists or others who fail to comply with the laws of war, Common Article 3 provides basic "protective parity" in the form of minimal safeguards to all persons in a conflict. See Richemond-Barak, "Nonstate Actors in Armed Conflict."

32 Ibid., 108–110. Also see Renee De Nevers, "Private Military Contractors and Changing Norms for the Laws of Armed Conflict," in Banks, *New Battlefields/Old Laws*, Chapter 7.

33 Ibid., 109.

34 Jensen, "Direct Participation in Hostilities," 92.

35 In the so-called "Torture Memos," three legal memoranda drafted by U.S. Justice Department official John Yoo for Assistant Attorney General Jay Bybee and given to the CIA for guidance on interrogation techniques, the suggestion was made that certain "enhanced interrogation methods" might be permissible when used in "the war on terrorism."

36 The United States distinguished between the prisoners held at Guantanamo following 9/11 and those held in Iraq during the Second Gulf War. Although the United States said the POW provisions of the Geneva Convention applied in the latter case, they did not apply in the former case. The U.S. was criticized for abusing and humiliating prisoners at Abu Ghraib prison in Iraq in violation of the Geneva treaties, and later apologized. See Seymour Hersh, "The Gray Zone," *New Yorker*, May 24, 2004; and Alberto Gonzalez, "The Rule of Law and the Rules of War," *New York Times*, May 15, 2004. On torture, see Malcolm D. Evans, "How Has the Prohibition of Torture Survived 11 September 2001," in Robert P. Barnidge, ed., *The Liberal Way of War* (London: Ashgate, 2013), 15–36.

37 Geoffrey Corn, "Extraterritorial Law Enforcement or Transnational Counterterrorist Military Operations," in Banks, *New Battlefields/Old Laws*, 24.

38 Charles Dunlop was among the first to use the term "lawfare," although he used it to mean a strategy for states to employ whereby adherence to international humanitarian law might help achieve military objectives. Charles J. Dunlap, "Lawfare Today and Tomorrow," in Raul Pedrozo and Dana Wollschlaeger, eds, *International Law and the Changing Character of War* (U.S. Naval War College International Law Studies, vol. 87, 2011), 315–325.

39 Osama bin Laden: Statement by the UN Rapporteurs on Summary Executions and on Human Rights and Counter-Terrorism, issued by the UN Office of the High Commissioner for Human Rights, May 6, 2011.

40 Draft Memorandum from White House Counsel Alberto R. Gonzalez to President George W. Bush (January 25, 2002); "Decision re Application of the Geneva Convention on Prisoners of War to the Conflict with al Qaeda and the Taliban."

41 Report of the Special Rapporteur on Extrajudicial, Summary or Arbitrary Executions (Alston Report), UN General Assembly Doc. A/HRC/14/24/Add.6, May 28, 2010, 3.

42 Kirchner, "Modern International Humanitarian Law," 249.

43 See speech by John Brennan, Assistant to the President for Homeland Security and Counterterrorism, "Strengthening Our Security by Adhering to Our Values and Laws," delivered at Harvard University School of Law, September 16, 2011; and speech by Eric Holder, U.S. Attorney-General, delivered at Northwestern University School of Law, March 5, 2012.

44 Richard Goldstone, the South African jurist who headed the UN commission that investigated war crimes in the 2008 Israeli–Palestinian Gaza conflict, speaking at the

Yale Club on October 4, 2011, stated that he agreed with the U.S. position that it was at war and entitled to target and kill terrorists as combatants, although he was concerned whether there was sufficient judicial oversight of the CIA's targeted killing program. See David Kaye, "International Law Issues in the Department of Justice White Paper on Targeted Killing," American Society of International Law Insights (February 15, 2013).

45 Report of the Special Rapporteur (Alston Report), 3. Also see Report of the Special Rapporteur on Extrajudicial, Summary or Arbitrary Executions (Heyns Report), UN General Assembly Doc. A/68/382, September 13, 2013.

46 Virginia Nesmith, "Landmines Are A Lingering Killer," *St. Louis Post-Dispatch*, December 31, 1995.

47 See Scott Shane, "The Moral Case for Drones," *New York Times*, July 15, 2012; and Kirchner, "Modern International Humanitarian Law," 237.

48 Report of the Special Rapporteur (Alston Report), 25. Also see Report of the Special Rapporteur (Heyns Report), 6.

49 Walzer, *Arguing About War*, 101.

50 "Drone Strikes Kill, Maim, and Traumatize Too Many Civilians, U.S. Study Says," CNN, September 25, 2012.

51 The 10 percent figure is cited in ibid. The 4 percent figure is cited in Shane, "The Moral Case for Drones," which concludes that "even if the highest estimates of collateral deaths are accurate, the drones kill fewer civilians than other modes of warfare."

52 Report to the Security Council on the Protection of Civilians in Armed Conflict, UN Doc. S/2001/331, March 2001, 1.

53 Report of the Special Rapporteur (Heyns Report), 4.

54 Rosa Brooks, "Drones and the International Rule of Law," *Ethics and International Affairs*, 28, no. 1 (2014): 83.

55 Report of the Special Rapporteur (Heyns Report), 22.

56 For various perspectives on the legality of drones, see Brooks, "Drones and the International Rule of Law": 83–103; Susan Breau, "Civilian Casualties and Drone Attacks: Issues in International Humanitarian Law," in Robert P. Barnidge, ed., *The Liberal Way of War* (London: Ashgate, 2013), 115–138; and Mary Ellen O'Connell, "The International Law of Drones," American Society of International Law Insight (November 12, 2010).

4

ON CONCLUDING A WAR

The Absence of *Jus Post Bellum* Rules

Just as the longstanding scholarly interest in "why wars begin"[1] recently has been supplemented with a growing body of scholarship on "why wars end,"[2] so, too, has the literature on *jus ad bellum* (as well as *jus in bello*) expanded of late to include ***jus post bellum*** questions. The latter questions have to do not so much with how to bring an immediate cessation of hostilities but rather how to produce a post-conflict peace that is sufficiently "just" as to be durable, so that hostilities do not recur.

The Aftermath of War as an Afterthought

It may seem odd, but the aftermath of war has been largely an afterthought, receiving relatively little attention by international legal scholars until only very recently. As Michael Walzer has said, *jus post bellum* – the set of norms following the end of a conflict, governing the achievement of a stable peace – is "the least developed part of just war theory."[3] Brian Orend agrees, noting that "there is a robust set of rules for resorting to war (*jus ad bellum*) and for conduct during war (*jus in bello*) but not for the termination phase of war."[4] Orend calls on the international community "to remedy this glaring gap in our ongoing struggle to restrain warfare."[5] It should be obvious that what transpires at the end of a war is at least as important as what occurs earlier. It is not merely that "the aftermath of war is crucial to the justice of the war itself"[6] but that "the way a war is fought and *the deeds done in ending it* live on in the historical memory of societies and may or may not set the stage for future war. It is always the duty of statesmanship to take this longer view [italics mine]."[7] There is no better example of this proposition than the punitive Treaty of Versailles after World War I, widely blamed for fueling German revanchism, the rise of Adolf Hitler, and the onset of World

War II. Although "the duty of peace must outweigh the duty of justice," and there can be "an excruciating tradeoff" at times, generally peace and justice tend to go together rather than being mutually exclusive.[8]

The issues that arise at the end of a war include such matters as how to restore the sovereignty of a conquered country, whether to impose regime change or in some way remake the political institutions of the latter state, whether to conduct war crimes trials, whether to seek reparations from the defeated foe or impose economic and other sanctions, and whether victors are obligated to contribute to the reconstruction of the economy and infrastructure of countries devastated by war. Although these sorts of questions would seem to apply mainly to interstate wars, they could apply to civil wars as well.[9] For instance, the issue of **regime change** has come up in both the context of interstate war (e.g., the Allies had to decide how far to go in eliminating all members of the Nazi regime in Germany and remaking the political system of Japan after World War II) and the context of intrastate war (e.g., the NATO forces engaged in humanitarian intervention in the Libyan civil war in 2011 had to decide how far to go in helping the rebels to overthrow the Gaddafi government). Since civil wars are more frequent today than interstate wars, *jus post bellum* rules will have to be adapted to those kinds of wars if they are to be relevant to the contemporary international system.

The problem is there are virtually no rules. As Orend observes, "there has never been an international treaty to regulate war's final phase."[10] Customary law does not help much either. Part of the difficulty here is that there may be a fine line between the final phase of a conflict and the fighting that preceded it. The United States has had to confront *jus post bellum* issues in Iraq, Afghanistan, and other such conflicts, where the "kinetic" phase of actual combat operations may last only weeks and give the appearance of victory, yet the hard part is putting down the resistance movement that follows and coming up with a successful "exit strategy." Recall George W. Bush's premature declaration of "mission accomplished" on the USS *Abraham Lincoln* on May 1, 2003, less than two months after the Second Gulf War had begun; American troops were to be bogged down in Iraq, suffering over 4,000 casualties, before finally leaving eight years later.

In describing the changing face of war the United States experienced in Iraq, John Donnelly suggests how warfighting is morphing into "**mootwa**" (military operations other than war) and in the process is posing *jus post bellum* types of questions:

> When Donald H. Rumsfeld became Defense secretary at the start of the Bush administration … what he did not foresee was a guerrilla war in the ancient streets of Baghdad that would tie down his Army for years and cost him his job. Iraq required more foot soldiers than the Pentagon had thought, and to be successful, those soldiers had to do jobs for which they were ill-prepared: negotiating with local sheiks, managing municipal governments,

fixing sewers, defusing mobs, keeping the lights on, and understanding tribal and religious quarrels.

For the Army, the new doctrine [focusing much more on irregular, guerrilla conflicts] means a seismic culture shift. It will still have guns and tanks, but it will also need more people skilled in languages, public affairs, economic development, even anthropology. Instead of grudgingly accepting the task of nation-building ... the new Army will have to embrace the role.

"These conflicts [according to Secretary of Defense Robert Gates, Rumsfeld's successor] will be fundamentally political in nature. Success will be less a matter of imposing one's will and more a function of shaping behavior." [According to the Army and Marine Corps field manual], the "center of gravity" in counterinsurgency is the mass of civilians ... . Winning them over – rather than just killing insurgents – is the key to success.[11]

The main architect of the "**counterinsurgency**" (COIN) doctrine in Iraq was General David Petraeus, who felt it was a preferred alternative to a "counter-terrorism" strategy that mainly aimed to kill insurgents. Dan Caldwell describes Petraeus's strategy, noting he supported selling Iraqi oil in order to "finance projects to rebuild local schools, medical clinics, and other basic reconstruction projects known in the Army as 'SWET': sewage, water, electricity, trash disposal."[12] Among the rules of counterinsurgency warfare he articulated was "return real control of the government to locals as soon as possible."[13]

The idea of a *counterinsurgency* strategy aimed at winning the "hearts and minds" of the local, native population was not altogether new – it had been tried in Vietnam, with poor results – but it had taken on added importance, given the "new warfare."[14] U.S. policymakers seemed to understand that achieving any durable peace in many of the conflicts in which the United States might be embroiled (Kosovo, Afghanistan, and the like) would require both "nation-building" and "state-building." The former refers to bringing about national reconciliation among warring factions. The latter refers to everything from repairing roads and other infrastructure to reestablishing a court and policing system to trying to install "democracy at gunpoint" in a society that has never known democratic governance.[15] About Somalia, Secretary of State Madeleine Albright acknowledged at the time (in the early 1990s) that the United States was engaged in "an unprecedented enterprise aimed at nothing less than the restoration of an entire country."[16] The United States proved to be not up to the challenge for various reasons, not the least of which was the minimal existence of state capacity and functioning governing institutions to begin with.

Around the same time as the ill-fated U.S. humanitarian intervention mission in Somalia, in his *Agenda for Peace* proposals presented in 1992, UN Secretary-General Boutros Boutros-Ghali introduced the concept of "peacebuilding" as an important new mission for the UN in failed or devastated states.[17] Whereas "peacekeeping" (traditionally performed by UN blue-helmeted troops inserted as a neutral buffer in war zones) mainly addressed the establishment of physical security, "peacebuilding" addressed larger concerns about human security. The 2000 *Report of the Panel on United Nations Peace Operations* (the Brahimi Report) suggested the enormous range of activities that peacebuilding missions might entail. Somewhat echoing the challenges embodied in U.S. counterinsurgency doctrine, the Report stated:

> These operations face challenges and responsibilities that are unique among United Nations field operations. No other operations must set and enforce the law, establish customs services and regulations, set and collect business and personal taxes, attract foreign investment, adjudicate property disputes and liabilities for war damage, reconstruct and operate all public utilities, create banking systems, run schools, pay teachers, and collect the garbage ... . In addition to such tasks, these missions must also try to rebuild civil society and promote basic respect for human rights, in places where grievance is widespread and grudges run deep.[18]

Whether pursued unilaterally or through a multilateral institution such as the United Nations, the effort to promote a just, durable peace in modern conflicts that satisfies *jus post bellum* standards articulated by Walzer and others is clearly a huge undertaking. The difficulties of nation-building and state-building have caused some second thoughts in Washington about the viability of counter-insurgency doctrine and in UN circles about the realities of peacebuilding.[19] Still, if we are serious about creating the conditions necessary for long-term peace, we cannot avoid *jus post bellum* issues.

The Development of *Jus Post Bellum* Rules: What Would A Just Peace Look Like?

Based on the work of Michael Walzer, Brian Orend has attempted to "construct a general set of plausible principles to guide communities seeking to resolve their armed conflicts fairly." "The first step," he says, "is to answer the question: What may a participant rightly aim for with regard to a just war? What are the *goals* to be achieved by the settlement of the conflict? [italics mine]"[20] Walzer and Orend set the bar quite high when conceptualizing the elements of a just peace. For Orend, "the just goal of a just war, once won, must be a more secure and more just state of affairs than existed prior to the war."[21] For Walzer, it is "restoration plus."[22] So restoring the status quo is not enough.

Orend lists various specific goals. First, assuming that one party to the conflict started the violence, the aggression must be rolled back, with the victim of the aggression reestablishing whatever political independence and territorial integrity might have been compromised and the aggressor forfeiting any unjust gains it had made. Second, the aggressor should have to pay some amount of restitution for the suffering it has caused the victim, which should be proportional to the degree of damage done and commensurate with what the aggressor is capable of paying; the compensation should be paid by those political and military elites most responsible for the aggression rather than by the aggressor's population generally, and should not unduly punish the latter through economic or other sanctions. Third, there may be a need for some demilitarization of the aggressor sufficient to provide assurance from another attack in the future. Fourth, in extreme cases only ("if the actions of the aggressor during war were truly atrocious, or if the nature of the regime at the end of the war is so heinous that its continued existence poses a serious threat to international justice and human rights"), there may be need for "political rehabilitation" – regime change – to be forcibly brought about; the party imposing regime change has a special obligation to insure that the successor regime is a major normative improvement on the one that committed the aggression. Fifth, war crimes trials may be held to prosecute and punish the aggressor for *jus ad bellum* violations (committed by leaders of the regime) as well as *jus in bello* violations (committed by military commanders and soldiers); true justice requires that the victim side be held accountable, also, for any *jus in bello* infractions committed.[23]

Paul Diehl and Daniel Druckman have focused on the role of United Nations "peace operations" (both peacekeeping and peacebuilding) in leading to not merely conflict "abatement and containment" but actual **settlement**. [24] Although their work only tangentially touches the subject of *jus post bellum*, they also list a number of goals that should be pursued in order to achieve a successful outcome that avoids a prolongation and recurrence of the conflict, particularly in cases of civil war. They note that it is not enough for the violence to end as a result of a "hurting stalemate" or the parties all being exhausted from the fighting; a lasting settlement normally requires a resolution of the underlying, root grievances.[25] An agreement once reached must be properly implemented; for example, "of the sixteen peace agreements negotiated to end civil wars in the early 1990s, six were successfully implemented, and four were only partially successful."[26]

They discuss the aims of "the new peacekeeping" missions, which are hard to distinguish from peacebuilding; these include election supervision, democratization, humanitarian assistance, "DDR" (disarmament, demobilization and reintegration of all armed forces into the society), and human rights protection.[27] Regarding election supervision, there is a need not only for competitive parties with various factions represented on the ballot but also outside monitoring or other mechanisms to insure all protagonists can have confidence in the procedures and outcome of voting; the test of success will be turnout levels and, where power-sharing does not result, whether the defeated side accepts defeat or returns to the battlefield. Democratization refers to press freedom, transparent governmental institutions, the rule of law, and strengthening of interest groups, labor unions, and other elements of civil society. Humanitarian assistance should aim to relieve suffering and improve the quality of life for the local population. DDR may entail weapons collection and repatriation of ex-combatants into the national fabric. Regarding "postconflict peacebuilding," Diehl and Druckman include goals ranging from removing landmines to restoring electricity and other public services to building a well-functioning judicial system to promoting "reconciliation between the warring parties" and "transforming attitudes and relationships so that armed conflict is no longer considered to be a mechanism for dispute resolution."[28]

In his treatment of *jus post bellum* "rules," Gary Bass discusses many of the same elements mentioned by Orend and other authors. The victor's obligations include "cleaning up the battlefields" (e.g., de-mining a bomb-littered landscape), "economic reconstruction" (assisting in "the restoration of a shattered economy and society to its prewar status, or at least pulling it out of the rubble"), and, in some cases, "political reconstruction." The obligations of the vanquished, particularly when the latter was the aggressor, include payment of reparations, which "should be compensatory, not vindictive," with the burden falling as much as possible on "war supporters and profiteers" rather than the entire society being punished for aggression.[29]

Regarding "political reconstruction," Bass asks: "To what extent are victorious states justified in the political reconstruction of a society? Are there moral grounds for getting rid of threatening politicians and their supporters, reorganizing a society so that it will be less prone to aggression or slaughter – making it something very different from what it was before the war?"[30] In other words, when is *regime change* appropriate as part of *jus post bellum*? Echoing Orend, Bass argues that only "in the most extreme cases" is "there a compelling argument for a *jus post bellum* duty for foreigners to reconstruct a defeated country."[31] He has in mind here "genocidal states," such as Nazi Germany. With Walzer, he argues that "mere aggression" and "mere dictatorship" are not sufficient grounds to justify regime change. Walzer's logic is that state sovereignty is critical to the ordering principles of the international system, and thus must be respected and restored at the end of a conflict, trumping the felt need to remake a regime however odious the latter might be and no matter the aggression committed (as long as the regime does not cross the line and commit genocide or comparable atrocities).[32]

Bass adds, "There may also be a case for a more limited kind of foreign reconstruction in cases where a just war has left a defeated country on the verge of anarchy," in other words where a country has become a "failed state."[33] Libya is an interesting case, where, in 2011, the dictatorial regime of Muammar Gaddafi brutally suppressed a revolt by engaging in indiscriminate slaughter of civilians (albeit not genocide), before a UN-authorized humanitarian intervention by NATO led to his violent demise and regime change, which in turn left Libya essentially a **failed state**. How might *jus post bellum* apply to Libya? In *Fixing Failed States*, Ashraf Ghani and Clare Lockhart, identify 10 "functions" failed states must be able to perform if they are to maintain stability: the rule of law, a monopoly on the use of force, administrative control of the government bureaucracy, transparent use of public funds, the development of citizens' potential, well-defined citizenship rights, infrastructure development, a well-regulated free market, proper management of public resources, and effective bond and government lending.[34] To what extent does the international community have an obligation to follow up regime change in Libya with repairing what has become a failed state? And to what extent would such external involvement infringe on Libya's sovereignty? Such questions have arisen in the past whenever proposals have been floated for the United Nations to create a new "Failed States Council" to replace the now-moribund UN Trusteeship Council that had been established in 1945 to facilitate the decolonialization process.

Whether reconstructing strong states (genocidal regimes such as Nazi Germany) or failed states (anarchical entities such as Libya or Somalia), "reconstruction is, of course, a horribly difficult task." In the former case "the point is to dispose of cruelty, not to build a utopia," while in the latter case one may have to settle for creating some minimal semblance of a functioning polity and society.[35]

Applying *Jus Post Bellum* Rules: Easier Said Than Done

Aside from the sheer challenge of trying to reconstruct whole societies in a post-conflict situation, including some that were not remotely whole to begin with, there are other more fundamental problems inherent in applying *jus post bellum* norms. *Jus post bellum* rules, by definition, operate at the end of a conflict. Yet, in conflicts such as the "war on terror" conducted by the United States and other actors, there may be no end in sight; notwithstanding Fred Charles Ikle's book title *Every War Must End*,[36] the "new warfare" includes conflicts that at best may be frozen or only sporadically are renewed in isolated bursts of violence.

Even when there is an end to or winding down of a conflict, there is usually a tension between, on the one hand, a victor wanting to do the "right thing" in terms of political and economic reconstruction and, on the other hand, over-staying one's welcome and being accused of "occupation" and imposing one's cultural and other values on the remade state and its people. The United States, for example, was accused of "occupation" in both Iraq and Afghanistan as it tried to stabilize and democratize both countries after its invasion following 9/11 (although "victory" proved elusive). In the case of Afghanistan during the 1980s, as recounted in the film "Charlie Wilson's War," the United States was criticized for abandoning that country and leaving it in rubble in the wake of helping the *mujahideen* oust the Soviet army with CIA-supplied Stinger missiles; yet, had the United States maintained a presence there, it no doubt would have invited criticism as an occupying power, perhaps being accused also of cultural imperialism had it attempted to change the sexist, patriarchical culture of that society. Even when reconstruction is done in the name of *jus post bellum* after a humanitarian intervention, this same sort of damned if you do, damned if you don't dilemma arises. It is hard enough for a state such as the United States to convince its own taxpayers to foot the bill for nation-building and state-building in a place like Afghanistan; it is still harder to convince the people of Afghanistan that your only interest is in their self-determination.

Conclusion: Selection of Cases Examining the Laws of War in Action

In order to get a better handle on how the "new warfare" complicates the workings of international law, it is helpful to look at some specific cases in recent history. One must be careful extrapolating generalizations from single cases, but they are useful in illustrating what might otherwise strike the reader as mere theoretical ideas.

When using case studies, one is immediately faced with the decision as to what cases to employ to demonstrate various aspects of the puzzle under investigation. Here we are most interested in the problems arising in relation to three sets of issues or situations: *jus ad bellum, jus in bello,* and *jus post bellum.* As we have suggested in Part Two, many conflicts today include all three of these elements as overlapping challenges. Many contemporary conflicts also involve a mix of interstate, intrastate, and extrastate violence. The U.S. war in Afghanistan is a good example of such complexity that defies easy categorization.

Thus, in selecting cases for examination in Part Three, aimed at showing the difficulties the "new warfare" presents for the application of rules of war, I struggled with where best to place a particular case. My main concern was to pick cases that vividly showed the strategic, moral, and, especially, legal dilemmas increasingly experienced by actors attempting to adhere to the traditional norms surrounding warfare; there was no neat logic as to which chapter a case appeared in.

In Chapter 5, which focuses on *jus ad bellum* questions, I chose to discuss "The Second Gulf War and Anticipatory Self-Defense," "The Osama bin Laden Raid and the War on Terror," and "Kosovo and the Responsibility to Protect," since I felt these cases all dealt with interesting dimensions of the regime governing the resort to the use of armed force. In Chapter 6, which focuses on *jus in bello* questions, I decided to discuss "The U.S. Drone Campaign: The Legality of Targeted Killings," "The Israeli-Palestinian Gaza War of 2008–2009: Engaging in Asymmetrical Warfare," and "The Second Congo War: Rebels, Gangs, and Armies in Civil-International Strife," since these offered special insights into what uses of force are permissible during an armed conflict. In Chapter 7, which focuses on *jus post bellum* questions, I used the "Intervention in Libya" since that conflict raises interesting issues regarding how a just and durable peace can be realized amidst total chaos.

Chapter 4 Discussion Questions

1. What is meant by *jus post bellum*?
2. What are the key issues that arise at the end of a war which relate to creating the conditions conducive to a post-conflict durable peace? What generally are the elements of a "just peace"?
3. How can international law help contribute to "peacebuilding"?

Notes

1 Among the classic works on the causes of war are Quincy Wright, *A Study of War*, 2nd edn (Chicago, IL: University of Chicago Press, 1965) and Kenneth N. Waltz, *Man, the State, and War* (New York: Columbia University Press, 1959); also see the many works in the Correlates of War project, such as J. David Singer and Melvin Small, *The Wages of War, 1816–1965* (New York: John Wiley, 1972).

2 On the causes of peace, on how wars end, see Tansa George Massoud, "Review Essay: War Termination," *Journal of Peace Research*, 33, no. 4 (1996): 491–496; and Jung In Jo, "The UN's Effectiveness in Post-Civil War Peace Durability," *Journal of International and Area Studies*, 13, no. 1 (2006): 23–35.

3 Michael Walzer, *Arguing About War* (New Haven, CT: Yale University Press, 2004), 161.

4 Brian Orend, "Justice After War," *Ethics and International Affairs*, 16 (Spring 2002): 43. Also, see Brian Orend, *War and International Justice: A Kantian Perspective* (Waterloo: Wilfrid Laurier University Press, 2000), especially 217–263.

5 Orend, "Justice After War," 43.

6 Gary J. Bass, "Jus Post Bellum," *Philosophy and Public Affairs*, 32, no. 4 (2004): 384.

7 John Rawls, *The Law of Peoples* (Cambridge, MA: Harvard University Press, 1999), 96.

8 Bass, "Jus Post Bellum," 405.

9 See Orend, "Justice After War," 56.

10 Ibid., 43.

11 John M. Donnelly, "Small Wars, Big Changes," *CQ Weekly*, January 28, 2008.

12 Dan Caldwell, *Vortex of Conflict* (Stanford, CA: Stanford University Press, 2011), 233.

13 Ibid., 259.

14 On earlier counterinsurgency efforts in Vietnam and elsewhere, see Max Boot, *The Savage Wars of Peace: Small Wars and the Rise of American Power* (New York: Basic Books, 2002); David Galula, *Counterinsurgency Warfare: Theory and Practice* (New York: Praeger, 1964); and John Nagl, *Learning to Eat Soup with A Knife: Counterinsurgency Lessons from Malaya and Vietnam* (Chicago, IL: University of Chicago Press, 2002).

15 See Jeffrey Pickering and Mark Peceny, "Forging Democracy at Gunpoint," *International Studies Quarterly*, 50 (September 2006): 539–560. The authors find, based on an empirical analysis of U.S. military interventions since World War II, that multilateral interventions under UN auspices are more likely to succeed than unilateral American interventions.

16 Quoted in Michael Mandelbaum, *The Case for Goliath* (New York: PublicAffairs, 2005), 74.

17 Boutros Boutros-Ghali, *An Agenda for Peace*, UN Doc, A/47/277 and S/24111, 1992.

18 Quoted in Donald Puchala et al., *United Nations Politics* (New York: Pearson, 2007), 140–141. See Michael N. Barnet et al., "Peacebuilding: What Is In A Name?," *Global Governance*, 13, no. 1 (2007): 35–58.

19 On U.S. policy, see Fred Kaplan, "The End of the Age of Petraeus: The Rise and Fall of Counterinsurgency,"*Foreign Affairs* (January/February, 2013): 75–90. On UN efforts to improve peacebuilding, see Puchala et al., *United Nations Politics*, 150.

20 Orend, "Justice After War," 44.

21 Ibid., 45.

22 Michael Walzer, *Just and Unjust Wars*, 3rd edn (New York: Basic Books, 2000), 119.

23 Orend, "Justice After War," 45–54.

24 Paul F. Diehl and Daniel Druckman, *Evaluating Peace Operations* (Boulder, CO: Lynne Rienner, 2010). Also see Michael W. Doyle and Nicholas Sambanis, *Making War and Building Peace* (Princeton, NJ: Princeton University Press, 2006); and Virginia Page Fortna, *Does Peacekeeping Work?: Shaping Belligerents' Choices After Civil War* (Princeton, NJ: Princeton University Press, 2008).

25 Diehl and Druckman, *Evaluating Peace Operations*, 43.
26 Ibid., 46.
27 Ibid., 63 and Chapter 4.
28 Ibid., 111 and Chapter 5. Charles Call, in *Why Peace Fails: The Causes and Prevention of Civil War Recurrence* (Washington, DC: Georgetown University Press, 2012), stresses the importance of including all groups in governance, especially where ethnic cleavages and identity politics have been the key source of a conflict.
29 Bass, "Jus Post Bellum," 406–409.
30 Ibid., 396.
31 Ibid.
32 Walzer, *Just and Unjust Wars*, 113.
33 Bass, "Jus Post Bellum," 403.
34 Ashraf Ghani and Clare Lockhart, *Fixing Failed States* (Oxford: Oxford University Press, 2008), 125–163.
35 Bass, "Jus Post Bellum," 403.
36 Fred Charles Ikle, *Every War Must End*, 2nd edn (New York: Columbia University Press, 2005).

PART 3

The Laws of War

Are They Still Relevant?

On the Second Gulf War:

> The problem here is that there will always be some uncertainty about how quickly he [Saddam Hussein] can acquire nuclear weapons. But we don't want the smoking gun to be a mushroom cloud.
>
> U.S. National Security Advisor Condoleezza Rice, explaining in September 2002 (months before the American invasion of Iraq) why the Bush administration felt it had enough evidence and reason to launch a preemptive attack

> If the preemptive attack is for the purpose of taking away WMDs from irrational or insane governments, then a preemptive strike does not violate the international rule of law but rather saves it.
>
> Anthony D'Amato, Professor of International Law, Northwestern University, May 1, 2003

> The notion of justified preemption runs counter to international law, which sanctions the use of force in self-defense only against actual, not potential, threats.
>
> Henry Kissinger, *Chicago Tribune*, August 11, 2002

> The right of anticipatory self-defense ... certainly does not include the right to a preventive war.
>
> Boleslaw A. Boczek, *International Law: A Dictionary*

On the War on Terror:

There are times when waging war is not only morally permitted, but morally
necessary, as a response to calamitous acts of violence, hatred, and injustice.
This is one of those times.

> "What We're Fighting For: A Letter from America," statement of 60
> American scholars (including Michael Walzer, Theda Skocpol, Samuel
> Huntington, and Amitai Etzioni) issued in February 2002, offering a "just
> war" defense of the war against terrorism following 9/11

The Obama administration's defense of its expanding global wars boiled
down to the assertion that it was in fact at war; that the authorities granted
by the Congress to the Bush administration after 9/11 to pursue those
responsible for the attacks justified ... ongoing strikes against "suspected
militants" across the globe – some of whom were toddlers when the Twin
Towers crumbled to the ground – more than a decade later.

> Jeremy Scahill, "Epilogue: Perpetual War," in *Dirty Wars*

[The 2011 Navy Seals raid to capture Osama bin Laden] aimed to remove an
enemy who had been trying every day to attack the United States. ... I
haven't the slightest doubt it was entirely appropriate for American forces to act.

> John Paul Stevens, retired U.S. Supreme Court Justice, remarks at
> Northwestern University, May 12, 2011

He [bin Laden] was the head of al Qaeda, an organization that had conducted
the attacks of September 11th. It's lawful to target an enemy commander
in the field.

> Eric Holder, U.S. Attorney General during the Obama administration

On humanitarian intervention in Kosovo in 1999:

Nothing contained in the present Charter shall authorize the United Nations
to intervene in matters which are essentially within the domestic jurisdiction
of any state.

> United Nations Charter, Article 2(7)

International law is able to provide no satisfactory answer concerning the
validity of humanitarian intervention in Kosovo or elsewhere. ... The [UN]
Charter was violated by NATO's intervention in Kosovo.

> Michael Glennon, *Limits of Law, Prerogatives of Power: Intervention in Kosovo*

What we did there was not legal, but it was right.

> Madeleine Albright, former U.S. Secretary of State in the Clinton administration, National Public Radio interview on September 26, 2013

On the Israeli–Palestinian Gaza War of 2008–2009:

Both Israel and Palestinian militant groups committed war crimes and acts that were likely crimes against humanity during the fighting in the Gaza Strip ... a United Nations fact-finding mission [the Goldstone Commission] has concluded... . The mission believed the Israeli military operation was "directed at the people of Gaza as a whole." ... On the other side, Palestinian rocket fire into southern Israel ... failed to distinguish between civilians and soldiers, causing "terror."

> *Haaretz*, September 15, 2009

On the general responsibility of a state to help repair damage done in another state whose polity and economy it has played a role in destroying:

The Pottery Barn rule: You break it, you own it.

> Attributed to U.S. Secretary of State Colin Powell, after the American invasion of Iraq in 2003

These things happened. They were glorious and they changed the world ... and then we f— up the endgame... . We never figured out how to deal with the peace.

> The film *Charlie Wilson's War*, on how the United States helped bring down the Soviet Union in Afghanistan during the 1980s but then abandoned the country rather than help rebuild it

5

APPLYING *JUS AD BELLUM* RULES TO THE NEW WARFARE

Cases

In Chapter 2, we examined the body of international law governing *jus ad bellum*, the circumstances under which it is legal to resort to the use of armed force, and noted many questions that have arisen in applying these rules to contemporary warfare. In this chapter, I will employ three case studies of recent conflicts to follow up that discussion and illustrate in greater detail the kinds of problems we confront today.

The Second Gulf War and Anticipatory Self-Defense

The **Second Gulf War** started as an interstate war between the United States and Iraq, evolved into a civil war involving sectarian strife between Shiite and Sunni Muslims and Kurds, and became further complicated by the participation of transnational terrorist networks.

On March 19, 2003, the United States invaded Iraq, initiating a "shock and awe" aerial bombardment campaign, accompanied by the dispatch of more than 100,000 ground troops. (There was never any formal declaration of war; instead the George W. Bush administration relied on a joint resolution of Congress passed in October 2002, authorizing "the use of United States armed forces against Iraq" if the President felt it necessary.) Eventually, 39 countries contributed troops to what the Bush administration called a "coalition of the willing," ranging from three soldiers deployed by Iceland to 46,000 deployed by the United Kingdom.[1] The goal was to topple the regime of Saddam Hussein. Within a month of the invasion, Saddam fled and went into hiding, his giant statue in Baghdad's Firdos Square taken down on April 9; he was subsequently captured and executed. Coalition forces suffered fewer than 200 combat fatalities by the time that President Bush made a triumphant appearance aboard the *USS*

Abraham Lincoln on May 1 to declare "Mission Accomplished." The victory celebration proved to be premature, as the United States found itself for the next eight years bogged down in an asymmetrical war, fighting various insurgent and terrorist groups contesting the interim government the United States had installed, before finally leaving in December 2011, after suffering over 4,000 combat deaths and the country still in turmoil. Our primary concern here is not how the war ended but how it began, in particular the claim by the United States that it had a right to engage in the "preemptive use of armed force."

The story begins with the First Gulf War. Iraq had invaded Kuwait in August 1990 and had attempted to annex that country, the first time any UN member had sought to eliminate another member of the international community. This triggered a U.S.-led coalition (Desert Storm), authorized under Chapter VII by UN Security Council Resolution 678 in November 1990, that forced Iraq's retreat and surrender. Iraqi leader Saddam Hussein agreed to the terms of UN Security Council Resolution 687 passed in 1991, which, in exchange for a cease-fire that permitted him to remain in power, required him to renounce any biological, chemical, or nuclear weapons (WMDs) programs and to permit UN inspectors (UNSCOM) onto Iraqi soil to monitor disarmament. Over the next decade, however, Iraq frustrated the UN weapons search with half-hearted compliance, forced the inspectors to leave in 1998, and refused to account for its weapons stocks, including chemical weapons Saddam was known to have used against Iran in the 1980s and against his own people, the Kurds, in 1988. There were other UN Security Council resolutions passed after the First Gulf War, such as restrictions on the sale of Iraqi oil (aimed at limiting proceeds that could underwrite Iraqi weapons development) and restrictions on Iraqi aircraft flying over Kurdish villages in northern Iraq (aimed at limiting oppression against the Kurds); as with UNSCOM, Saddam played a cat-and-mouse game in evading UN mandates.

Following the al Qaeda terrorist attack on the United States on September 11, 2001, the Bush administration became increasingly concerned about Iraq's suspected WMD capabilities and links to terrorist groups in the Middle East. In November 2002, Washington persuaded the UN Security Council to pass Resolution 1441, giving Saddam "a final opportunity" to allow the inspectors back to do their job and also demanding a "full disclosure" statement of his weapons programs by January, warning of "serious consequences" if he did not comply. When Saddam continued to obstruct full cooperation and compliance, the United States attempted at the eleventh hour to get another Security Council resolution passed explicitly authorizing the use of armed force against Iraq, but failed to gain the necessary support from council members France, Russia, and China, who all threatened to veto the proposal. The United States finally went ahead anyway with the invasion, dubbed "Operation Iraqi Freedom," in March 2003. (Supposedly, Washington initially had considered calling the mission "Operation Iraqi Liberation," except for concerns that the "OIL" acronym might invite howls from critics about crasser U.S. motives.)

If one evaluates the U.S. invasion of Iraq in moral, practical, and legal terms, the strongest case can be made on *moral* grounds. Saddam Hussein was as brutal a dictator as one could find, drawing comparisons with Adolph Hitler. It is estimated he was responsible for more than 300,000 mass graves discovered by coalition forces upon entering Iraq.[2] He had state-of-the-art torture chambers and allowed no dissent against his rule. According to one author, "the whole country was like an illuminated prison yard."[3] Moreover, as noted earlier, Iraq under Saddam was the first country to use lethal chemical weapons in an interstate conflict since World War I, in violation of the 1925 Geneva Protocol, when he used them against Iran in the 1980s. Also in the 1980s, his cousin Ali Hassan al-Majid ("Chemical Ali") conducted a campaign of genocide and ethnic cleansing against Kurds in northern Iraq that included over 5,000 Kurdish civilians killed in chemical strikes in the town of Halabja. Aside from his brazen attempt to annex a UN member state in Kuwait during the First Gulf War, Iraqi armies burned 700 oil wells in Kuwait during the conflict, causing massive atmospheric pollution.[4] In short, Saddam was rightly seen as a ruthless dictator internally and serial aggressor externally, seemingly providing ample moral grounds for legitimizing humanitarian intervention and regime change, not unlike Slobodan Milosevic, the Serb dictator deposed by the Clinton administration a few years earlier following the NATO intervention in Kosovo (discussed later in the chapter).[5] That there was no immediate likelihood of Saddam resuming acts of genocide and aggression owed only to the sanctions that had been imposed on Iraq, constraints that contained numerous loopholes Saddam was attempting to exploit.

Much has been written about the wisdom of the U.S. invasion and whether it made any *practical* sense, in terms of serving American security and other interests. The general view is that the Iraq War shares with Vietnam the distinction of being perhaps the greatest debacle in the history of American foreign policy, given the huge cost of the war in dollars (a total of over $1 trillion) and lives (over 100,000 Iraqi and other casualties in addition to the thousands of American servicemen killed or wounded) and the failure to achieve most of the stated objectives other than the overthrow of Saddam. Many have argued that Iraq became a distraction and diversion of resources from what should have been the main battleground after 9/11 – Afghanistan. However, at the time the invasion decision was taken, it did not seem so wrongheaded. There were many observers on the eve of war who shared Kenneth Pollack's view, stated in *The Threatening Storm*, that "the only prudent and realistic course of action left to the United States is to mount a full-scale invasion of Iraq to smash the Iraqi armed forces, depose Saddam, and rid the country of weapons of mass destruction."[6]

True, no WMDs ultimately were found in Iraq. Still, if you were George W. Bush sitting in the Oval Office in March of 2003, it would not be wholly unreasonable to take the view that in a post-9/11 world an American president no longer had the luxury of waiting for perfect or near-perfect intelligence before acting, and that there was every reason to believe Iraq either had WMD capabilities (at the very least chemical weapons) or, if programs had been suspended, they could be reconstituted quickly. The director of the CIA told the President it was a "slam dunk" Saddam had such weapons.[7] Virtually every intelligence service in the world said as much. Typical was the statement by an analyst with the Carnegie Endowment for International Peace: "Iraq continues to possess several tons of chemical weapons agents, enough to kill thousands and thousands of civilians or soldiers."[8] Saddam himself cultivated such assumptions, probably in an effort to maintain Iraq's status and reputation as a regional power. The 12,000 page "full disclosure" report he submitted in response to UN Resolution 1441 appeared to be "nothing more than recycled reports, plagiarized documents, and outright lies."[9] Although Bush was accused of "lying" about the existence of WMDs, he and his staff were more likely guilty of "groupthink" in presuming such.[10] On the inherent uncertainty of intelligence, especially when some WMDs can be hidden in basements and garages, one observer perhaps said it best in noting "the laughable contradiction of the Senate Intelligence Committee criticizing the Bush administration for acting on third-rate intelligence [in going to war], even as the 9/11 Commission criticized it for not acting on third-rate intelligence [in failing to anticipate the 9/11 attack]."[11]

It was also true that, although Saddam was accused by the Bush administration of sponsoring terrorism – he was reportedly paying the families of Islamic jihadist suicide bombers $25,000 each for attacks on Israeli civilians – there was never any direct link established to al Qaeda and the 9/11 attacks. Nonetheless, in his State of the Union speech in January 2002, the President told Americans that Iraq (along with Iran and North Korea) was a member of "the axis of evil, arming to threaten the peace of the world. By seeking weapons of mass destruction, these regimes pose a grave and growing danger. They could provide these arms to terrorists, ... I will not wait on events while dangers gather." As far back as the Clinton administration, Congress had passed the Iraq Liberation Act in 1998 (signed by Clinton) that stated: "It should be the policy of the United States to support efforts to remove the regime headed by Saddam Hussein from power in Iraq and to promote the emergence of a democratic government to replace that regime."[12] After 9/11, regime change to some seemed all the more imperative. There was the hope that the overthrow of Saddam would help "drain the swamp," that is, change the landscape of the Middle East by producing the first Arab, Islamic democracy in the region that could serve as an alternative model to the dictatorial regimes under which terrorism had taken root. The administration underestimated the challenge of trying to "forge democracy at gunpoint" in a place like Iraq, with its many ethnic and religious cleavages and no prior experience with democratic institutions.[13] If a moral case could be made in support of the war decision, a cost-benefit analysis of the wisdom of the decision would leave one much more skeptical.

What about the question that is most relevant to this book: Was it *legal*? Was the decision by the United States to resort to armed force against Iraq compatible with *jus ad bellum* rules?

The Bush administration claimed its behavior was legal based mainly on two arguments.[14] First, it tried to argue that it was essentially engaged in a "collective security" operation under Chapter VII of the UN Charter, in that it was enforcing a series of resolutions passed by the UN Security Council that Saddam had flouted; the Security Council had repeatedly charged Iraq with being "in material breach" and "in flagrant violation" of its obligations.[15] Washington contended that both Resolution 678 in 1990 and Resolution 1441 in 2002 gave any member the necessary authority to carry out military sanctions against Iraq. Niall Ferguson noted that "considering the list of Saddam's violations of international law and his manifest contempt for the UN Security Council resolutions he had inspired – seventeen in just four years – the only mystery is why Iraq was not invaded before 2003."[16] Richard Haass concluded that the Iraq invasion "was legal, or in any event was surely closer to being legal than the Kosovo operation,"[17] since in the latter case Russia never supported any Security Council resolution condemning Serbia and the Milosevic regime whereas it did vote to punish Iraqi aggression in 1990. However, the problem with this argument is that the 1990 resolution applied to the previous war and the Bush administration was never able to get explicit approval in 2002 to use armed force against Saddam the second time around, as the Security Council resolution only referred vaguely to "serious consequences" that would follow from continued Iraqi noncompliance. Hence, most legal experts rejected the first argument.

The second argument used to justify the invasion, which became known as the Bush Doctrine, was discussed briefly in Chapter 2. In his annual report on "The National Security Strategy of the United States" presented to Congress in September 2002, President Bush claimed the United States had a right to engage in the *preemptive* use of armed force in "self-defense" against any state or other actor which was thought to possibly pose a threat to American security in the future, even before the threat "was fully formed." The counterargument offered by critics was that no such extensive right of anticipatory self-defense could be found in the UN Charter; and to the extent any such right existed at all, the burden was on the state claiming such a right to demonstrate the seriousness of the threat. Critics argued that the attack on Iraq was more a *preventive* war against a distant threat at best rather than a preemptive war against an immediate threat of the sort that could conceivably trigger the self-defense provision of the UN Charter.[18] Given the fact that no attack by Iraq was imminent, there was no certain evidence it still possessed WMDs, and there was no proven connection between Iraq and the 9/11 terrorists, it was hard for Washington to meet the aforementioned *Caroline* test that the need to act was "instant, overwhelming, and leaving no choice of means, and no moment of deliberation." Hence, UN Secretary-General Kofi Annan called the U.S. invasion "illegal," along with most international lawyers.[19]

The dilemma here is that there can be a fine line between a preemptive and preventive war, especially given the inherent imperfection of intelligence; it is a line that lawyers may find easier to operationalize than practitioners responsible for a nation's security, especially when the price of underreacting to a threat is so much higher in an age of WMDs. As Michael Walzer puts it, due to "weapons of mass destruction or delivery systems that allow no time for arguments about how to respond ... perhaps the gulf between preemption and prevention has now narrowed so that there is little ... difference between them."[20] On the one hand, perhaps it was reasonable for the Bush administration to take the position that, after 9/11, the United States could not afford to be a "sitting duck" waiting for a state or nonstate actor to initiate a WMD attack on New York City or another American target before responding. Yet, on the other hand, the loose, expansive definition of self-defense implied in the Bush Doctrine figured to unravel the entire Charter regime that had been developed to control the outbreak of war.

In the Iraq case, most analysts have argued that it was highly unlikely that Iraq itself would have initiated a WMD attack against the United States even if it had possessed such weapons, since it would have been suicidal. In other words, the United States could have handled the Iraqi threat the same way it successfully handled the constant threat of a Soviet first strike nuclear attack during the Cold War – through *deterrence*, i.e., relying on the threat of retaliation as a means to dissuade the enemy from committing aggression. However, nonstate actors armed with WMDs, perhaps serving as proxies for Baghdad (having obtained "loose nukes" through accidental leakage or through direct transfer from the Iraqi military), would have been another matter altogether. It is generally understood that, while deterrence can work against *states*, it is less effective against *nonstate* actors, in particular shadowy, mobile terrorist organizations, whose addresses are less verifiable and which are therefore less vulnerable to a reprisal; not only is it hard to locate and target terrorists hiding in caves or mountain retreats, but how does one deter a suicide bomber who welcomes death? In 2004, the UN Secretary-General's High-Level Panel on Threats, Challenges, and Change attempted to address this problem by calling for legalizing the preventive use of armed force (to eliminate the potential for horrific terrorist attacks) as long as such use of force was authorized by the UN Security Council. Not surprisingly, President Bush dismissed the proposal, stating that "I will never turn over our national security decisions to leaders of other countries."[21]

The inadequacy of *jus ad bellum* rules given the new realities associated with "the new warfare" can be most plainly seen in the following hypothetical scenario. What if U.S. intelligence sources found strong evidence of an al Qaeda cell in Pakistan plotting to blow up the Brooklyn Bridge or Statue of Liberty in New York City (or, even worse, planning to launch an anthrax attack on the city)? If the attack is merely in the planning stage and has not yet been implemented, can the American military use armed force to attempt to destroy the cell, or must the U.S. wait until the attack is more "imminent"? This leads us to consider a second case study – the 2011 raid that resulted in the death of Osama bin Laden, as part of the "War on Terror."

The Osama bin Laden Raid and the War on Terror

The **Afghanistan War** that began three weeks after the terrorist attack of September 11, 2001 is the longest war in American history; most combat troops were scheduled to be withdrawn by late 2014, with the war ended by late 2016.[22] We must note that it is only the longest war if one does not count what the Pentagon after 9/11 dubbed "The Long War" – the **Global War on Terror**, which has no end in sight.[23] It is hard to imagine eliminating the last terrorist. As one U.S. government report stated, "Victory against terrorism will not occur in a single definable moment. It will not be marked by the likes of a surrender ceremony on the deck of the *USS Missouri* that ended World War II."[24] Instead, victory will consist of the management of terrorism so that what incidents occur are isolated and relatively minor in lethality and destructiveness.

The 2011 American raid that killed **Osama bin Laden**, the al Qaeda leader who masterminded the 9/11 attack, was just one "battle" in the larger "war," albeit perhaps the single greatest success thus far. Here we will examine not only the legal conundrums raised by that incident but also the host of legal questions relating to *jus ad bellum* concerns that have arisen around the War on Terror generally, questions that go well beyond anticipatory self-defense.

Osama bin Laden was born in 1957, the 17th son of 24 sons and 54 children total of Muhammad bin Laden, a rich Saudi construction magnate. By his early 30s, he had turned to terrorism as his life's work and had helped found al Qaeda ("The Base"), motivated by radical Islamic fundamentalist teachings he had been exposed to as a youth, inspired by the success of jihadist fighters against the Soviet Union in Afghanistan during the 1980s, and fueled by resentment against the United States military presence in the Muslim holy lands of Saudi Arabia (at the invitation of the Saudi government) after the First Gulf War. The first al Qaeda strike against the United States interests occurred in 1992 with the bombing of a hotel in Yemen. What followed was a series of attacks leading up to 9/11, including a truck bomb attack on the World Trade Center in New York City in 1993 that injured over a thousand people, attacks on American embassies in Kenya and Tanzania in 1998, and the suicide bombing of the *USS Cole* docked in Yemen in 2000. Al Qaeda issued what amounted to a declaration of war in 1998, when it proclaimed that "to kill the Americans and their allies – civilians and military – is an individual duty for every Muslim who can do it in any country in which it is possible."[25]

On **September 11, 2001**, between 9:00 am and 11:00 am, as many as 3,000 people – mostly Americans but also foreign nationals from dozens of other countries – perished when the twin towers of the World Trade Center in New York City collapsed after being struck by two airplanes flown by al Qaeda operatives; the Pentagon Building in the nation's capital was hit by a third plane, also resulting in substantial loss of life; and a fourth plane crashed in rural Pennsylvania before it could reach its intended destination. Al Qaeda had planned the attack from Afghanistan, whose Taliban government had harbored Osama bin Laden and his followers. Afghanistan refused to surrender them to U.S. authorities when the Bush administration requested their capture and extradition following the 9/11 incident. Immediately after 9/11, the UN Security Council passed Resolution 1368, recognizing the U.S. "inherent right of individual or collective self-defense" and expressing the council's "readiness to take all necessary steps to respond to the terrorist attacks of 11 September 2001, and to combat all forms of terrorism." The United States subsequently, within one month of the attack, launched air and ground strikes against the Taliban and al Qaeda, quickly eliminating the Taliban and dispersing al Qaeda, although bin Laden managed to escape. A new Afghan government was put in place, supported by some 100,000 American and NATO troops deployed to engage in counterterrorism operations in Afghanistan and throughout the region. The Global War on Terror had begun.[26]

It took a decade for the United States to locate and hunt down its prime target, Osama bin Laden. On the night of May 1, 2011, two U.S. military helicopters carrying 23 elite troops from Navy SEAL Team Six took off covertly from Afghanistan and entered Pakistan air space undetected, their destination a house in the town of Abbottabad near a major Pakistani military academy; they were joined by two other support helicopters. Based on intelligence extracted by the CIA from detainees at the Guantanamo Bay naval base prison in Cuba, bin Laden had been connected to a courier who had made repeated trips to the home, and it was determined that the al Qaeda leader was hiding on the third floor of the structure along with members of his family. Apparently, some thought had been given to informing the Pakistan government of the mission and getting its approval, but Washington did not trust that the raid could be kept secret; Pakistan was known to have a dysfunctional government, where one part of the government (the ISI intelligence service) was sympathetic to terrorists while another part (the military establishment) was supportive of U.S. counterterrorism efforts, so that sharing information and seeking Pakistani permission risked undermining the operation. In the early hours of May 2, in total darkness and wearing night vision goggles, the SEALS landed in the compound and within 20 minutes stormed the building, broke through the security gates, shot bin Laden's guards along with the courier and bin Laden's son, and finally killed bin Laden. There is some debate as to whether they ever considered taking him alive – it was unclear if he was armed and prepared to surrender – but the presumption is that the mission called for terminating him rather than capturing him. The computer files the SEALS collected revealed that bin Laden "had been developing plans to assassinate Obama and [General David] Petraeus, to pull off an extravagant September 11 anniversary attack, and to attack American trains."[27] The mission ended with the helicopters taking off with bin Laden in a body bag, the corpse eventually given Muslim burial rites and dumped into the Arabian sea. Pakistan protested U.S. violation of its sovereignty, but others had to wonder how the government could not have been aware of bin Laden's presence within a mile of the Pakistan Military Academy and whether Islamabad had been complicit in sheltering him.

From a *moral* standpoint, few could blame the United States for seeking retribution against bin Laden, given the atrocities he committed; nor, from a *practical* standpoint, was it questionable whether the al Qaeda leader was an important target to eliminate, given his charismatic allure in the jihadist world. But was it *legal*? Pakistan was not alone in criticizing the United States for violating international law. There were many questions raised about the legality of the raid. In examining these questions, it is akin to peeling away the layers of an onion, starting with the broader elements on the surface and then penetrating deeper.

In Chapter 2, Michael Glennon was quoted as saying that "law cannot regulate acts that it is unable to place in categories. ... If use of force is to be made subject to law, we must be able to sort it into categories."[28] What category does the War on Terror, which was the context for the bin Laden raid, fit into? Is it an "armed conflict" under the UN Charter? Were the resolutions passed by the UN Security Council in the immediate aftermath of 9/11, acknowledging the right of the United States to use armed force against the 9/11 perpetrators in "self-defense" and justifying the invasion of Afghanistan, meant to give the U.S. a carte blanche invitation to fight terrorists in an infinite future on an infinite battlefield, whenever and wherever Washington decided to act? Was Jeremy Scahill, the author of *Dirty Wars*, right to question this interpretation, when he railed against a "borderless, permanent global war" waged by the United States? Or was he ignoring the reality of "force without war" today, when so many conflicts involve geographically scattered and temporally sporadic fighting? Scahill has commented: "The Obama administration's defense of its expanding global wars boiled down to the assertion that it was in fact at war; that the authorities granted by the Congress to the Bush administration after 9/11 to pursue those responsible for the attacks justified ... ongoing strikes against 'suspected militants' across the globe – some of whom were toddlers when the Twin Towers crumbled to the ground – more than a decade later."[29] But was not the War on Terror ongoing, with lots of unfinished business, such as the apprehension of Osama bin Laden? In justifying the bin Laden raid and other counterterrorism actions, Obama's Attorney-General, Eric Holder, said this:

> We are a nation at war. ... Because the United States is in an armed conflict, we are authorized to take action against enemy belligerents under international law. ... And international law recognizes the inherent right of national self-defense. None of this is changed by the fact that we are not in a conventional war. Our legal authority is not limited to the battlefields in Afghanistan. ... We are at war with a stateless enemy, prone to shifting operations from country to country.[30]

Even with Osama bin Laden gone, other al Qaeda affiliates and offshoot groups are still at large plotting further attacks on the United States. Indeed, they are scattered across several countries and regions, such as al Qaeda of the Arabian Peninsula (AQAP) in Yemen, al Qaeda of the Islamic Maghreb in Mali and Algeria (AQIM), and al-Shabaab in Somalia. There are also rival terrorist groups, notably the Islamic State of Iraq and Syria (ISIS) seeking a takeover of those states and causing bedlam elsewhere. At what point is the battlefield considered "hot," constituting a war zone for purposes of international law? How "imminent" does the threat have to be for a proactive American response against these adversaries to meet the *Caroline* test and qualify as "self-defense"? And even if the United States has a right to use force in self-defense against terrorists, what about its obligation not to violate the sovereignty of a UN member state in the process? After the bin Laden raid, Pakistan's Prime Minister said, "Our people are rightly incensed on the issue of violation of sovereignty as typified by the covert U.S. air and ground assault on the Osama hideout in Abbottabad."[31] On the matter of whether the United States must get Pakistani (or Yemeni or Somali) approval before using force on their territory against nonstate actors, the onus is on the United States, if it acts unilaterally, to show that the host government is either unable or unwilling to exercise its state responsibility in denying safe haven to actors who threaten international security. Washington seemed to be acting legally in the case of the bin Laden raid, but such determinations are often unclear in many instances.[32]

There are other *jus ad bellum* issues as well, some of which overlap with *jus in bello* issues. Related to Glennon's point about having to sort use of force cases into the right "categories," there are some who would argue that bin Laden really was a criminal rather than a combatant and, thus, should have been handled as a police suspect subject to arrest and taken into custody rather than as an enemy on the battlefield "killed in action." In other words, putting the raid in the "armed conflict" category would be wrong, not because of timing but because of the nature of the action. In Chapter 3, we discussed the "warfare vs. lawfare" debate and whether terrorism should be considered a military security matter subject to the laws of war or rather a law enforcement problem subject to the rules associated with the criminal justice system. Prior to 9/11, when al Qaeda was emerging as a terrorist threat, the United States initially tended to treat terrorist attacks (such as the 1993 attack on the World Trade Center) mainly as crimes calling for the deployment of the FBI and investigative police agencies. However, this changed with 9/11, when Bush launched the Global War on Terror, to be fought primarily through the national security establishment.

Still, the "lawfare vs warfare" debate continues. Following the bin Laden raid, Attorney-General Holder insisted that "the operation against bin Laden was justified as an act of national self-defense." Citing the example of the U.S. attempt to shoot down the plane of Japanese Admiral Yamamoto over the Pacific during World War II, he noted, "It's lawful to target an enemy commander in the field."[33] Law professor Steven Ratner has countered, "A lot depends on whether you believe Osama bin Laden is a combatant in a war or a suspect in a mass murder. [In the latter case] you would only be able to kill a suspect if they represented an immediate threat [e.g., if they were about to shoot a bystander or policeman]."[34] UN officials have pushed for the application of the lawfare model, urging that "the norm should be that terrorists be dealt with as criminals, through legal processes of arrest, trial, and judicially decided punishment. ... In respect of the recent use of deadly force against Osama bin Laden, the United States should disclose ... if the planning of the mission allowed an effort to capture bin Laden."[35] The legality of "targeted killings" will be discussed more extensively in the next chapter, when we focus on the challenges that drone strikes pose for the functioning of *jus in bello* rules. Meanwhile, the reader can be left to ponder whether the killing of bin Laden was a "targeted killing" (what some might call "targeted assassination") as opposed to a combat fatality suffered by an enemy officer in a firefight.

Before moving to the next chapter, there is one last case study to discuss – the 1999 war in Kosovo. Whereas in the bin Laden case, the United States was accused of violating a country's sovereignty in the name of "self-defense," in the Kosovo case the United States was accused of violating sovereignty in a different way, in the name of "humanitarian intervention."

Kosovo and the Responsibility to Protect

In Chapter 2, we cited UN Secretary-General Kofi Annan's pronouncement that the protection of human rights must "take precedence over concerns of state sovereignty" and that sovereignty cannot provide "excuses for the inexcusable."[36] This view was elaborated by the 2001 International Commission on Intervention and State Sovereignty, which stated: "Where a population is suffering serious harm, as a result of internal war, insurgency, repression or state failure, and the state in question is unwilling or unable to halt or avert it, the principle of non-intervention yields to the international responsibility to protect."[37] Especially where a government was committing atrocities against its own people, Annan argued, the international community had a "responsibility to protect" the victims, including possible military intervention, which became known as the "R2P" doctrine.[38] R2P remains a controversial concept, given that it is squarely at odds with perhaps the most fundamental principle of the Westphalian state system. As one commentator notes, "the starting point of international relations is the existence of states, of *independent* political communities [italics mine]."[39] By "independent" is meant sovereign units, whose governments by definition are entitled to exercise control over their internal affairs. As noted earlier, the UN Charter, Article 2 (7) goes so far as to state: "Nothing contained in the Charter shall authorize the United Nations to interfere in matters which are essentially within the domestic jurisdiction of any state."

Nowhere has the R2P norm aroused more contentious debate than in regard to the **Kosovo War of 1999**. The Kosovo War was a civil war pitting Kosovo Albanian rebels, based in a province within Serbia, against the government of Serbia and Montenegro (the Federal Republic of Yugoslavia). The conflict became internationalized when NATO forces intervened in March 1999 to stop Serb ethnic cleansing of Kosovars, mounting an aerial bombardment campaign that lasted over two months before ending in June. Kosovo went on to claim independent statehood, but has not yet been fully recognized by the international community.

In order to understand the war, which involved complex ethnopolitical conflict, one must go back to 1918, when Yugoslavia was created after World War I, fashioned out of Serbia and the Austro-Hungarian and Ottoman empires. It was never truly a "nation"; instead it was a crazy-quilt, jerry-built state, consisting mainly of Serbs, Croats, Slovenes, Albanians, and assorted other nationality groupings divided by language, religion, and other cultural differences. After World War II, the Communist leader Josip Broz Tito was able to bring a degree of unity and cohesion to Yugoslav politics, even as tensions continued to boil beneath the surface. Tito created a federation of six republics – Serbia, Croatia, Slovenia, Bosnia-Herzegovina, Montenegro, and Macedonia. Within Serbia, two autonomous provinces were created. One was Kosovo, considered the "cradle of the Serbian nation," which until the Ottoman conquest in the fourteenth century had been predominantly Serbian but by the 1970s was almost 80 percent ethnic Albanian. After Tito died in 1980, Yugoslavia started to fall apart amid economic and political turmoil, as the individual republics each sought greater autonomy while Kosovo itself sought to become a republic. Slobodan Milosevic came to power in Serbia in 1989, and proceeded to fan the flames of Serb nationalism not only within Serbia but also among ethnic Serbs in Bosnia, Croatia, and the other republics as well as in Kosovo. Between 1990 and 1995, a civil war ensued throughout Yugoslavia and did not end until Yugoslavia became extinct and five new states had been established – Serbia and Montenegro, Croatia, Slovenia, Bosnia-Herzegovina, and Macedonia.[40]

Meanwhile, the status of Kosovo had been left unresolved. Kosovo was still an independent province within Serbia, but found its autonomy increasingly undermined by Milosevic, who saw himself as protecting the minority Serb population there from an oppressive Albanian majority. As tensions grew throughout the 1990s, and Kosovo demanded independence, Milosevic cracked down on the Albanian separatists, who then formed the Kosovo Liberation Army (KLA). Full-scale civil war broke out by 1998 between the KLA and the Serb military, which used "freelance paramilitary groups," including "common criminals" to carry out mass atrocities.[41] As Milosevic's massacre and ethnic cleansing of Albanians escalated, the United States and its European allies tried to persuade the UN Security Council to become involved in what was seen as a humanitarian crisis. The Security Council adopted Resolution 1199 in September 1998, expressing "grave concerns" about Serb atrocities, although both sides were contributing to the violence. Due to the threat of a Russian veto, the United States was unable to get the Security Council to take stronger action in the form of humanitarian intervention. Finally, NATO decided to act on its own, commencing an aerial bombing campaign in March 1999 that lasted until June 1999, when a peace agreement was signed. Overall, more than 2,000 missiles were fired and thousands of bombs dropped by Allied warplanes on Serb military targets as well as bridges, factories, power stations, and communication centers, eventually punishing Serbia into submission. An estimated 10,000 civilians were killed and over 500,000 people displaced from their homes, mostly Kosovar Albanians. Due mainly to the decision not to commit ground forces and to rely solely on air power against weak Serb air defenses, the United States and its NATO allies suffered virtually no combat fatalities despite some 30,000 sorties flown. As a postscript, NATO then dispatched a peacekeeping mission (KFOR) to restore order and forge a peace between Serbs and Kosovars. Regime change occurred, as Milosevic was charged by the International Criminal Court for the Former Yugoslavia with committing crimes against humanity and died in his cell before a verdict could be reached. The final chapter has not been written, as Kosovo's declaration of independence has been only partially recognized by the UN membership and an uneasy peace prevails in the region, with neither Serbs nor Albanians showing signs of ending their mutual animosity.[42]

The general view of the NATO action in Kosovo was that, in the words of the International Independent Commission for Kosovo, "the NATO military intervention was illegal but legitimate."[43] As U.S. Secretary of State Madeleine Albright later confessed, "What we did there was not legal, but it was right."[44] Whatever the moral justification, the fact that the action was never authorized by the UN Security Council has opened it to considerable criticism as a violation of international law and a dangerous precedent for powerful states to claim the right to meddle in the affairs of weaker states.[45] Indeed, some worry about such intervention even if it is blessed by the Security Council. Michael Walzer argues that the "presumption against intervention is strong," based on "opposition to imperial politics and [a] commitment to self-determination."[46] As one third-world spokesperson has said, "We do not deny that the United Nations has the right and duty to help suffering humanity. But we remain extremely sensitive to any undermining of our sovereignty, not only because sovereignty is our last defense against the rule of an unequal world but because we are not taking part in the decision-making process of the Security Council."[47] Certainly it is highly unlikely that any of the Perm Five would allow the UN or any other external actor to engage in humanitarian intervention in its own affairs.

There are other problems raised by the Kosovo intervention and humanitarian intervention in general. First, intervention is costly in both manpower and money. Although "the UN can help states to pool the costs and risks of humanitarian intervention,"[48] is there enough blood and treasure to intervene militarily wherever people are oppressed or where a failed state is neglecting to meet the basic needs of its people? Freedom House counts 48 countries as "not free" and another 59 as only "partly free," so that over half the nation-states in the world potentially could be candidates for intervention based on their lack of democracy; moreover, the annual Failed States Index compiled by *Foreign Policy* counts dozens of "failed" or at least "fragile" states in the world.[49] Even if we agree that humanitarian intervention should be reserved for only the most egregious cases of human rights violations, there is not always a global consensus behind this; with regard to as heinous a crime as genocide, witness UN inaction in the face of the slaughter of Tutsis by Hutus in Rwanda in the 1990s and the Darfur tragedy in the Sudan in the early twenty-first century. Even if morality and legality are on your side, it would seem unwise to intervene unless one believes one can make a positive difference in the conflict, particularly where armed intervention must overcome civil strife fueled by a complex cauldron of ethnic, racial, religious, and other divisions. In the case of Kosovo, there is evidence that intervention at least initially aggravated ethnic cleansing; and efforts at creating a durable peace have yet to bear fruit, as Kosovo remains a Balkan "powderkeg."[50] Finally, there is still resentment among Serbs and others over perceived bullying by NATO countries that dropped lots of bombs without putting their own forces at much risk, violating the norm advanced by Walzer: "You can't kill unless you are prepared to die."[51]

Due to the considerable criticism it attracted, Kosovo had a somewhat chilling effect on subsequent calls for humanitarian intervention. Although the UN Security Council did authorize military intervention in Libya in 2011, in order to prevent the slaughter of civilians by Libyan dictator Muammar Gaddafi in the violent uprising against his regime, not all Security Council members who voted for the resolution intended for the mandate to extend to regime change; when the resulting NATO air campaign led to Gaddafi falling from power, Russia and China complained that "R2P" had been abused. This made it all the more difficult to get Security Council approval for humanitarian intervention against the murderous regime of Syrian leader Bashar al-Assad as the death toll mounted in the Syrian civil war that started in 2011.[52] Meanwhile, Russian leader Vladimir Putin invaded Ukraine in 2014, under the pretext of engaging in humanitarian intervention on behalf of a predominantly Russian population in Crimea against an ultranationalist government in Kiev that was privileging non-Russian language and culture; when he proceeded to back the independence of Crimea (which then opted for annexation by Moscow), he claimed his behavior differed little from that of the United States and NATO in Kosovo, which was also marked by the illegal use of armed force and the dismemberment of a UN member state.

The future of humanitarian intervention remains uncertain. The concept of humanitarian intervention, while a noble notion intended to address the worst sorts of atrocities committed on the planet, has further complicated efforts to apply *jus ad bellum* rules in contemporary world politics.

Conclusion

Although Steven Pinker and others contend that war is "going out of style," someone has forgotten to tell much of humanity, even in the Northern hemisphere, on the European continent (in places like the former Yugoslavia), a supposed "zone of peace," where – unlike "zones of turmoil" in the Middle East, Africa and elsewhere in the South – organized savage fighting is no longer supposed to happen.[53] Thomas Friedman's "golden arches theory of conflict prevention" posits that "when a country reaches the level of economic development where it has a middle class big enough to support a McDonald's network," it loses its stomach for war. Friedman has found virtually no instance where two countries that have a McDonald's restaurant have gone to war against each other.[54] He considers the Kosovo War an exception that proves the rule, since, even though both Serbia and the United States/NATO countries consumed Big Macs, the allies shed little of their own blood in the war, while after only 78 days the Serbs "wanted McDonalds re-opened much more than they wanted Kosovo re-occupied."[55] It would appear that the Russian invasion of Georgia in 2008 and the Ukraine in 2014 would be other exceptions that prove the rule, insofar as they were relatively rare examples of interstate hostilities and seemed barely to qualify as "wars."

Of course, what is or is not a "war" is increasingly open to debate, at least in legal terms. I have tried to use the Second Gulf War, the bin Laden raid and the War on Terror, and the Kosovo War to show the changing nature of war and the accompanying challenges experienced in observing *jus ad bellum* principles. These three case studies also raise *jus in bello* issues as well. The Second Gulf War, for example, included controversy over U.S. treatment of Iraqi POWs at Abu Ghraib prison in Iraq. The War on Terror raised similar concerns about the status and treatment of terrorist detainees at Guantanamo and the use of torture against them (whether waterboarding and other "enhanced interrogation" methods were used to extract the intelligence leading to bin Laden's hideout); there was also the question of whether bin Laden should have been treated as a criminal rather than a combatant and, if he was rightly considered a combatant, whether the United States violated *hors de combat* principles in killing him while he lay wounded. The Kosovo War raised questions about whether NATO air strikes adequately honored the principle of distinction (between civilian and military targets) and whether the Serb leadership was guilty of crimes against humanity in its ethnic cleansing of Albanians.

In the next chapter, we now turn to a focused examination of three other case studies that offer a window into the challenges associated with applying *jus in bello* rules today.

Chapter 5 Discussion Questions

1.   Do a legal analysis of the resort to armed force by the United States in 2003, when the Bush administration decided to intervene in Iraq, starting the

Second Gulf War. What legal arguments did the Bush administration attempt to use to justify its action? Was the intervention legal? If not legal, was it moral? Smart?

2. Do a legal analysis of the 2011 American raid that killed Osama bin Laden. What legal arguments did the Obama administration attempt to use to justify its action? Was the raid legal? If not legal, was it moral? Smart?

3. Do a legal analysis of the humanitarian intervention engaged in by the United States and its NATO allies during the Kosovo War of 1999. What legal arguments did the Clinton administration attempt to use to justify its action? Was the intervention legal? If not legal, was it moral? Smart?

Notes

1 Dan Caldwell, *Vortex of Conflict* (Stanford, CA: Stanford University Press, 2011), 215. For cases studies of the Second Gulf War, in addition to Caldwell, see David Kinsella, *Regime Change: Origins, Execution, and Aftermath of the Iraq War*, 2nd edn (Belmont, CA: Thomson Wadsworth, 2007); Frank P. Harvey, *Explaining the Iraq War* (Cambridge: Cambridge University Press, 2012); Thomas E. Ricks, *Fiasco: The American Military Adventure in Iraq* (New York: Penguin, 2006); and Bob Woodward, *Plan of Attack* (New York: Simon & Schuster, 2004).

2 Niall Ferguson, *Colossus* (New York: Penguin, 2004), 164.

3 Robert D. Kaplan, "Haunted by Hussein, Humbled By Events," *Los Angeles Times*, April 17, 2006.

4 David J. Scheffer, "Use of Force After the Cold War," in Louis Henkin et al., *Right v. Might* (New York: Council on Foreign Relations Press, 1991), 141–143. Also, see Note 25 in Chapter 3.

5 It must be said that the United States itself could be considered morally challenged, having supported Saddam's rise to power in 1979 and provided him with initial access to chemical weapons.

6 Cited in Ferguson, *Colossus*, 155. Pollack has since had second thoughts about the war. Many prominent "realist" scholars from the start opposed the war, with several dozen (such as John Mearsheimer, Kenneth Waltz, and Stephen Walt) putting their signatures on a full-page anti-war advertisement published in the *New York Times* on September 26, 2002. However, showing the complexity of the decision, many equally prominent scholars associated with the "idealist" or "liberal" school (such as Joseph Nye and Michael Ignatieff), known for dovish proclivities, at least initially supported going to war, persuaded by the need to overthrow a maniacal tyrant.

7 Cited in Woodward, *Plan of Attack*.

8 The quote is from Jon Wolfstahl, cited in "Experts: Iraq Has Tons of Chemical Weapons," CNN, accessed April 22, 2014 at www.archives.cnn.com/2002/WORLD/meast/09/02/iraq.

9 The characterization of the "full disclosure" report belongs to Marvin Zonis of the University of Chicago. The evidence for WMDs is discussed in Kinsella, *Regime Change*, 13–15. Also, see "Saddam Hussein Sowed Confusion About Iraq's Arsenal As A Tactic of War," *New York Times*, October 7, 2004, which reported on how Saddam purposely wanted to leave the impression he still had a WMD capability in order to deter Iran and maintain regional influence.

10 Many critics argued that, at the very least, the Bush administration cherry-picked and skewed the data to support its agenda. A special presidential commission appointed in 2005 to examine why no WMDs were found issued a blistering report about U.S.

intelligence failures. See Walter Pincus, "WMD Commission Releases Scathing Report," *Washington Post*, March 31, 2005. It should be noted that there was a postscript, as the *New York Times* on October 15, 2014 reported some remnants of "abandoned" deteriorated chemical weapons stocks belatedly found in Iraq.

11 The quote is from Charles Hill, accessed April 22, 2014 at www.powerlineblog.com/archives/007246.

12 Kinsella, *Regime Change*, 10–11.

13 On the difficulty of imposing democracy on a society lacking such institutions, see Jeffery Pickering and Mark Peceny, "Forging Democracy at Gunpoint," *International Studies Quarterly*, 50 (September 2006): 539–560. Also see Note 15 in Chapter 4.

14 For Bush's legal defense of the war, see his UN speech reported in the *New York Times*, September 22, 2004.

15 See Adam Roberts, "The Use of Force," in David M. Malone, ed., *The UN Security Council* (Boulder: Lynne Rienner, 2004), 140.

16 Ferguson, *Colossus*, 154.

17 Richard N. Haass, *The Opportunity* (New York: Public Affairs, 2005), 185. Also see Roberts, "The Use of Force," 140.

18 Abraham D. Sofaer, in "The Best Defense?: Preventive Force and International Security," *Foreign Affairs*, 89, no. 1 (January/February 2010): 112, notes that "despite the illegality and the risks involved, states have used unauthorized force for preventive purposes in well over 100 instances since the UN Charter was signed in 1945." However, what distinguished the U.S. use of such force in 2003 was President Bush's justification expressed in a formalized pronouncement that seemed to articulate a new legal norm; other states may have acted similarly in the past, including the United States, but without their action accompanied by any pronouncements.

19 "UN Chief Ignites Firestorm by Calling Iraq War 'Illegal,'" *New York Times*, September 17, 2004. On whether the invasion could be considered a "just war" under international law, see Kinsella, *Regime Change*, 26–35; and Michael Walzer, *Arguing About War* (New Haven, CT: Yale University Press, 2004), 160–161.

20 Walzer, *Arguing About War*, 147.

21 Presidential debate on October 13, 2004. Haass, *The Opportunity*, 177, also questions how realistic it is to expect any country to entrust its national security to the UN Security Council.

22 "U.S. Troops to Leave Afghanistan by End of 2016," announced by President Obama and reported in *New York Times*, May 27, 2014. As of this writing, it is unclear whether the 2016 deadline will be met, given ongoing security concerns in Afghanistan.

23 During the Bush administration, "The Long War" was also referred to as "The Global War on Terror." The Obama administration dropped both names for the conflict, preferring to characterize it as "Overseas Contingency Operation." See "'Global War on Terror' Is Given New Name," *Washington Post*, May 25, 2009.

24 *National Strategy for Combatting Terrorism* (Washington, DC: February 2003), 12.

25 World Islamic Front, "Jihad Against Jew and Crusaders," February 23, 1998; cited in Glenn Hastedt et al., *Cases in International Relations: Pathways to Conflict and Cooperation* (Thousand Oaks, CA: CQ Press, 2015), 98.

26 It is widely accepted that the UN resolutions following 9/11 provided legal support for the U.S. invasion of Afghanistan against al Qaeda and the Taliban, although few legal experts took this as an open-ended invitation to fight a Global War on Terror. See Rosa Brooks, "Drones and the International Rule of Law," *Ethics and International Affairs*, 28, no. 1 (2014): 83–103.

27 Nicholas Schmidle, "Getting Bin Laden," *The New Yorker*, August 8, 2011. Details of the raid are derived from Schmidle and various news sources.

28 See Note 28 in Chapter 2.

29 Jeremy Scahill, *Dirty Wars* (New York: Nation Books, 2013), 520.

30 Remarks delivered by U.S. Attorney-General Eric Holder at Northwestern University, March 5, 2012. Likewise, John Brennan, Assistant to the President for Homeland Security, speaking at the Harvard Law School on September 16, 2011, said that the U.S. may "take action against al Qaeda and its associated forces without doing a separate self-defense analysis each time."

31 Yousaf Raza Gilani, "Pakistan PM's Speech on Osama bin Laden," *International Business Times*, May 9, 2011.

32 On the thorny legal issues raised by armed attacks by nonstate actors and the culpability of states that purposely or inadvertently provide sanctuary to those actors, see Louise Arimatsu, "Spatial Conceptions of the Law of Armed Conflict," in Robert P. Barnidge, ed., *The Liberal Way of War* (London: Ashgate: 2013), 167–188; Report of the Special Rapporteur on Extrajudicial, Summary Or Arbitrary Executions (Alston Report), UN General Assembly Doc. A/HRC/14/24/Add.6, May 28, 2010, 11–12; and Report of the Special Rapporteur on Extrajudicial, Summary or Arbitrary Executions (Heyns Report), UN General Assembly Doc. A/68/382.

33 See the Holder citation in Note 30 above.

34 Andrew Longstreth, "Analysis: Legal Questions Remain Over Bin Laden Killing," *Reuters*, May 9, 2011.

35 Osama bin Laden: Statement by the UN Special Rapporteurs on Summary Executions and on Human Rights and Counter-Terrorism (Christof Heyns and Martin Scheinin), accessed April 25, 2014 at www.ohchr.org/EN/Countries/ENACARegion/Pages/USIndex.aspx.

36 See Note 31 in Chapter 2.

37 Report of the International Commission on Intervention and Sovereignty (2001), XI.

38 The R2P doctrine was further developed in the 2004 report of the "United Nations Secretary-General's High-Level Panel on Threats, Challenges and Change" and in Kofi Annan's 2005 report "In Larger Freedom: Towards Development, Security and Human Rights for All."

39 Hedley Bull, *The Anarchical Society* (New York: Columbia University Press, 1977), 8

40 On the history of Yugoslavia before and after the death of Tito, see Dennison Rusinow, ed., *Yugoslavia: A Fractured Federalism* (Washington, DC: Woodrow Wilson Center Press, 1988); and Susan Woodward, *Balkan Tragedy* (Washington, DC: Brookings Institution, 1995).

41 On how Kosovo typified the "new wars," see Mary Kaldor, *New and Old Wars*, 2nd edn (Stanford, CA: Stanford University Press, 2007), 99.

42 For an overview of the Kosovo conflict, see Andrew J. Bacevich and Eliot A. Cohen, *War Over Kosovo: Politics and Strategy in A Global Age* (New York: Columbia University Press, 2001); and Ivo H. Daalder and Michael E. O'Hanlon, *Winning Ugly: NATO's War to Save Kosovo* (Washington, DC: Brookings Institution Press, 2001).

43 Independent International Commission on Kosovo, *The Kosovo Report* (2000), 2 and 186. Also, see Ruti Teitel, "Kosovo to Kadi: Legality and Legitimacy in the Contemporary International Order," *Ethics and International Affairs*, 28, no. 1 (2014): 105–113; and Bruno Simma, "NATO, the UN, and the Use of Force: Legal Aspects," *European Journal of International Law*, 10, no. 1 (1999): 1–22.

44 National Public Radio Interview on September 26, 2013, reported in *Washington Examiner*, September 26, 2013.

45 On the fallout from the Kosovo War, see Michael J. Glennon, *Limits of Law, Prerogatives of Power: Intervention After Kosovo* (New York: Palgrave, 2001). On the concerns of Third World states, see especially 158–162.

46 Walzer, *Arguing About War*, 68.

47 Remarks made by Algerian President Abdelaziz Bouteflika, quoted in Barbara Crosette, "UN Chief Wants Faster Action to Halt Civil Wars and Killings," *New York Times*, September 21, 1999.

48 Mark Stein, "Unauthorized Humanitarian Intervention," *Social Philosophy and Policy*, 21 (Winter 2004): 14.

49 See Freedom House, *Freedom in the World 2014*, accessed June 26, 2014 at www.free domhouse.org/report/freedom-world/freedom-world-2014#; and Foreign Policy and Fund for Peace, *Failed States Index 2013*, accessed June 26, 2014 at www.foreignpolicy. com/articles/2013/06/24/2013_failed_states_interactive_map.

50 See Ted Galen Carpenter, "The Kosovo Powderkeg," *The National Interest* (December 5, 2011); and "Kosovo, Still Messy After All These Years," *New York Times*, October 27, 2005.

51 Walzer, *Arguing About War*, 99–101.

52 On the Libyan and Syrian situations, see J. Craig Barker, "The Responsibility to Protect: Lessons from Libya and Syria," in Robert P. Barnidge, ed., *The Liberal Way of War* (London: Ashgate, 2013), 63–85; Michael N. Schmidt, "Legitimacy Versus Legality Redux: Arming the Syrian Rebels," *Journal of National Security Law and Policy*, 7 (2014): 139–159; and Saira Mohamed, "The UN Security Council and the Crisis in Syria," American Society of International Law *Insights*, 16 (March 26, 2012).

53 Max Singer and Aaron Wildavsky, in *The Real World Order*, revised edn (Chatham, NJ: Chatham House, 1996), 3, speak of the world as divided into two halves – "one part is zones of peace, wealth and democracy … and the other part is zones of turmoil, war, and development."

54 Thomas L. Friedman, *The Lexus and the Olive Tree* (New York: Farrar, Straus, Giroux, 1999), 196.

55 Thomas L. Friedman, "Was Kosovo World War III?," *New York Times*, July 2, 1999.

6

APPLYING *JUS IN BELLO* RULES TO THE NEW WARFARE

Cases

In Chapter 3, we examined the body of international law governing *jus in bello*, which prescribes the conduct that is acceptable during the waging of armed conflict. We offered an overview of the history of regime-development in this area and the kinds of problems posed by the new warfare. It was noted that *jus in bello* rules try to place limits on who and what can be targeted, how combatants as well as noncombatants can be treated, and the kinds of weapons that can be used. At the core of such rules, often referred to as "international humanitarian law" (IHL), are the concepts of distinction, necessity, and proportionality. As in the previous chapter, we will use three case studies here to delve more deeply into these matters and elucidate the many difficulties today experienced by actors attempting to apply the laws of war, particularly *jus in bello* rules. In the words of William Banks,

> Twenty-first century forms of conflict ... are fostering new questions about the legitimacy of the international humanitarian law corpus. The challenge is thus to balance reform with preserving these venerable international legal instruments to ensure their longevity, relevance, and continued success in humanizing the battlefield – including maintaining the balance ... between states' security aims and the human rights community's commitment to minimize unnecessary suffering on the newest battlefields.[1]

The U.S. Drone Campaign: The Legality of Targeted Killings

Although "targeted killings" have a fairly lengthy history,[2] targeting via "unmanned aerial vehicles" or "remotely piloted aircraft," otherwise known as

drones, is a recent addition to the art of warfare. As early as World War I, with the invention of the airplane, military planners were already envisioning the potential uses of drones for purposes of both reconnaissance and targeting. By the late twentieth century, the United States had developed models of its Predator and Reaper drones that could stay aloft and monitor activity over a target for more than a dozen hours at a time, controlled by ground crews stationed at distant sites thousands of miles away. As a weapon, they offered the special advantage of being able to kill intended targets in a timely fashion, with relatively little military intrusion (obviating both conventional boots on the ground and massive air power), thus seemingly minimizing loss of life both for the attacking forces as well as the local population. 9/11 and the War on Terror provided the catalyst for drones becoming a staple of the U.S. arsenal.

The first reported U.S. drone attack outside a regular combat zone was November 3, 2002. A Hellfire missile was fired from a Predator by Central Intelligence Agency operatives based at CIA headquarters in Langley, Virginia, aimed at a car in Yemen that was carrying six passengers, including a senior al Qaeda leader who was wanted for the *USS Cole* bombing in 2000.[3] All six passengers were killed. Over the next several years, drones became the centerpiece of American counterterrorism strategy. Between 2004 and 2014, according to some accounts, it is estimated that the United States was responsible for roughly 1,000 drone attacks in Afghanistan, Pakistan, Yemen, Somalia, and a few other countries.[4] Aside from the main combat theatre of Afghanistan, the great bulk of these attacks, some 400 strikes, were in Northwest Pakistan, aimed at eliminating al Qaeda and Taliban leaders thought to be hiding there.[5] Whereas George W. Bush ordered fewer than 50 drone strikes while in office, Barack Obama authorized over 400 in his first term alone;[6] one organization that tracks such data reported that drone strikes were occurring every four days in the Obama administration, compared to only once every 40 days during the Bush administration, reflecting the former's tenfold increase in the use of the technology.[7] Although Obama cut back on drone usage somewhat in his second term, in reaction to criticisms over the amount of collateral damage being caused, drones continued to be a major arm of his counterterrorism policy.

Estimates of the number of incidents are somewhat sketchy, since they are based on hard-to-verify information from anonymous American officials, foreign governments, foreign press organizations, human rights groups, and militants themselves, each of which often has an agenda or incomplete data. Accurate counts of casualties are all the more difficult to track, particularly trying to distinguish between combatants versus civilians killed or injured. Consistent with the statistics presented earlier in Chapter 3,[8] Daniel Byman of the Brookings Institution, writing in 2013, noted that "according to data compiled by the New America Foundation, since Obama has been in the White House, U.S. drones have killed an estimated 3,300 al Qaeda, Taliban, and other jihadist operatives in Pakistan and Yemen ... [including] over 50 senior leaders," while only "between

150 and 500 civilians have been killed by drones during Obama's administration."[9] On the other hand, "the Bureau of Investigative Journalism reports that in 2011 alone, nearly 900 noncombatants, including almost 200 children, were killed by U.S. drone strikes. Columbia Law School's Human Rights Clinic also cites high numbers of civilian deaths."[10] A study by Stanford Law School and New York University School of Law, "Living Under Drones," disputed Obama administration contentions that virtually no civilian deaths could be traced to drones and found that "the number of 'high-level' targets killed as a percentage of total casualties is extremely low – about 2%."[11] Byman concludes, "The truth is that all the public numbers are unreliable. Who constitutes a civilian is often unclear; when trying to kill the Pakistani Taliban leader Baitullah Mehsud, for example, the United States also killed his doctor [who was not targeting American forces but was nonetheless abetting a known terrorist]."[12]

Earlier I had noted the thorny problem of how to treat "a farmer by day and a fighter by night" when applying the norm of "distinction." The same goes for "a doctor by day and a fighter by night." Who exactly is fair game as "participating in hostilities"? And, relating to "proportionality," how much unintended collateral damage is permissible in pursuit of a high-value target? Drone strikes only further complicate the issue of who can be targeted, under what circumstances, and with how much lethality. In one celebrated case, in 2009, a U.S. Hellfire missile killed Pakistan Taliban leader Hakimullah Mehsud (thought to have been involved in both the 2008 Marriott Hotel bombing in Islamabad and the 2007 assassination of Prime Minister Benazir Bhutto) along with his wife, mother- and father-in-law, seven bodyguards, and a lieutenant. One critic claims that the United States violated international humanitarian law, since Mehsud was receiving an intravenous transfusion at the time and thus should have been spared as an enemy *hors de combat*.[13]

Drone attacks pose a host of moral, legal, and practical (strategic) questions. John Brennan, President Obama's Homeland Security and Counterterrorism Advisor and a key figure in the bin Laden raid, defended the U.S. drone policy as satisfying all conceivable criteria, calling the strikes "legal, ethical and wise."[14] Again, some go so far as to argue on *moral* grounds that using drones "to go after terrorists not only was ethically permissible but might be ethically obligatory, because of their advantages in identifying targets and striking with precision. ... All the evidence we have so far suggests that drones do better at both identifying the terrorist and avoiding collateral damage than anything else we have." The basis for the latter observation is that, even if one accepts the high-end estimate of 20 percent of drone casualties being civilians, that is less than the civilian toll typically produced by conventional warfare.[15] Still, many critics are unimpressed with the notion that "compared with a 500-pound bomb dropped from an F-16, the grenadelike warheads carried by most drones create smaller, more precise blast zones."[16] There remain profound moral questions about whether drones represent a dehumanizing, dishonorable mode of fighting – facilitating, even encouraging, low-risk killing fields that border on long-distance executions. Their use has been called "lawful but awful."[17]

Beyond moral considerations, drones may offer *practical* advantages in the short term but in the long term may prove strategically costly, if they result in more use of armed force than would otherwise occur, if they alienate foreign governments and publics, if they breed more terrorists, and if they set a precedent that irresponsible governments or nonstate actors will abuse down the road as the technology becomes more widespread.[18]

It is the *legal* issues surrounding drones that are among the most intriguing and problematic. I touched upon these briefly in Chapter 3, but they deserve fuller discussion. There is nothing inherently illegal about drones per se as instruments of war. Just as UN Special Rapporteur Heynes has concluded that "there is broad agreement that drones themselves are not illegal weapons,"[19] Mary Ellen O'Connell, a professor of international law at Notre Dame University, likewise calls drones "a lawful battlefield weapon" as long as used properly.[20] What constitutes proper use is open to debate, however, with O'Connell and other critics arguing that U.S. drone strikes often violate both *jus ad bellum* and *jus in bello* norms[21] while Michael Schmitt of the U.S. Naval War College and others find the United States generally in compliance with international law.[22]

In addition to Obama Homeland Security Advisor John Brennan, Eric Holder, Obama's Attorney-General, also defended the legality of American drone strikes. In his 2012 Northwestern University speech, referenced in the discussion of the bin Laden raid in Chapter 5, Holder addressed both *jus ad bellum* issues and *jus in bello* issues. Regarding the former, he relied on both the post-9/11 authorization to use armed force by the U.S. Congress as well as the authorization by the UN Security Council, grounded in the UN Charter's right of self-defense, as a basis for claiming that the War on Terror constituted an ongoing "armed conflict" in which the United States had a right to use "lethal force" against any "enemy belligerent" posing an "imminent threat of violent attack," no matter the locale, even in countries whose government had not consented to such actions, if it was determined that the latter was "unable or unwilling to deal effectively" with the threat. Regarding *jus in bello* concerns, specifically "targeted killings," Holder stated that they did not violate international law (international humanitarian law) or U.S. domestic law (constitutional or criminal law) bans on assassinations or arbitrary executions, since targets were carefully vetted and overseen by a Foreign Intelligence Surveillance Court, were limited to "senior-level" terrorist operatives (if outside a "hot" battlefield and "actively engaged in planning to kill Americans"), and were selected for killing where "capture" was deemed "infeasible." Moreover, most controversially, Holder justified even the targeting of American citizens overseas if they met the criteria.[23]

In a 2010 speech to the American Society of International Law, U.S. State Department Legal Advisor Harold Koh insisted that the United States made every effort to comply with *jus in bello* principles, including "the principle of distinction, which requires that attacks be limited to military objectives and that civilians or civilian objects shall not be the object of the attack" and "the principle of proportionality, which prohibits attacks that may be expected to cause incidental loss of civilian life [or] injury to civilians ... that would be excessive in relation to the concrete and direct military advantage anticipated." He rejected the notion that drone strikes amounted to "unlawful extrajudicial killings," arguing that a state "that is engaged in an armed conflict ... is not required to provide targets with legal process before the state may use lethal force."[24] President Obama himself, in a 2013 speech on "Drone Policy" at the National Defense University, remarked similarly: "America's actions are legal. We were attacked on 9/11. ... So this is a just war – a war waged proportionally, in last resort, and in self-defense."[25]

O'Connell disagrees. She maintains that only in a specific locale such as post-9/11 Afghanistan could an "armed conflict" (a "hot" battlefield with sustained fighting between combatants) be said to exist, where the laws of war therefore applied; only there could one rightly assess whether U.S. drone strikes did or did not meet international humanitarian law requirements. In other words, she argues that in Pakistan, Yemen, and most places where the United States has fired drones, these have been outside the normal theatre of conflict; hence, the use of armed force in these instances is not subject to the laws of war but rather the rules associated with law enforcement and criminal justice, i.e., the "lawfare" rather than "warfare" paradigm applies.[26]

Referring to American drone strikes in Western Pakistan in particular, O'Connell states: "These attacks cannot be justified under international law" since "drones launch missiles or drop bombs, the kind of weapons that may only be used lawfully in armed conflict hostilities ... . [There] was no armed conflict on the territory of Pakistan because there was no intense armed fighting between organized armed groups. ... The so-called 'global war on terror' is not an armed conflict."[27] Elaborating, she comments:

> Drones are not lawful for use outside combat zones. Outside such zones, police are the proper law enforcement agents and police are generally required to warn before using lethal force. [Even if Pakistan or Yemen were to give the United States permission to engage in drone strikes], states cannot consent to a right they do not have. States may not use military force against individuals on their territory, when law enforcement measures are appropriate.[28]

Moreover, she contends that, even where an armed conflict exists and laws of war apply, such as Afghanistan, the U.S. is "failing to follow important battlefield rules" relating to "necessity, proportionality, and humanity."[29]

UN Special Rapporteurs for Extrajudicial, Summary or Arbitrary Executions (Philip Alston and Christof Heyns) have echoed O'Connell's view that in most cases the lawfare model is the more appropriate way to conceptualize and evaluate the legality of "targeted killings."[30] This assumes that terrorism is a crime rather than a national security threat, and that due process and other norms of exemplary criminal justice systems should apply. However, it is not likely that MPs (military police) or other cops can be entrusted with capturing al Qaeda terrorists abroad; instead, some sort of military force will likely be required. As Geoffrey Corn notes, "Organized militaries are not conversant with the law enforcement framework, and, as a general proposition, armed forces are not trained to conduct law enforcement operations."[31]

These issues came to a head with the targeted killing of Anwar al-Awlaki, a U.S. citizen killed on September 30, 2011, when he and three other passengers traveling in a car in northern Yemen were hit by a Hellfire missile fired from a CIA-operated Predator drone. Al-Awlaki, born to Yemini parents in New Mexico in 1971, and thus possessing American citizenship, had become a radical Muslim cleric promoting jihadist violence against the United States. As an imam at a mosque in Falls Church, Virginia in 2001, he had preached to three of the 9/11 hijackers. By the mid-2000s, he had gone to Yemen and become an al Qaeda member, using the Internet to spread anti-American hatred. He was wanted by both the United States and the Yemini government, especially after being connected to Nidal Hasan, the U.S. Army psychiatrist found guilty of the 2009 mass shootings on the Fort Hood, Texas military base, as well as the Nigerian "Underwear Bomber" who had tried to blow up Northwest Airlines Flight 253 on Christmas Day, 2009. In 2010, President Obama had included him on a CIA "kill list," an unprecedented action against an American citizen, sparking outrage from constitutional law and civil liberties groups in addition to raising *jus ad bellum* and *jus in bello* international law questions. Some critics argued that Obama's entire drone program ignored the executive order banning assassinations signed by President Ford in 1976, although the order did not apply to "wartime" activities. Others argued that al-Awlaki's death amounted to execution without trial in violation of the U.S. Constitution's Fifth and Sixth Amendments, human rights treaties, and international humanitarian law, while the Obama administration maintained that he was a dangerous national security threat whose capture and prosecution was not possible and whose targeting met both U.S. domestic law criteria as well as international law criteria. According to the administration, his American citizenship did not negate the fact he was an enemy combatant in an armed conflict who could be targeted based on strong intelligence data, while the drone attack had the blessing of the Yemini government and met the standard of military necessity and other norms.

Here, again, readers are left to reach their own judgments as to whether al-Awlaki should have been treated as a criminal subject to arrest and a jury trial or whether the warfare model applied. Such are the kinds of debates occurring today. A related debate is whether "CIA personnel who conduct targeted drone killings are committing war crimes because they, unlike the military, are [non-uniformed] 'unlawful combatants'."[32] Although few would find support for this in IHL, there is growing pressure on the United States to shift primary responsibility for the drone program away from the CIA to the Department of Defense, on the grounds of transparency, that "drone operations be placed in institutions that are able to disclose to the public the methods and findings of their intelligence, criteria used in selection of targets ... and an official record regarding the persons killed."[33]

Some observers favor doing away with the drone program altogether, for reasons having to do with fear of weapons proliferation. Although, as of 2014, only the United States, Israel, and the United Kingdom are believed to have used armed drones, more than 70 countries now have some type of drone.[34] Nonstate actors, either terrorist groups or drug cartels, may not be far behind. Peter Bergen has said that "the time has come for some kind of international convention on the legal framework surrounding the use of such weapons."[35] Others maintain that "such an arrangement would not necessarily require new international laws; rather, it would necessitate a more broadly accepted understanding of which existing laws apply and when and a faithful and transparent adherence to them."[36]

Clearly, the United States has a special responsibility to provide leadership in addressing the legal issues surrounding not only targeted killings but the larger problem of restoring parameters around the use of armed force generally. As former UN Rapporteur Philip Alston has written, "If other states were to claim the broad-based authority that the United States does, to kill people anywhere, anytime, the result would be chaos."[37] Israel finds itself in a somewhat similar situation, dealing with a seemingly never-ending, unconventional conflict that makes adherence to traditional rules very difficult, inviting criticism that it is an outlaw state undermining world order. We now turn to the Gaza War of 2008–2009 between Israelis and Palestinians, a case that further illustrates how hard it is today to fight wars that are not "dirty."

The Israeli–Palestinian Gaza War of 2008–2009: Engaging in Asymmetrical Warfare

The **Gaza War of 2008–2009**, between Israel and Hamas (the governing authority of Palestinians living in the Gaza Strip), is one of three such wars that have been fought in the past decade. The Gaza War of 2008–2009 (Israeli code name "Operation Cast Lead") lasted three weeks; the Gaza War of 2012 ("Operation Pillar of Defense") lasted one week; and the Gaza War of 2014 ("Operation Protective Edge") lasted seven weeks. Although it is the 2008–2009 war we focus on here, all three episodes raised similar questions about the workings of international law in asymmetrical warfare situations.

The 2008–2009 Gaza War cannot be understood apart from the much larger Israeli–Palestinian conflict that has been ongoing for decades. In the space of a few pages, we cannot possibly summarize the entire conflict, only provide some basic historical context for the case study.[38]

The conflict is between two peoples who each have their own narrative and version of events. The dispute has proven intractable, with each side seemingly having a claim to the land (a small patch of real estate in the Middle East between the Mediterranean Sea and the Jordan River), both harboring legitimate grievances, and together contributing to a failed resolution. The many cycles of violence sparked by the dispute remind one of the two brothers engaged in constant fighting who complain to their father that "it all started when he hit me back!" Since this chapter deals with *jus in bello* rather than *jus ad bellum* issues, we are less interested here in how the conflict started than in how it has been conducted; but it is hard to separate out these sets of issues.

From the Israeli perspective, the origins of the conflict go back millennia, as Israelis trace their claim to the land to biblical times 5,000 years ago, to Abraham, Moses, and the ancient Hebrews. The Palestinians trace their own claims almost as far back, to the ancient Canaanites. With the destruction of the Second Temple in Jerusalem by the Romans in 70 CE, the Jews became dispersed all over the world – the so-called Diaspora. It was not until the late nineteenth century, through what became known as the Zionist movement in Europe, that Jews envisioned returning to their homeland and reestablishing a Jewish state there. By that time, however, Palestinians and other Arabs were the dominant population living in that location, ruled then by the Ottoman Empire (Turkey). A key event was the Balfour Declaration, issued by the British government in 1917, during World War I, whereby Britain promised Jews their own homeland in Palestine. Once World War I ended, with Turkey defeated and the United Kingdom administering Palestine under a League of Nations "mandate" during the Interwar Period, the British tried to satisfy the aspirations of both the Jews and the Palestinians for their own states but found themselves embroiled in a growing territorial dispute. By 1945, the Arab population in the area numbered over 1 million, while the Jewish population numbered roughly 500,000 (their numbers having swelled due to immigration of Jews fleeing the Nazi Holocaust during World War II). To the Jews, the Holocaust in Germany and Europe justified their demands for a homeland where they could be safe. To the Palestinians, they argued that the British never had the right to promise away land that was not theirs, that Arabs should not be made to pay for Europe's sins, and that this was yet another example of Western imperialism.

The United Nations General Assembly addressed the issue by voting in 1947 to partition Palestine into two new states, one Jewish (the state of Israel) and one Arab (the latter encompassing the West Bank of the Jordan River as well as the Gaza Strip adjoining the Mediterranean), with Jerusalem to be an international city under joint control. While Jews accepted the partition plan and agreed to give Palestinians within their borders full Israeli citizenship, Arabs rejected the plan. Israel declared its independence in May 1948. Full-scale war broke out,

with the Arab states of Egypt, Syria, Jordan, and Lebanon fighting against partition and encouraging Palestinians living within Israel to join in the fight. Israel
defeated the Arab armies, with Palestinians displaced from their homes and settled
in refugee camps, as an armistice left Jordan exercising sovereignty over the West
Bank (including East Jerusalem) and Egypt over the Gaza Strip.

This territorial arrangement remained intact until the Six-Day War in June
1967. Israel, faced with several Arab armies mobilizing on its border and the
Straits of Tiran closed to Israeli shipping, attacked first, claiming self-defense.[39]
Thanks to its air superiority, the war was a huge triumph for Israel; it seized the West
Bank from Jordan (including East Jerusalem, giving it control of the entire city) and
the Gaza Strip (plus the Sinai Peninsula) from Egypt, along with the Golan
Heights from Syria. In the Camp David Accords of 1978, brokered by U.S. President Jimmy Carter, a peace agreement was reached between Israel and Egypt
that returned the Sinai to Egypt. However, Israel ever since has continued to
control the other captured territories, including East Jerusalem, the West Bank,
and the Gaza Strip, which Palestinians consider constituting a Palestinian state
under illegal Israeli "occupation." United Nations Security Council Resolution
242 in 1967 called for Israel to return to its pre-1967 borders in return for Arabs
and Palestinians recognizing Israel's right to exist, but neither side has met its
obligations. Even though the international community has urged a "two-state
solution," Israel has restricted Palestinian self-governance and expanded settlements
beyond the 1967 boundaries, while the Palestinians have refused to formally
recognize Israeli statehood.

The Israeli–Palestinian conflict has taken numerous twists and turns in recent
years, with peace efforts alternating with flare-ups of violence. Israel's military
presence in the Palestinian territories, including checkpoints that limited Palestinian movement, led in 1987 to the first "Intifada" (uprising) and the creation of
Hamas, a militant Islamic fundamentalist group that Israel, the United States, and
the European Union have labeled a "terrorist" organization due to its attacks on
civilians. Hamas has competed for Palestinian leadership with Fatah, a faction
headed by Mahmoud Abbas, the Palestine Liberation Organization successor to
the late Yassir Arafat, with both opposing Israeli occupation but Fatah adopting
less violent resistance tactics. Following the Israeli army's unilateral disengagement
from the Gaza Strip in 2005, Hamas won a Palestinian election that made it the
governing authority over Palestinian inhabitants of Gaza, while Fatah ruled over
Palestinians in the West Bank. With the Hamas charter calling for the extermi-
nation of the state of Israel and Hamas periodically firing rockets at Israeli towns
and villages, Israel responded in 2007 with a naval, air and land blockade aimed at
limiting arms and other strategic goods into Gaza, although Hamas in turn built a
series of underground tunnels for smuggling munitions and launching raids into
Israel. Each side accused the other of instigating violence.

Such was the backdrop of the Gaza War that began on December 27, 2008
and ended on January 18, 2009. The finger-pointing followed the familiar pattern

of Israel insisting it had to engage in aerial strikes to stop rocket fire into Israel and arms smuggling into Gaza, with the resulting carnage and damage to Palestinian civilians and buildings (homes, schools, mosques, and hospitals) prompting Hamas to intensify its own rocket attacks on Israeli civilians, thereby causing Israel eventually to mount a ground invasion that further exacerbated the destruction of Palestinian neighborhoods.

Although it is hard to find accurate, reliable data from neutral sources, it is estimated that in the lead-up to the war, each side fired thousands of rockets and mortar rounds, with Palestinian casualties far outnumbering Israeli casualties due to the latter's more sophisticated military technology as well as civil defense capabilities. An Egyptian-brokered cease-fire in June 2008, calling for a six-month lull in fighting based on Hamas committing to stopping its military buildup and rocket attacks on Israel, and Israel committing to easing the blockade and stopping military raids in Gaza, collapsed, with each side, again, accusing the other of bad faith. Israel officially initiated "Operation Cast Lead" on December 27, with a massive air campaign that, according to Israel Defense Force (IDF) sources, targeted Hamas headquarters and government offices, police stations, homes of Hamas commanders, and weapons storage sites. Hamas followed with a rocket barrage against major cities in Southern Israel, including Ashdod and Beersheba. On January 3, Israel mounted a ground operation against militants operating in cities in the Gaza Strip that continued until Israel declared a unilateral cease-fire on January 17. By the time it was over, the war had claimed well over 1,000 Palestinian fatalities and thousands more injured, compared to Israeli fatalities in single digits, although hundreds were either wounded or suffering from severe anxiety from the threat of rockets.[40]

Which side in the Gaza War could claim the high ground in terms of acting morally, legally, and sensibly? *Morally* speaking, each side can lay claim to "injustices." It is difficult to assign moral superiority when so many innocent lives were lost or threatened on both sides. On the one hand, as Israeli President Shimon Peres said at the outset of Operation Cast Lead, "We cannot permit that Gaza will become a permanent base of threatening and even killing children and innocent people in Israel for God knows why."[41] On the other hand, the sheer firepower employed by Israel, with its vastly bigger military machine, resulted in a wildly disparate ratio of Palestinian to Israeli casualties, leaving Israel open to charges that its use of force was "excessive" and the contest "unfair." That, along with the characterization of Israel's control over the Palestinian territories and blockade of Gaza as "occupation," tended to make the Palestinians appear to be the "victim" in the eyes of many observers. In terms of world public opinion, Israel, a democracy, found itself having to settle for, at best, a verdict of moral equivalency with a group branded as a "terrorist" organization. Many also questioned whether Israel's policy of attacking Gaza was strategically *wise*, since, while it may have won the battle, in decimating Hamas at least in the short run, it arguably lost the war, insofar as media coverage showing demolished Palestinian cities gave the Palestinian cause a PR victory. Whether it was worth the price paid by the Palestinians remained itself questionable, though, as a Palestinian state has yet to be established and fully recognized by the international community.

The *legal* issues were especially perplexing. Although there was widespread agreement that Israel's resort to armed force in response to Hamas belligerency, including the latter's frequent rocket attacks, could be justified as "self-defense," the nature and extent of force used was problematic and was criticized for violating various *jus in bello* rules pertaining to necessity, distinction, and proportionality.[42] Hamas also was criticized for violations of international humanitarian law. Indeed, the 2009 **UN Fact-Finding Mission on the Gaza Conflict** (the **Goldstone Report**), established by the UN Human Rights Council and chaired by South African jurist Richard Goldstone, accused both Israel and the Palestinian authorities of "possible war crimes and crimes against humanity,"[43] although the great bulk of the criticism was reserved for Israel, given the more severe devastation it inflicted.

Israel was castigated for many transgressions, such as extending the blockade to include restrictions on the import of food and medicines into Gaza, in violation of the 1949 Fourth Geneva Convention.[44] The report gave special attention to Israel's targeting actions during the war, noting that "in a number of cases Israel failed to take feasible precautions required by customary law [reflected in the 1977 Additional Protocol I] to avoid or minimize incidental loss of civilian life, injury to civilians, and damage to civilian objects." The report added: "Deliberate actions of the Israeli armed forces ... indicate the intention to inflict collective punishment on the people of the Gaza Strip," in violation of the Fourth Geneva Convention.[45] The number of Palestinian fatalities, based on figures provided by Gaza and Israeli sources, was estimated to be between 1,166 and 1,444, with "the percentage of civilians among those killed ... [raising] very serious concerns about the way Israel conducted the military operations in Gaza."[46] According to the Israeli government, due to an elaborate early warning system, there were only four Israelis killed (three civilians and one soldier) as a result of Hamas rocket attacks in Southern Israel, along with nine IDF soldiers killed during the fighting in Gaza.[47]

Many specifics were cited in the Goldstone Report. For example, Israel was criticized for:

- shelling such nonmilitary targets as the Palestinian Legislative Council building, two hospitals, and Gaza's main prison, along with six police stations (killing over 200 policemen), even though Israel maintained some of these structures housed Hamas munitions and the Gaza police were integrated into the Hamas security forces.
- firing into heavily populated areas where it could be anticipated there would be considerable "collateral damage" in the form of civilian casualties, without significant military advantage to be gained; even though Israel may have

made some effort to warn Gaza residents in advance to evacuate, through air-dropping of leaflets and other means, the report contended that Israel had not done enough to distinguish civilians from combatants and to minimize casualties.

- shelling one home in which 29 family members were killed.
- using certain types of weapons, such as white phosphorous, likely to inflict extraordinary suffering (even if in the latter case there was no ban on its use).
- detaining Palestinians in "degrading conditions" and in some cases subjecting them to "harsh interrogations and beatings."
- destroying "industrial infrastructure, food production, water installations, sewage treatment plants, and housing."[48]

Meanwhile, the report also noted transgressions committed by the Gaza authorities. Since 2001, the Palestinians had launched approximately 8,000 rockets and mortars into Southern Israel. During the Gaza War, in addition to the three civilians killed, over 1,000 Israelis were injured and schools and other buildings damaged.[49] As the report stated, "There is no justification in international law for the launching of rockets and mortars that cannot be directed at specific military targets into areas where civilian populations are located. Indeed, Palestinian armed groups, among them Hamas, have publicly expressed their intention to target Israeli civilians ... . [This] breaches the fundamental principle of distinction."[50]

Judge Goldstone subsequently retracted his view that Israel had *deliberately* targeted civilians "as a matter of policy," contending that evidence made available after publication of the report suggested otherwise.[51] Hamas leaders were in no position to deny culpability in directly aiming at Israeli civilians. In Goldstone's words, "That the crimes allegedly committed by Hamas were intentional goes without saying – its rockets were purposely and indiscriminately aimed at civilian targets. ... That comparatively few Israelis have been killed by the unlawful rocket and mortar attacks from Gaza in no way minimizes the criminality." He added that "the laws of armed conflict apply no less to non-state actors such as Hamas than they do to national armies. Ensuring that non-state actors respect these principles ... is one of the most significant challenges facing the law of armed conflict."[52]

If Hamas was most guilty of ignoring the principle of "distinction," Israel arguably was most guilty of violating the principle of "proportionality." Hamas's main sin was not only aiming at civilians (at Israeli towns and villages) but hiding behind civilians (using their own population as "human shields"). Israel's main sin, at least to many critics, was overreacting with excessive force that, even if not explicitly aimed at civilians, was bound to kill or injure large numbers relative to the likely military gain. Barnidge captures the "great complexities of asymmetrical warfare":

During Operation Cast Lead, the urban spaces of Gaza became its fighting spaces, with the attendant intermingling of civilians and combatants in close quarters. Civilian residences were taken over and used by Palestinian forces for tactical military advantage, for attacking the IDF and as weapons depots, and mosques were used for military purposes that included the storage of Kalashnikov assault rifles, improvised explosive devices, Qassam rockets, an antiaircraft gun, and ammunition. Even a zoo in Gaza was found to have been used ... to store a rocket-propelled grenade and light arms.[53]

Similar observations were reported in the Gaza wars of 2012 and 2014. One can sympathize with the predicament that Israeli commanders faced in countering this sort of adversary – spare hospitals, schools, mosques, and other civilian refuges and thus concede military advantage to the enemy and expose your troops and own people to harm, or strike such targets and thus risk human rights groups condemning your actions and inviting charges of war crimes for committing atrocities. Hamas leaders saw the predicament differently – play by the rules and, as the weaker side, you are likely to lose. This kind of environment is not very hospitable to the functioning of international law. One can only hope that actors will learn to factor into their calculus the frequent futility of violence and the utility of developing a reputation for being law-abiding and valuing human life. In any event, actors will need to adapt as best they can to "the new warfare." The rules may also have to be adapted as well.

The Second Congo War: Rebels, Gangs, and Armies in Civil-International Strife

There are few better examples of the complex intermingling of international, intranational, and extranational violence and the haphazard operation of the laws of war than the **Second Congo War**, sometimes referred to as "Africa's World War."[54] The war, which began in 1998 and officially ended in 2003 but still is not entirely resolved, has involved nine African countries and over two dozen different armed groups. It has resulted in the bloodiest conflict since World War II – over 5 million deaths, half of whom are children, who have died not only from military attacks but from disease, malnutrition, and other deprivations associated with the war.

The conflict has centered on an ongoing civil war in the Democratic Republic of the Congo (DRC, formerly known as the Republic of Zaire between 1971 and 1997), which is the second largest country in Africa, with a population of roughly 80 million and a land area of almost 1 million square miles, a highly impoverished society despite possessing vast mineral resources (diamonds, gold, nickel, zinc, cobalt, and coltan). The neighboring states that have been brought into the conflict are Rwanda, Uganda, and Burundi (who have mostly supported the rebels in the Congo against the Kinshasa government), along with

Zimbabwe, Angola, Namibia, Chad, and Sudan (who have generally supported the Kinshasa government). The role played by these nations, along with various nonstate actors such as the Lord's Resistance Army and M23, is discussed below, but not before providing some brief historical background.

The Belgian Congo achieved independence from Belgium in 1960, with the founding of the DRC.[55] The father of Congolese independence, Patrice Lumumba, was overthrown in a violent coup that year, replaced by Mobutu Sese Soko, who renamed the country Zaire. His long autocratic, corrupt rule ended in 1997, during the First Congo War. The First Congo War was triggered by the massive genocide in neighboring Rwanda in 1994, when the majority Hutu who were in power at the time massacred 800,000 countrymen, mostly members of a rival ethnic group, the Tutsis. The Tutsis then gained control of the Rwandan government and, in their retaliation against the Hutu, caused many of the latter to flee across the border to seek sanctuary in eastern Zaire. The First Congo War, starting in 1996, saw Rwanda arming ethnic Tutsis in eastern Zaire (the Banyamulenge) in order to combat Hutu militias operating out of the same region who were engaging in cross-border raids into Rwanda. Since the Mobutu government seemed unable or unwilling to disband the Hutu militias that had taken refuge on Congo territory, Rwanda engaged in military intervention and engineered a coup in 1997 that replaced Mobutu with a new leader, Laurent Kabila, who restored the country's name as the Democratic Republic of the Congo. When, in 1998, Kabila attempted to reduce Rwandan influence in Congo affairs, including the presence of ethnic Tutsis in eastern Congo, Rwanda broke ranks with Kabila and invaded the DRC again, starting the Second Congo War. Uganda and Burundi joined in as allies of Rwanda against the DRC, with Zimbabwe, Angola, Namibia, Chad, and Sudan supporting the DRC.

Rwanda's involvement could be traced not only to its complex internal ethnic politics but other factors as well, which included long-standing territorial claims in the Congo, a desire to expand regional influence, and the attraction of the Congo's rich mineral resources. Other states were driven by a similar mix of ethnic or sectarian, security, and economic concerns. The combination of weak states and local, tribal rivalries encouraged the formation of many different armed groups who participated in the Second Congo War as substate or transnational actors, in some cases fighting each other and in other cases fighting national armies. Some of these groups wore uniforms, and others did not. Some could be characterized as "guerrillas" or "paramilitary" units or "militia," while others were little more than roving "gangs," and still others were "terrorist" organizations. They were all irregular forces and exemplars of what Max Boot has called "invisible armies,"[56] except they were all too visible to the countless victims they raped, pillaged, and murdered. Armed with machetes along with more sophisticated weaponry (financed by the seizure and sale of "conflict diamonds" and other precious minerals), these groups – whose members numbered in the hundreds or thousands – wreaked havoc in the countryside and threatened capital cities as well, their motives ranging from sheer looting to score-settling to a desire to take over the government. The atrocities they committed were often matched by atrocities committed by government forces in what seemed to many a wholly anarchic environment.

One of the most active nonstate actors was the Patriotic Forces for the Liberation of Congo (FPLC), which, led by Thomas Lubanga Dyilo, was a rebel group operating in North Kivu in the northeast corner of the Congo that aimed to take control of the rich gold and diamond resources there. Dylio was arrested in 2005 and tried by the **International Criminal Court (ICC)** in The Hague, the body established in 1998 by the Rome Statute to prosecute individuals alleged to have committed war crimes, crimes against humanity, and genocide; in 2012, he was the first person ever convicted by the ICC, charged with war crimes – engaging in enlistment of child soldiers, murder and torture – and sentenced to 14 years imprisonment. Another group was the Democratic Forces for the Liberation of Rwanda (FDLR), the Rwandan Hutu militia that had regrouped in the eastern Congo after Rwanda's Tutsi government forced them to flee from Tutsis seeking revenge for the genocide the Hutus had committed in 1994; although wary of their presence in the Congo, the DRC government at times has allied with them to counter the influence of Tutsis. The National Congress for the Defense of the People (CNDP) was the counterpart to the FDLR, organized to protect Tutsis from Hutus in eastern Congo but also serving as a proxy for the Rwandan government. The Mai-Mai groups were small local groups in the DRC formed to resist Tutsi expansion into the Congo. The Lord's Resistance Army, which aimed to establish a Christian theocracy across the region, terrorized villages in the Congo, Uganda, Sudan, and elsewhere until the ICC issued an indictment against their founder, Joseph Kony, and others for carrying out abductions and mutilations, forcing the leaders into hiding. M23 was a rebel group composed mostly of disaffected or forcibly recruited DRC soldiers that formed late in the conflict, supported by Rwanda and Uganda until the two countries agreed to withdraw their support.

It was hoped that the Lusaka Peace Agreement signed in 1999 had put an end to the Second Congo War, but peace remained elusive, with a UN peacekeeping force (MONUC) sent to the Congo to restore calm. Laurent Kabila was assassinated by a bodyguard in 2001, his son Joseph succeeding him as DRC President. The Pretoria Accord, signed in 2003, officially ended the war, but problems persist in trying to reintegrate rebel forces into Congo society and maintaining harmony among the DRC and neighboring states.[57]

The Congo conflict may not be a "permanent" war, but it is an enduring one. Whether it meets the legal definitional test of an "armed conflict" – and, if so, whether it is "international" or "non-international" – may be a moot point to its myriad victims, but it does throw into question what laws of war apply. All of the governments that have been party to the conflict have been corrupt dictatorships to varying degrees, which have routinely violated the human rights of their own people and, also, whose forces often have been guilty of violations of international humanitarian law in their treatment of foreign combatants and civilians. However, their offenses generally have been dwarfed by the atrocities committed by rival warlords commanding nonstate actors. I have noted the ICC conviction of Thomas Lubanga Dylio, leader of the FPLC, for conscripting children and forcing them to participate in hostilities. Other rebel leaders have been charged with various war crimes and crimes against humanity that have included rape and sexual slavery, attacks against the civilian population, torture, and murder. If it has been difficult at times to distinguish combatants from civilians, it also has been difficult to sort out the different participants in order to determine whether they should be treated as criminals, POWs, or unlawful combatants. Human Rights Watch has vividly described the brutality of the Congo conflict and the blurring of state and nonstate actor behavior:

> M23 rebels and Congolese army soldiers raped scores of women and committed other war crimes during the rebels' occupation of Goma [a DRC provincial capital] in late 2012. ... M23 rebels raped at least 36 women and girls in and around Goma, including at least 18 wives of army soldiers and a 10-year-old girl. ... The night after they withdrew from Goma, the M23 attacked a camp for displaced people. They raped at least 13 women living in the camp and looted dozens of huts. ... [There were] at least 76 cases of rape of women and girls by Congolese army soldiers from November 20 to 30 [in various towns and villages]. The victims included women as old as 60 and girls as young as 13. ... Some of the victims were gang raped in front of their husbands and children by several soldiers operating together.[58]

Among the many questions that surfaced in the Congo conflict were issues concerning **child soldiers**. Nowhere has the "child soldier" problem been more prevalent and posed more "challenges for international humanitarian law and international criminal law" than in Africa.[59] The 1977 Additional Protocol I on Protection of Victims of International Armed Conflicts prohibits recruitment of children under the age of 15 into armed forces and affords them special protections should they be involved in hostilities and captured. The 1989 **Convention on the Rights of the Child** (ratified by virtually every UN member, including the Democratic Republic of the Congo) reinforces the protections in Additional Protocol I.[60] Despite these legal instruments, many children, in some cases as young as eight years of age, joined armed groups in the Congo either voluntarily or forcibly. It is estimated that some 30,000 children were used by regular armies or irregular forces in the conflict, comprising up to 40 percent of some militias.[61] The usual moral, strategic, and legal quandaries arose: To what extent could one avoid targeting children if they were directly participating in hostilities on a particular side or were being used as human shields to gain military advantage? If caught on the battlefield and implicated in abetting atrocities, could they be subject to prosecution, imprisonment, and possibly execution, or treated as juveniles entitled to more favorable treatment? And what should be the penalty for those guilty of enlisting children?

Conclusion

It is hard to imagine a messier war than the Second Congo War. But it was only messier by degree compared to other cases we have examined, not qualitatively different from those. Aside from the many *jus in bello* questions surrounding the conduct of war, the Congo conflict, as with other conflicts, also raised *jus post bellum* questions – what might it take to create a "just" and durable peace? The subject of *jus post bellum* is revisited in the next chapter, also through the help of a case study.

Chapter 6 Discussion Questions

1. Discuss the legality of "targeted killings," specifically the use of drones. President Obama's Homeland Security and Counterterrorism Advisor has called them "legal, ethical, and wise." Give your evaluation of the U.S. policy, particularly whether terrorists should be treated as "combatants" in the context of rules governing warfare or, instead, as "criminals" in the context of rules governing law enforcement.
2. Discuss the legality of Israeli and Palestinian behavior during the 2008–2009 Gaza War, particularly regarding their observance of the rules of distinction, necessity, and proportionality.
3. Discuss how the Second Congo War exemplifies "the new warfare," and how international humanitarian law was flouted by many of the participants.

Notes

1 William C. Banks, *New Battlefields/Old Laws: Critical Debates on Asymmetric Warfare* (New York: Columbia University Press, 2011), 14.
2 See Uri Friedman, "Targeted Killings: A Short History," September 1, 2012, accessed July 3, 2014 at www.cfr.org/middle-east-and-north-africa/foreign-policy-targeted-killings-short-history.
3 There is some disagreement over where the first CIA drone attack occurred, depending on whether one is referring to a "combat zone" or not. Most studies cite the 2002 Yemen incident. See Report of the Special Rapporteur on Extrajudicial, Summary or Arbitrary Execution (Alston Report), UN General Assembly Doc. A/HRC/14/24/Add.6, May 28, 2010, 7; Susan Breau, "Civilian Casualties and Drone Attacks: Issues in International Humanitarian Law," in Robert P. Barnidge, Jr., ed., *The Liberal Way of War* (Burlington, VT: Ashgate, 2013), 115; and Rosa Brooks, "Drones and the International Rule of Law," *Ethics and International Affairs*, 28, 1 (2014): 89. Some studies instead point to a 2002 drone strike in Afghanistan, with bin Laden the intended target; see John Sifton, "A Brief History of Drones," *The Nation* (February 27, 2012).
4 See Sarah Kreps and Micah Zenko, "The Next Drone Wars: Preparing for Proliferation," *Foreign Affairs*, 93, no. 2 (March/April 2014): 71; and Bureau of Investigative Journalism, "Drone Warfare," accessed July 8, 2014 at http://www.thebureauinvestiga

ttes.com/category/projects/drones/drwar-drones. Also see statistics reported in Martin S. Flaherty, "The Constitution Follows the Drone: Targeted Killings, Legal Constraints, and Judicial Safeguards," *Harvard Journal of Law and Public Policy*, 2 (Winter 2015): 213.

5 Bureau of Investigative Journalism, "Drone Strikes in Pakistan," accessed July 8, 2014 at www.thebureauinvestigates.com/category/projects/drones/drones-pakistan. Also see New America, "Drone Wars Pakistan: Analysis," accessed July 8, 2014 at http://secur itydata.newamerica.net/drones/pakistan/analysis; and The Long War Journal, "Charting the Data for US Airstrikes in Pakistan, 2004–2014," accessed July 8, 2014 at www. longwarjournal.org/pakistan-strikes.php.

6 Daniel Byman, "Why Drones Work," *Foreign Affairs*, 92, no. 4 (July/August 2013): 32.

7 American Security Project, "The Strategic Effects of A Lethal Drones Policy," accessed July 8, 2014 at www.americansecurityproject.org/asymmetric-operations/the-stra tegic-effects-of.

8 See Chapter 3, Notes 50 and 51.

9 Byman, "Why Drones Work": 33 and 36. Also see Flaherty, "The Constitution Follows the Drone": 213. Flaherty states that "approximations of civilian deaths in drone strikes fall between a high of 35 percent to a low of six percent."

10 Ibid., 35.

11 "Drone Strikes Kill, Maim, and Traumatize Too Many Civilians, U.S. Study Says," CNN, September 25, 2012.

12 Byman, "Why Drones Work": 36.

13 The case is recounted in Breau, "Civilian Casualties and Drone Attacks," 124. Breau does a good job of not only reporting statistics on drone casualties but also examining the complex issues of distinction and proportionality.

14 "Homeland Security Advisor Speaks About Ethics of White House Strategy," American History TV, accessed July 9, 2014 at http://series.c-span.org/History/Events/ Homeland-Security-Advisor-Speaks.

15 The quoted comment belongs to Bradley Strawser, a professor at the Naval Postgraduate School, cited in Scott Shane, "The Moral Case for Drones," *New York Times*, July 15, 2012.

16 Byman, "Why Drones Work": 34.

17 The quote is from Harold Koh, the U.S. State Department Legal Advisor under President Obama, cited in Rosa Brooks, "Cross-Border Targeted Killings: 'Lawful But Awful'?" *Harvard Journal of Law and Public Policy*, 2 (Winter 2015): 213. Also, see "Drone Strikes Kill, Maim, and Traumatize Too Many Civilians, U.S. Study Says"; and Shahzad Bashir and Robert Crews, *Under the Drones* (Cambridge, MA: Harvard University Press, 2013).

18 On the pros and cons of the wisdom of the U.S. drone policy, see a special issue of *Foreign Affairs*, 92, no. 4 (July/August 2013), "Death From Above: Are Drones Worth It?," including Daniel Byman, "Why Drones Work: The Case for Washington's Weapon of Choice" and Audrey Kurth Cronin, "Why Drones Fail: When Tactics Drive Strategy."

19 See Note 53 in Chapter 3.

20 Mary Ellen O'Connell, "Lawful Use of Combat Drones," testimony before the Subcommittee on National Security and Foreign Affairs, U.S. House of Representatives, April 28, 2010.

21 See ibid.; Mary Ellen O'Connell, "Unlawful Killing with Combat Drones: A Case Study of Pakistan, 2004–2009," Notre Dame Legal Studies Paper No. 09–43, accessed July 9, 2014 at http://ssrn.com/abstract=1501144; Mary Ellen O'Connell, "The International Law of Drones," American Society of International Law Insight, vol. 14, no. 16 (November 12, 2010); and Mary Ellen O'Connell, "The Questions Brennan Can't Dodge," *New York Times*, February 7, 2013. Brooks, "Drones and the

International Rule of Law," 89, notes that, at the very least, "drone strikes – or, more accurately, the post-9/11 legal theories underlying such strikes – constitute a serious … assault on the generally accepted *meaning* of certain core legal concepts, including 'self-defense,' 'armed attack,' 'imminence,' 'necessity', 'proportionality,' 'combatant,' 'civilian,' and 'hostilities'."

22 See Michael N. Schmitt, "Extraterritorial Lethal Targeting: Deconstructing the Logic of International Law," *Columbia Journal of Transnational Law*, 52 (November 2013): 79–114; and Robert P. Barnidge, "A Qualified Defense of American Drone Attacks in Northwest Pakistan Under International Humanitarian Law," *Boston University International Law Journal*, 30 (2012): 409–447.

23 Remarks delivered by U.S. Attorney-General Eric Holder at Northwestern University on March 5, 2012, accessed July 9, 2014 at www.justice.gov/iso/opa/ag/speeches/ 2012/ag-speech-1203051.html; see Note 30 in Chapter 5.

24 Remarks delivered by U.S. State Department Legal Advisor Harold Koh before the American Society of International Law on March 25, 2010, accessed July 10, 2014 at www.state.gov/s/l/releases/remarks/139119.htm.

25 Barack Obama's speech at National Defense University, May 23, 2013; see "Obama's Speech on Drone Policy," *New York Times*, May 23, 2013.

26 The "warfare" vs. "lawfare" debate was discussed in Chapter 3 (see Notes 37–45) and Chapter 5 (see Notes 33–35).

27 O'Connell, "Unlawful Killing with Combat Drones."

28 O'Connell, "Lawful Use of Combat Drones."

29 Ibid.

30 See Chapter 3, Notes 39 and 45.

31 Geoffrey S. Corn, "Extraterritorial Law Enforcement or Transnational Counterterrorist Military Operations," in Banks, *New Battlefields/Old Laws*, 40.

32 Alston Report, 21.

33 Report of the Special Rapporteur on Extrajudicial, Summary or Arbitrary Executions (Heyns Report), UN General Assembly Doc. A/68/382, September 13, 2013, 21.

34 Kreps and Zenko, "The Next Drone Wars": 72.

35 Peter Bergen, "A Dangerous New World of Drones," CNN, October 2, 2012.

36 Kreps and Zenko, "The Next Drone Wars": 70.

37 Philip Alston, "Statement of UN Special Rapporteur on U.S. Targeted Killings Without Due Process," American Civil Liberties Union, accessed July 12, 2014 at www.aclu.org/national-security/statement-un-special-rapporteur-us-targeted-killings- without-due-process.

38 Among the many histories of the Israeli–Palestinian conflict, see Ian Bickerton and Carla Klausner, *A History of the Arab-Israeli Conflict*, 6th edn (Upper Saddle River, NJ: Pearson, 2009); Alan Dowty, *Israel/Palestine* (Cambridge: Polity Press, 2008); and Deborah J. Gerner, *One Land, Two Peoples*, 2nd edn (Boulder, CO: Westview, 1994).

39 The "self-defense" claim remains controversial. See the discussion in Chapter 2 and Note 40.

40 Many statistics on casualties, drawn from different sources, can be found in the case study by Robert P. Barnidge, Jr., "The Principle of Proportionality Under International Humanitarian Law and Operation Cast Lead," in Banks, *New Battlefields/Old Laws*, 182–183. See especially the statistics reported in *Report of the United Nations Fact-Finding Mission on the Gaza Conflict* A/HRC/12/48 (2009), also known as the Goldstone Report, named after the chairman of the study group; and Amnesty International, *Israel/Gaza: Operation "Cast Lead": 22 Days of Death and Destruction* (2009).

41 Israel Ministry of Foreign Affairs, "Statement by President Shimon Peres on IDF Operation in Gaza," December 28, 2008; accessed July 12, 2014 at www.mfa.gov.il/

MFA/Government/Speeches+by+Israeli+leaders/2008/Statement+by+President_Per
es_IDF_operation__Gaza_28-Dec-2008.htm

42 *Jus ad bellum* and *jus in bello* issues often have been conflated in the Israeli–Palestinian
conflict. For example, the United Nations has acknowledged that, in light of Hamas
rocket attacks, Israel's blockade can be justified legally as an act of "self-defense"; but it
has criticized the manner in which Israel at times has implemented the blockade.
When Israeli commandos in 2010 boarded a Turkish flotilla suspected of carrying
weapons destined for Gaza and killed nine passengers, a UN report condemned Israel
for "excessive" use of armed force even though there was evidence that Israeli forces
were under attack. See "Report Finds Naval Blockade by Israel Legal But Faults
Raid," *New York Times*, September 1, 2011.

43 Goldstone Report, 413.

44 Ibid., 16, 24–26, and 82ff.

45 Ibid., 413 and 416.

46 Ibid., 17. UN Special Rapporteur Richard Falk, in his February 11, 2009 report to the
UN Human Rights Council, found "a total of 1,434 Palestinians were killed, of
whom 235 were combatants. Some 960 civilians reportedly lost their lives, including
288 children and 121 women." In contrast, Israeli IDF sources concluded in a different
study that, of the Palestinian fatalities who could be identified, "there were approximately
two combatants killed for every noncombatant killed." Cited in Barnidge, "The Principle
of Proportionality," 182. On Israeli efforts to minimize casualties, see Richard Kemp,
"Gaza's Civilian Casualties: The Truth Is Very Different," Gatestone Institute, August 3,
2014; accessed June 11, 2014 at www.gatestoneinstitute.org/4570/gaza-civilian-casualties.

47 Goldstone Report, 17.

48 Ibid., 17–24. A critical Israeli response to the Goldstone report is offered by Moshe
Halbertal in "The Goldstone Illusion", *New Republic*, November 6, 2009.

49 Ibid., 31. Also, see 419–420.

50 Ibid., 365. The report (page 366) went so far as to find the Palestinian "commission of
an indiscriminate attack on the civilian population of Southern Israel a war crime, and
may amount to crimes against humanity."

51 Richard Goldstone, "Reconsidering the Goldstone Report on Israel and War Crimes,"
Washington Post, April 1, 2011. The other members of the Mission continued to stand
by the report's initial findings.

52 Ibid. Hamas did deny the "war crimes" allegation in a 52-page report it submitted to
the United Nations in 2010, claiming that the killing of three Israeli civilians in rocket
attacks during the Gaza War "was an accident and military installations had been targeted." "Hamas Gives UN Response to Gaza War Crimes Report," *New York Times*,
February 3, 2010.

53 Barnidge, "The Principle of Proportionality," 184.

54 For background, see Gerard Prunier, *Africa's World War: Congo, the Rwandan Genocide,
and the Making of a Continental Catastrophe* (New York: Oxford University Press, 2009).
Anup Shah, "The Democratic Republic of the Congo," accessed May 20, 2014 at
www.globalissues.org/article/87/the-democratic-republic-of-congo; and Anthony
Gambino, *Congo: Securing Peace, Sustaining Progress* (New York: Council on Foreign
Relations Press, 2008).

55 On the history of colonial rule in the Congo, see Adam Hochschild, *King Leopold's
Ghost* (New York: Houghton Mifflin, 1999).

56 See Note 9 in Chapter 1.

57 Persistent problems are discussed in Jason K. Stearns, "Helping Congo Help Itself:
What It Will Take to End Africa's Worst War," *Foreign Affairs*, 92, no. 5 (September/
October 2013): 99–112.

58 "DR Congo: War Crimes By M23, Congolese Army," Human Rights Watch, February 5, 2013; accessed May 20, 2014 at www.hrw.org/prim/news/2013/02/05/dr-congo-war-crimes-m23-congolese-army.
59 Hilly Moodrick-Even Khen, "Children As Direct Participants in Hostilities: New Challenges for International Humanitarian Law and International Criminal Law," in Banks, *New Battlefields, Old Laws*, 133–149.
60 On the evolution of rules governing child soldiers, see Noelle Quenivet, "The 'New Wars' of Children or On Children?," in Robert P. Barnidge, ed., *The Liberal Way of War* (London: Ashgate, 2013), 139–165. Also, see Peter W. Singer, *Children At War* (New York: Pantheon Books, 2005); Michael G. Wessells, *Child Soldiers: From Violence to Protection* (Cambridge, MA: Harvard University Press, 2006); and Scott Gates and Simon Reich, eds, *Child Soldiers in the Age of Fractured States* (Pittsburgh, PA: University of Pittsburgh Press, 2010).
61 See Wessells, *Child Soldiers*, 12; Claude Rakisits, "Child Soldiers in the East of the Democratic Republic of the Congo," *Refugee Survey Quarterly*, 27 (2008): 108–122; and "Child Recruitment Remains Endemic in Democratic Republic of Congo, UN Says in New Report," United Nations, October 24, 2013.

7

APPLYING *JUS POST BELLUM* RULES TO THE NEW WARFARE

Cases

Chapter 4 examined *jus post bellum* questions, namely what rules of international law apply to the termination of conflicts, where the challenge is forging a just peace, that is, one that is likely to be durable. I noted that the difficulty here is not so much that the rules have become more problematical in their application to "the new warfare" but rather that the rules are virtually nonexistent. I also noted that scholars have recently begun to give increased attention to this situation in an effort to remedy the problem.[1] As Carsten Stahn states, "the increased interweaving of the concepts of intervention, armed conflict and peace-making in contemporary practice makes it necessary to complement the classical rules of *jus ad bellum* and *jus in bello* with a third branch of the law, namely rules and principles governing peace-making after conflict."[2]

Jus post bellum presumes that post-conflict peace-making must be accompanied by peacebuilding – addressing the long-term conditions associated with a lasting peace, which can include both structural changes (ranging from such seemingly mundane matters as demining the countryside, repair of roads and other infrastructure, and reestablishing basic services to more daunting matters such as political institution-building) as well as attitudinal changes (relating to normative conceptions of justice on the part of the society facing post-conflict reconstruction). In many societies that have emerged from war, the peacebuilding project entails not merely reconstruction but construction, where state- and nation-building has to start almost from scratch, given the low level of development (state capacity and national identity) that might have existed prior to the conflict and might have triggered the conflict.[3] Regime-change may be the toughest challenge, if the society lacks any history of strong institutions much less democratic ones and if outsiders do not want to be seen as "occupiers" imposing change on the populace. What is the role of international law in all this?

In Chapter 4, I noted the lament voiced in "Charlie Wilson's War" that the United States abandoned Afghanistan in the 1990s after a decade of contributing to the physical destruction of the country in the process of helping to save it from Soviet domination. Walzer contends that "when the war was over, Afghanistan was left in a state of anarchy and ruin. At that point, the Americans walked away and were certainly wrong, politically and morally wrong, to do so."[4] However, the United States had invited itself in, and had to be wary of wearing out its welcome.

After returning to Afghanistan following the 9/11 terrorist attacks, in order to defeat al Qaeda and the Taliban, the United States was faced once again with the quandary of how long to stay, as it sought to wind down its longest war in history and remove most of its forces by 2016. The United States had gotten UN Security Council authorization immediately after 9/11 to combat the terrorists who had used Afghanistan as a base of operations, although it was never intended as an open-ended authorization to remain in Afghanistan indefinitely. The government in Kabul that succeeded the Taliban turned to the United States for assistance in rebuilding the country, but it was a government essentially installed by Washington. Peter Bergen captured the challenge facing the United States:

> Afghanistan was supposed to be the model: a quick war and a thorough renovation of the country's infrastructure and political system. ... We should be clear about what would constitute a realistic victory in Afghanistan. Even our most concerted efforts will not turn it into Belgium, but we can prevent it from becoming a safe haven for al Qaeda, stop the Taliban from threatening the population, bring security to much of the countryside, and wean farmers away from the poppy trade by expanding the legitimate economy. The achievement of these goals would set the country back on the road to relative peace and prosperity where it was headed in the 1970s before the Soviet invasion.[5]

Bergen acknowledged the scale of the challenge, noting it would take at least 30 years to get Afghanistan just up to the level of state "capacity" even of Pakistan, which was experiencing its own severe political and economic problems. On the one hand, President Obama in 2014, worried about accusations of "occupation" and the limits of American power as well as the limits of the American public's patience for protracted conflicts, called for an end to the U.S. military presence within two years, stating that "we have to recognize Afghanistan will not be a perfect place and it is not America's responsibility to make it one. The future of Afghanistan must be decided by Afghans."[6] However, there was the lingering "**Pottery Barn**" (or "omelette") analogy suggested by Walzer and others, including General Colin Powell – if you break it, you own it.[7] That is, it is yours to fix. Still, this begged the question of how Afghanistan could be fixed when most people living within its borders did not think of themselves as

Afghans so much as Pashtuns (42 percent of the population), Tajiks (37 percent), Uzbeks (9 percent), and members of assorted other "nationality" groups.[8] Many observers argued that "fixing a failed state"[9] in Afghanistan's case meant not nation- or state-building but rather recognizing the preference of much of the people for political arrangements that honored traditional, tribal governance.[10] Clearly, "exit strategies" of intervening states must be carefully calibrated to take into account the values of the local population along with realities on the ground.[11] Despite spending close to a trillion dollars in Afghanistan since 2002, the United States had achieved few of its goals as of 2015, with many fearing that a premature exit might presage the country's relapse into full-scale civil war.[12]

Walzer maintains that "we cannot just walk away. Imagine a humanitarian intervention that ends with the massacres stopped and the murderous regime overthrown; but the country is devastated, the economy in ruins, the people hungry and afraid; there is neither law nor order nor any effective authority. The forces that intervened did well, but they are not finished. … Is it the price of doing well that you acquire responsibilities to do well again … and again?"[13] Imagine Libya.

Intervention in Libya

Chapter 4 made reference to the **2011 humanitarian intervention in Libya** that was authorized by the United Nations Security Council and which, in the process of overthrowing Muammar Gaddafi, produced the kind of collapsed state Walzer described above. The United States and other countries that had participated in the multilateral intervention exited immediately following the demise of Gaddafi, leaving a failed state behind and making practically no effort to fix it. How might *jus post bellum* principles and rules apply to this case?

Libya is an example of what Thomas Friedman has called "tribes with flags" – a collection of Middle East states (such as Iraq, Syria, Qatar, Yemen, and others) that are artificial creations of colonial mapmakers, whose boundaries bear no relation to any natural historical social-cultural identities of the sort associated with a "nation."[14] Ruled previously by the Ottoman Turks and then Italy, Libya achieved independence in 1951. Libya's people from the start tended to identify less with the state – with the central government in the capital – than with its various regions (Cyrenaica in the northeast, Fezzan in the south, and Tripolitania in the northwest). King Idris I attempted to govern the country until he was overthrown in a coup in 1969, led by a young 27-year-old army officer named Muammar Gaddafi. Over the next 42 years, the mercurial Gaddafi ruled with an iron hand, shifting between pan-Arab, anti-Western, and pro-Western policies but never succeeding in forging a unified nation-state. The common thread throughout his tenure was repression, as political parties, a free press, and other vestiges of democracy were suppressed. The economy had been kept afloat by the country's petroleum production, with oil revenues typically accounting for over half of its gross domestic product, 95 percent of its export earnings, and 90 percent of government income; but much of the country remained impoverished due to poor economic decision-making and governmental corruption. Although toward the end of his regime he had found favor with the United States in renouncing his support for terrorism, helping to fight against radical Islam, and terminating his WMD programs, he had relatively few friends, having alienated most of his Arab neighbors as well as most of his own people.

By 2011, the population of six million had become increasingly disaffected from the regime in Tripoli; and the "Arab Spring" that had started months earlier in Tunisia and Egypt and overthrown governments there had stirred similar unrest in Libya. The common Sunni Muslim religious affiliation and common Arab ethnicity of much of Libya's population disguised the fractured tribal identities that had long existed, with some 20 major tribal groups distributed across the country's three main geographical regions.[15] Gaddafi's main power base was in the northwest, where his clan was located and where the main oil production facilities were located as well. The cultural divisions combined with political dissension and economic problems to produce a powderkeg situation, resulting in mass protests in February 2011 centered in Benghazi and other cities in the northeast where tribal defections first occurred. A National Transitional Council (NTC) formed in opposition, claiming to be the legitimate representative of the Libyan people. What started as peaceful protests became a violent armed revolution that spread across the country, as rebels burned police stations and attacked security forces, which in turn led to Gaddafi promising to go "door to door" and "capture the rats" responsible for the uprising, vowing "everything will burn."[16]

Gaddafi's brutal crackdown on protestors, including air attacks on population centers, led the United Nations Security Council on March 17 to pass Resolution 1973 unanimously (with China, Russia, and a handful of Council members abstaining but not opposing). The resolution called on the Libyan government to put "a complete end to violence and all attacks against, and abuses of, civilians" and called upon UN member states to take "all necessary measures ... to protect civilians ... under threat of attack." A no-fly zone was established that authorized the international community to impose a ban against Gaddafi's air force flying over and strafing civilians. Although the resolution prohibited a foreign occupation force on Libyan territory, Libya was ordered to permit "the unimpeded passage of humanitarian assistance." Gaddafi proceeded to ignore the UN resolution and continued his attacks on dissidents. Led by NATO and supported by the Arab League, numerous air strikes were mounted against Gaddafi over the next several months. By September, the National Transitional Council gained international recognition as the de jure government of Libya, entitled to occupy Libya's UN seat. With the help of the UN "humanitarian intervention" forces, rebels were able to drive Gaddafi and his loyalists out of Tripoli and significantly degrade them. Gaddafi went into hiding around his hometown of Sirte and eventually was captured and ultimately killed in October, bringing an end to his rule.[17]

Some called the Libyan humanitarian intervention "a textbook application of R2P principles."[18] Others were not so sure.[19] On the one hand, there was the "moral clarity" that the international community had every reason to believe it was preventing a massacre from happening; and this time, unlike in Kosovo, humanitarian intervention had the explicit imprimatur of the United Nations.[20] However, the rub was that what had originally been a UN Security Council resolution authorizing the use of armed force only for the "protection of civilians" over time evolved into a push for "regime change" that culminated in Gaddafi's ouster. Aside from the legality of whether the United States and other NATO countries, in pummeling Gaddafi into submission and surrendering the reins of government, had exceeded their UN mandate, there was the matter of whether humanitarian intervention had left Libya in an improved state or had, if anything, added to the chaos in producing a collapsed state. Thus, alongside *jus ad bellum* questions were *jus post bellum* questions.

From the start, the National Transitional Council that replaced the Gaddafi regime was plagued by the internecine rivalries that had long simmered below the surface of Libyan politics. Gaddafi had been able to manage these conflicts through a combination of marital alliances and bribes along with coercion, but with his demise there was nothing to prevent them from being fully unleashed. As one observer noted, the revolutionary coalition was "fragmented along family, tribal, and local interests."[21] What was missing in the Libyan revolution that had been present to an extent in Egypt's overthrow of Hosni Mubarak were organized opposition groups in the form of trade unions, student activists, professionals, mass media, and other elements of civil society. What was also missing was the semblance of any state institutions that could help facilitate the transition. Instead, "an elite political leadership established itself at the top of a hitherto uncoordinated popular movement," with two sets of elites vying for control of the revolution; one were defectors from the Gaddafi regime, and the other were returning exiles from the regime of King Idris before the military coup had caused those families to flee the country.[22] Although some technocrats and members of the business community were included in the NTC, family, tribal, and regional/town affiliations were more important in determining the composition. Islamicists, long marginalized under Gaddafi's secular rule, also sought to shape the nature of the revolution and saw an opportunity in the chaos that ensued.

Thus, "the task to be accomplished ... amounted to nothing less than the establishment of a new state."[23] In the aftermath of the revolution, Libya generally descended into anarchy. The National Transitional Council gave way in August 2012 to an elected General National Congress (GNC), which was supposed to form a Constituent Assembly that would draft a new constitution. However, the work of the Congress was severely hampered by lack of cooperation between anti-Gaddafi militias that had not yet demobilized, many of whom had Islamist agendas or other narrow interests they were promoting, and the security forces controlled by the new government. Bombings and explosions in major cities were a commonplace occurrence along with abduction of lawmakers. On September 11, 2012, the U.S. ambassador to Libya, Christopher Stevens, was killed by militants belonging to the radical Islamist group Ansar al-Sharia who attacked the American consulate in Benghazi. When U.S. commandos captured a terrorist leader in eastern Libya suspected of having masterminded the ambassador's murder and returned him to the United States to stand trial, Libya complained about U.S. violation of Libyan sovereignty, while Washington invoked the same right it had invoked to apprehend Osama bin Laden in Pakistan. Libya's criminal justice system, barely functioning, did not inspire confidence in its verdicts. Indeed, thousands of Gaddafi loyalists and other detainees were still held by various armed groups. Libya challenged the jurisdiction of the International Criminal Court in The Hague that had indicted Gaddafi's son for crimes against humanity, demanding he be tried on Libyan soil, raising questions as to what courts were most appropriate to mete out post-conflict justice.

By 2014, Libya was the epitome of a failed state.[24] News headlines read, "Strife in Libya Could Presage Long Civil War," raising fears that the alternatives seemed limited to "a return to repressive authoritarianism or a slide toward Islamist extremism."[25] When rival militias fought for control of the Tripoli airport, with Islamist forces from the city of Misrata battling anti-Islamist militias from the town of Zintan, the United States closed its embassy along with other states who did likewise as they feared for the safety of their envoys; the United Nations evacuated its mission as well. Not only was the airport reduced to rubble, but so, too, were neighborhoods in an increasing number of towns and cities. Basic services, including sanitation and availability of gasoline for automobiles, deteriorated throughout the country. Oil production fell dramatically. A third of Libya's population had become refugees, streaming across the border into Tunisia. Outsiders only stoked the polarization, with Turkey and Qatar supporting the Islamists and Saudi Arabia, the United Arab Emirates, and Egypt supporting their opponents, although the battle lines were drawn around ethnic, tribal divisions and not only religion.[26] Meanwhile, Libya's problems were spilling over into neighboring Mali and other North African states, where terrorist groups armed with weapons caches left over from NATO's humanitarian intervention were threatening to make them failed states as well. A 16-nation UN-organized conference in Madrid in September 2014 failed to defuse the crisis. Governance remained split between a newly elected parliament recognized by the UN and based in Tobruk and an Islamist-dominated body (the remnants of the GNC) in control of Tripoli, where the Libyan ministries, central bank, and state oil company were located.[27] By 2015, the situation had become further complicated by the arrival of ISIS as another player in the civil war.[28]

It was anybody's guess whether Libya could be made whole much less made a stable, democratic state. At some point, some sort of improved order may come to the country, but it is doubtful that such an outcome will meet the kind of *jus post bellum* norms advanced by Michael Walzer and other scholars seeking to extend the "just war" tradition to the conclusion of conflicts. As of this writing, it is hard to see how any of the 10 "functions" that Ghani and Lockhart cite as necessary to "fixing failed states" can be performed by Libya in the foreseeable future, with or without outside help.[29] Moreover, the Libyan case arguably has not only set back *jus post bellum* thinking but also the R2P norm generally. The overreach of the humanitarian intervention mission, expanding the mandate from civilian protection to regime change, dampened the willingness of Russia and China and others to authorize another such mission in Syria, while the disastrous fallout from the mission dampened the enthusiasm of most other states for further such actions anywhere.[30] As much of a challenge as "the new warfare" poses for *jus ad bellum* and *jus in bello* rules, the contemporary landscape presents even more obstacles for the application of *jus post bellum* principles.

Conclusion

In Part Three, we have used several case studies to analyze what often seems a disconnect between the current laws of war and the contemporary conflicts in which they are applied. Clearly, there is a need for improved global governance in trying to control violence in an anarchic world. This has been an ongoing human project that has taken on special urgency today. If international regimes no longer fit the reality they are meant to regulate, they will gradually be discarded. They may be abandoned altogether, as actors wantonly ignore those prescriptions and fail to replace them with any new guideposts; or, preferably, there may be a conscious effort to repair and reformulate them in order to restore their utility. In Chapter 8, we look to the future and offer some concluding thoughts on how we might "rethink" *jus ad bellum, jus in bello,* and *jus post bellum* rules.

Chapter 7 Discussion Questions

1. Discuss the legality of the U.S./NATO humanitarian intervention in Libya in 2011, which led to the fall of Libyan dictator Muammar Gaddafi. What does international law have to say about outside actors imposing regime change on another country?
2. In the case of countries that have intervened militarily in another country, what are their obligations to contribute to the latter's political and economic reconstruction?
3. What lessons does the Libyan intervention offer in trying to implement *jus post bellum* norms?

Notes

1 In addition to the works cited in Chapter 4, see Carsten Stahn, "*Jus ad Bellum, Jus in Bello … Jus post Bellum?* – Rethinking the Conception of the Law of Armed Force," *European Journal of International Law*, 17, no. 5 (2006): 921–943; Stahn et al., eds, *Jus Post Bellum: Mapping the Normative Foundations* (New York: Oxford University Press, 2014); Matthew Saul, *Popular Governance of Post-Conflict Reconstruction: The Role of International Law* (Cambridge: Cambridge University Press, 2014); and the Jus Post Bellum Project at the University of Leiden, accessed July 20, 2014 at www.juspostbel lum.com/resources/1/JPB%20Mapping.

2 Stahn, "*Jus ad Bellum, Jus in Bello … Jus post Bellum?*": 921.

3 See the references to Diehl and Druckman in Notes 27 and 28 in Chapter 4.

4 Michael Walzer, *Arguing About War* (New Haven, CT: Yale University Press, 2004), 21.

5 Peter Bergen, "How Not to Lose Afghanistan (and Pakistan)," New American Foundation, October 10, 2008, accessed March 10, 2014 at http://newamerica.net.publica tions/policy/how_not_lose_afghanistan.

6 "Focus to Shift to Terror Threats Elsewhere," *New York Times*, May 28, 2014.

7 Powell's statement was cited in Bob Woodward, *Plan of Attack* (New York: Simon and Schuster, 2004), 150.

8 See U.S. Central Intelligence Agency, *CIA World Factbook* (Washington, DC: CIA, 2011); also, Thomas Barfeld, "Afghanistan's Ethnic Puzzle," *Foreign Affairs*, 90, no. 5 (September/October 2011): 54–65.

9 See Ashraf Ghani and Clare Lockhart, *Fixing Failed States: A Framework for Rebuilding A Fractured World* (Oxford: Oxford University Press, 2008), cited in Chapter 4, Note 34.

10 Thomas Barfeld, "Afghan Paradoxes," in Hy Rothstein and John Arquilia, eds, *Afghan Endgames: Strategy and Policy Choices for America's Longest War* (Washington, DC: Georgetown University Press, 2012), 54–55.

11 William Durch, "Exit and Peace Support Operations," in Richard Kaplan, ed., *Exit Strategies and State Building* (Oxford: Oxford University Press, 2012), 96.

12 Ahmad Rashid, "Afghanistan's Failed Transformation," *New York Times*, September 26, 2014.

13 Walzer, *Arguing About War*, 20–21.

14 Thomas Friedman, "The Key Question on Libya," *New York Times*, March 23, 2011.

15 The ethnic composition of Libya and other demographic characteristics are discussed in the *CIA World Factbook* (Washington, DC: Central Intelligence Agency, 2014). Also, see Wolfram Lacher, "Families, Tribes and Cities in the Libyan Revolution," Middle East Policy Council, accessed July 23, 2014 at www.mepc.org/journal/middle-east-p olicy-archives/families-tribes-and-cities-libyan.

16 Hebah Saleh and Andrew England, "Defiant Gaddafi Vows Fight to Death," *Financial Times*, February 23, 2011.

17 A historical case study of events is provided in Glenn Hastedt et al., "Libya's Uprising and the Responsibility to Protect," *Cases in International Relations* (Thousand Oaks, CA: CQ Press, 2015), 231–246.

18 Comment made by Madeleine Albright, cited in Thomas Weiss, *Governing the World?* (Boulder, CO: Paradigm Publishers, 2014), 29. For a positive view of the Libyan humanitarian intervention, see Ivo Daalder and James Stavridis, "NATO's Victory in Libya: The Right Way to Run an Intervention,"*Foreign Affairs* 91, no. 2 (March/April 2012): 2–7.

19 See David Rieff, "R2P, R.I.P.," *New York Times*, November 7, 2011; and J. Craig Barker, "The Responsibility to Protect: Lessons from Libya and Syria," in Robert P. Barnidge, ed., *The Liberal Way of War* (Burlington, VT: Ashgate, 2013), 63–85.

20 "The Lessons of Libya," *The Economist*, May 19, 2011.

21 Lacher, "Families, Tribes, and Cities."
22 Ibid.
23 Ibid.
24 Interestingly, on the annual rankings of failed ("fragile") states published by *Foreign Policy*, Libya in 2014 was ranked #42, well behind many other states which did not seem nearly as dysfunctional and collapsed. See www.foreignpolicy.com/fragile-sta tes-2014rankings, accessed July 23, 2014.
25 *New York Times*, August 25, 2014.
26 "Arab Nations Strike in Libya," *New York Times*, August 26, 2014.
27 "Libyan Tries to Solidify Rule Amid Turmoil," *Wall Street Journal*, September 18, 2014.
28 "Islamic State Takes Root Amid Libya's Chaos," *Wall Street Journal*, February 2, 2015.
29 See Note 34 in Chapter 4.
30 See Rief, "R2P, R.I.P."; and Barker, "The Responsibility to Protect: Lessons from Libya and Syria." Also, see Alan J. Kuperman, "Obama's Libya Debacle: How A Well-Meaning Intervention Ended in Failure," *Foreign Affairs*, 94, no. 2 (March/April 2015): 66–77.

PART 4

Conclusion

The Future of War, Peace, and Law

War is God's way of teaching us about geography.

Unknown source

The End of Geography

Subtitle of book by Richard O'Brien

The first time that states break a rule of international law, they apologize and claim that they were unaware the rule existed. The second time, they claim that the rule is ambiguous. The third time, they claim that the rule has changed.

Graham Allison

As they left the Garden of Eden, Adam turned toward Eve and said, "We live in an age of transition."

A remark attributed to former British
Prime Minister Harold Macmillan

PART 4

Conclusion

The Future of War, Peace, and Law

8

ADAPTING TO THE NEW FACE OF VIOLENCE

Graham Allison, the former dean of the John F. Kennedy School of Government at Harvard, once commented: "The first time that states break a rule of international law, they apologize and claim that they were unaware the rule existed. The second time, they claim that the rule is ambiguous. The third time, they claim that the rule has changed."[1] Allison's glib characterization of the weakness of international law may strike some as overly cynical. However, there is much to what he had to say. In fact, he could have added a fourth point: Sometimes, even if the law has not changed, it needs to, when it has become unworkable.

In the previous pages, I have tried to show that, given "the new warfare," the traditional laws of war have become increasingly problematical if not irrelevant. They are not working. They have always been erratically observed, but today especially they face special challenges. It is not just the changing nature of war, but also the changing nature of the Westphalian state system generally. If in the past it was joked that "war is God's way of teaching us about geography" – about places on the other side of the world that might otherwise have escaped our attention – today we may be witnessing "the end of geography" altogether, what James Rosenau has referred to as "boundary-spanning activities and processes" and others have called "the new feudalism," that is, increasingly blurred borders and messy political spaces.[2]

For our purposes here, we are not so much interested in multinational corporations and globalization, cyberspace, and other manifestations of Thomas Friedman's "flat world,"[3] but rather the "borderless global war" and other aspects of contemporary warfare that were the object of criticism in Jeremy Scahill's *Dirty Wars*, which was the starting point of this book.[4] "Cyberwarfare" (conducted by both state and nonstate actors) poses particularly difficult challenges for the laws of war and may require an entirely new body of law;[5] but that is beyond the scope of this book, as are the broader changes in the Westphalian system and their implications for world order. It is enough to grapple with the inadequacy of the laws of war when dealing with ISIS, Iraq, Afghanistan, and current conflicts.

Clearly, some rethinking of the rules is in order. How should we go about adapting international law to "the new warfare"?

What Rules Need Rethinking?

A number of questions were raised at the outset in Chapter 1 of the book, regarding such concerns as the legality of anticipatory self-defense, humanitarian intervention, targeted killings, drones, detention and treatment of captured prisoners without trial, and other issues. Previous chapters have attempted to analyze the problems these issues present today for actors facing hostilities, particularly those seeking to win at war even when "trying to do the right thing" as opposed to fighting "dirty." In considering what rules need rethinking, and what rethinking might look like, let us frame the discussion around the three areas of *jus ad bellum, jus in bello,* and *jus post bellum.* In all cases, we should be striving to develop rules that incentivize and reward what most of us would consider "good" behavior and that deter and punish what most of us would consider "bad" behavior.

Rethinking Jus Ad Bellum

Many observers have noted that the United Nations Charter, which is at the core of the international regime governing the resort to the use of armed force, is badly outdated given its "state-centric" set of assumptions. The Charter, drafted during World War II and ratified in the immediate aftermath of that war, presumed a world in which the main threat in the state system would remain aggression by one state against another state, usually taking the form of large-scale, sustained combat between organized armies over relatively well-defined fronts. Pinker and others have reported data indicating that such interstate wars are now few and declining in number. Max Boot has noted that, instead, "more small wars" will be the norm, particularly conflicts *within* states, where at least one of the parties is an *irregular* force.[6]

When Russia invaded neighboring Ukraine in 2014 and de facto annexed the Crimean peninsula, U.S. Secretary of State John Kerry understandably called it "an incredible act of aggression" that resembled "19th century behavior" of the sort many had assumed could not happen anymore in contemporary international relations.[7] Some analysts contended that Vladimir Putin's motivation was traditional Russian national interest in controlling the borders of its "near abroad" and the port that housed the Russian Black Sea fleet, suggesting geography apparently was still important to Putin. Others traced the action to domestic political concerns in Moscow about how Ukraine's Westward tilt toward the democracies of the European Union – Ukraine had been flirting with joining both the EU and NATO – might undermine Putin's dictatorial rule at home. Either way, the Russian action stunned NATO officials and others.

Still, arguably it was the exception that proved the rule, a rare case of seemingly old-fashioned territorial aggression.[8] It is worth noting that even this case had elements of the kind of complexity surrounding "the new warfare" we have been discussing here. The trigger for the conflict was an internal struggle within Ukraine between a pro-Russian government and Western-leaning dissidents, as well as ethnic divisions between the 60 percent of Crimea made up of ethnic Russians and the bulk of Ukraine's population consisting of non-Russians. Interestingly, once the pro-Russian government in Kiev was replaced in a coup, Putin invoked the right of "humanitarian intervention" aimed at protecting ethnic Russians in the Ukraine from purported oppression (drawing a parallel with the American humanitarian intervention to protect Kosovars in Serbia), as well as claiming Russian forces had been invited in by the just deposed Ukrainian government that had been overthrown in a civil war (which Putin maintained was still the legitimate government of the country). Thus, the rules governing interstate war became conflated with the rules governing civil wars and humanitarian intervention. Most legal analysts viewed Russian behavior through the prism of the UN Charter's Article 2 (4) proscription against aggression that violates the territorial integrity of any member state, but the situation was complicated by the blurring of intrastate and interstate hostilities.

Around the same time that Russia was attacking Ukraine in 2014, another development occurred that was not nearly as shocking, although nonetheless also was a cause of much alarm. That was the emergence of ISIS, the Islamic State of Iraq and Syria (also called the Islamic State of Iraq and al-Sham) and its attempt to gain control over large swaths of territory in the Middle East. ISIS started as "al Qaeda in Iraq" in 2004 and morphed into an independent radical jihadist movement that by 2014 had spread into neighboring Syria and was threatening Turkey and other states as well. Led by an emir named Abu Bakr al-Baghdadi and numbering several thousand fighters, ISIS proved to be a well-coordinated military machine that was ruthless in spreading its ultra-orthodox jihadist message; ISIS warriors slaughtered not only non-Muslims but also any Shiite or Sunni Muslims thought to be "infidels," and conducted beheadings of Western journalists as a warning to any countries contemplating military intervention against them. Having taken over territory the size of the United Kingdom, its ultimate aspiration was to establish a pan-Muslim caliphate ruling over all of Islam worldwide. As of this writing, the United States had mobilized a coalition of states to stop the advance of ISIS, with the effectiveness of the response yet to be determined.[9]

What was most puzzling was ISIS's calling itself a "state," when it seemed not to have any of the trappings of a state but, indeed, was clearly a nonstate actor engaged in terrorism, whose brutality was such that even al Qaeda had distanced itself from the group. As such, ISIS was unlikely to be recognized as a state by any member of the international community. Moreover, if somehow it ever did manage to take on the identity of a "state," which presumably would require the emir to have a fixed address in a capital (seat of government) somewhere, it would offer a much clearer target for the United States and other nations to aim at for purposes of deterrence or retaliation, so that the caliph might not be around very long. In any event, the Obama administration, in initiating air strikes against ISIS military targets in 2014, felt no need to get explicit authorization from either the U.S. Congress or the UN Security Council, as it operated on the assumption that the ISIS campaign remained part of the ongoing "war on terror," with its chronologically and spatially boundless parameters.

Both the Ukraine and ISIS cases added to the perplexities surrounding the question of what constitutes an "armed attack" today in world politics. Clearly, Article 2 (4) of the UN Charter needs revisiting. In an age of "low intensity" conflict, how big and sustained (as opposed to small and sporadic) must hostilities be to rise to the level of an "armed conflict" under the Charter? In the 1986 *Nicaragua vs. the United States* case, the World Court attempted to define the type of violence that would constitute "aggression" and would allow the "self-defense" clause of the Charter to be invoked. However, that ruling seems less and less relevant to "the new warfare," to situations of "force without war," where interstate, intrastate, and extrastate violence meld into each other.

International law needs to distinguish more clearly between these different categories of hostilities. The 1977 Additional Geneva Protocols I and II sought to mark off "international" armed conflicts from "non-international" armed conflicts and create different rules for each, but generally fell short in clarifying such classes of conflict and gaining widespread endorsement; meanwhile, no universally accepted definition of "terrorism" has yet materialized. In regard to terrorism, even if there is agreement that an adversary deserves the "terrorist" label, it can be hard to know *where* the "hot" battlefield begins and ends, as well as *when* the conflict itself begins and ends. Jeh Johnson, Pentagon General Counsel during the Obama presidency, specifically tried to give some definition to the U.S. "war on terror," when addressing the Oxford Union in 2012:

> The United States government is in an armed conflict against al Qaeda and associated forces. ... One week after 9/11, our Congress authorized our President to "use all necessary and appropriate force" against those nations, organizations, and individuals responsible for 9/11. ... But now that efforts by the U.S. military against al Qaeda are in their 12th year, we must also ask ourselves: how will this conflict end? The last day of the First World War was November 11, 1918, when an armistice was signed at 5:00 am in a railroad carriage in France... . The Second World War was concluded in the Pacific theatre in August 1945, with a ceremony that took place on the USS Missouri. ... We cannot and should not expect al Qaeda and its associated

forces to all ... sign a peace treaty with us. They are terrorist organizations. Nor can we capture or kill every last terrorist. ... I can offer no prediction about when this conflict will end, or whether we are, as Winston Churchill described it, near the "beginning of the end." I do believe there will come a tipping point – at which so many of the leaders and operatives of al Qaeda and its affiliates have been killed or captured ... such that the organization has been effectively destroyed. At that point, we must be able to say to ourselves that our efforts should no longer be considered an "armed conflict," rather a counterterrorism effort against individuals ... for which the law enforcement resources of our government are principally responsible.[10]

Aside from sowing further confusion over when to apply the warfare as opposed to lawfare paradigm, Johnson failed to address a host of other issues, such as the right of anticipatory self-defense, the right to attack nonstate actors in another state without the latter's permission, and the right to intervene in the internal affairs of a country at the behest of either the government or armed opposition groups.

With regard to the right of anticipatory self-defense, there is the need to build on the *Caroline* principle as a basis for distinguishing between the legal use of "preemptive" force and the illegal use of "preventive" force. As Grotius said, fear and suspicion of an adversary's intentions alone are not enough to justify the resort to armed force in self-defense. In an age of WMDs, hair-trigger judgments may have to be made as to when action is required in advance of an attack; the United States and other states understandably cannot be expected to wait until a mushroom cloud appears overhead or to cede to the UN Security Council the discretion to permit preemption, but the more solid intelligence one can muster to provide evidence of an imminent strike by an enemy, the greater one's anticipatory action will be viewed as legal.

As for the right to attack nonstate actors in another state without the latter's permission, such as American strikes against al Qaeda in Afghanistan before and after 9/11 or the killing of bin Laden in Pakistan, the rules governing "state responsibility" for denying safe haven to terrorists also need clarification and further elaboration. So does the definition of "terrorism," which remains elusive. Although we may never achieve a universally accepted definition of terrorism, the UN General Assembly and Secretary-General both have come close to one, which is anchored around the proscription of wanton violence against innocents (civilians and noncombatants). The international community needs to continue working on such a definition. In any event, states cannot be allowed to hide behind the principle of sovereignty as an excuse for enabling ISIS or any other such actor to operate freely and threaten other states.

A tougher question is whether states should be allowed to rely on the principle of sovereignty as a hedge against humanitarian intervention, as the Gaddafi regime tried to do in Libya in 2011. Here Article 2 (7) of the UN Charter needs revisiting, since presently it essentially bans interference in the internal affairs of member states and thus directly contradicts R2P. Although a noble attempt to prevent genocide and other horrendous acts committed by governments, R2P challenges the most fundamental ordering principles of the Westphalian system. After all, the one value that continues to command universal acceptance among governments is national sovereignty, eroded or not. At the very least, Security Council permission should be required for humanitarian intervention, even if it privileges the Perm Five. It would help if parameters were established, where R2P was limited to situations of extraordinary atrocities and where the primary mandate would be protection of the population, with regime change only as a last resort.

There is the larger issue of intervention in internal conflicts generally, whether on the side of the government or on the side of opposition groups and rebels. As a general rule, the principle of non-intervention should be reaffirmed and strengthened, particularly the rule against aiding subversion. Although as Boot says, it may be that "counterinsurgency is here to stay"[11] insofar as the United States or other countries may feel a need to intervene in internal conflicts to help governments deal with nonstate actors who threaten not only the latter regimes but other states as well, the rules governing such intervention need clarification.

Recall that, in addition to "self-defense," "collective security" is another justification for resorting to the use of armed force under the UN Charter. We have seen that Chapter VII of the Charter, requiring the support of the Security Council, rarely works. Yet, with some tweaking, perhaps greater use of Chapter VII might be possible. The prospects for peace and peaceful change can be greatly enhanced by the collective leadership provided by a dominant coalition of states able and willing to steer the system in a manner that not only serves their interests but wider interests as well. What comes to mind is an approach to world order modeled after the "concert of powers" scheme in an earlier era. The coalition must be broad enough to possess sufficient material resources to move the system and, also, to make a reasonable claim to the aura of legitimacy – it must have the necessary hard and soft power – but not so broad as to invite paralysis. It may be possible to put off for a while longer the single most contentious issue in UN reform, but the moment of decision cannot be avoided indefinitely on the future expansion of the Security Council. The current composition of the Council is the most glaring anachronism left over from the immediate post–World War II era.

A "prominent solution," as some have proposed, might consist of adding Japan and Germany (among the top three financiers of the organization) as permanent members; allocating a permanent seat each to Latin America, Asia, and Africa, with the regional caucus group in each case asked to develop selection procedures; and adding two nonpermanent seats from the developing world that would rotate biennially. A Security Council of 22 members, with each permanent member having a more circumscribed veto power, would seem the maximum size compatible with operability; although paralysis might still be a concern, there is much to be said for the organization not acting without the significant backing of major players in both the developed and developing worlds. Insofar as the expanded Security Council would likely represent over a majority of the world's people, as well as planetary product, military firepower, and UN budget contributions, the plan could claim to satisfy both realists and idealists in increasing the potential for collective security to become a more meaningful principle.

Of course, there remains the question, "will the need forge a way?"[12] This same question that applies to the need to rethink *jus ad bellum* rules applies also to *jus in bello* strictures.

Rethinking Jus In Bello

In referring at times to a "warfare vs. lawfare paradigm," I have presented this as a choice between two different ways of legally addressing conflict situations, one that treats violence as subject to the laws of war and the other that treats violence as subject to a criminal justice or law enforcement framework. Other scholars have used the terminology somewhat differently, using the word "lawfare" to mean the tactics often used by one side, usually the weaker one, to manipulate rules to their advantage in order to defeat the adversary. Much of this book has revolved around the dilemma faced by countries endeavoring to observe the laws of war when the enemy feels no such obligation. Jeremy Scahill and other critics of United States foreign policy tend to gloss over this dilemma, but it is a very real challenge for the United States or any other country engaged in hostilities these days. This is not to dismiss the legitimate concerns Scahill and others raise, only to acknowledge how difficult it is to avoid "dirty wars."

William Banks frames the problem as follows:

> Modern war is no longer characterized by "uniformed armies on a large plain, with civilians tucked away far behind enemy lines." Rather, military operations are now conducted in the contemporary operational environment, which assumes 360-degree operations against asymmetric opponents who strike at known weaknesses, *including a nation's compliance with the law of war* [italics mine].[13]

It is in the area of *jus in bello* rules that the dilemma is most evident and in need of attention – how does one observe the norms of distinction, proportionality, and military necessity without being a sucker or martyr?

For example, Israel claimed that the Gaza War of 2008–2009 started with Hamas's latest round of rocket attacks on Israeli villages. Israel further claimed that, although it killed over 1,000 Palestinians during the hostilities that followed, it had exercised great restraint and could have done far more damage, targeting as much as possible only those who were thought to be combatants, even if many innocent civilians were killed as well given the fact that the combatants, purposely or not, were often embedded in the civilian population, in some cases hiding in schools and hospitals. The Palestinians, in turn, not only blamed Israel for provoking the conflict, due to its occupation and blockade of Palestinian territory, but also cited the disproportionate casualties on their side relative to the Israeli side, and insisted the Israelis had violated the norm of distinction along with other norms. (The same accusations were traded again in the Gaza War of 2014, when Palestinians suffered over 2,000 deaths compared to some 100 Israeli fatalities.)

The norm is clear and needs to be reaffirmed by the international community, in keeping with the Fourth Geneva Convention: Regardless of who starts a war and how much "collateral damage" may occur, *each side is obligated to minimize civilian casualties, and under no circumstances is either side allowed to select civilians as their explicit, primary target or consciously hide behind civilians as human shields.* This means that conventional armies must take extra pains to discriminate between civilian and military targets, while irregulars must do likewise, so that terrorists and their apologists cannot rationalize terrorism as "the weapon of the weak." No matter weak or strong, no matter state or nonstate actor, no matter which side God is on, a leadership cannot wake up in the morning and ask "how many babies can we kill today?" and "how can we tempt the enemy to fire into a crowd?" If somehow that norm could be strengthened and more widely internalized, it would go a long way to not only humanizing war but also negating an advantage the ostensibly weaker side now enjoys in asymmetrical warfare.

On the subject of "targeted killings," they should not be considered "assassinations" or "extrajudicial executions" if done in the context of "war," again as long as one is targeting combatants ("participants in hostilities"). This still begs the questions having to do with when and where is a war underway (the "hot" battlefield problem), who is a combatant (the "farmer by day, fighter by night" problem) and other such not easily answerable questions. At the very least, the United States or any other country engaging in targeted killings, through drone strikes or some other use of force, should make every effort to improve intelligence capabilities, judicial-administrative oversight, and transparency in identifying targets, minimizing loss of life, and accounting for casualties. Existing rules should be strengthened to reflect these concerns and clarify issues (e.g., whether private contractors qualify as "combatants" who can be targeted, and how CIA drone operators should be treated). The more that those who conduct targeted killings can demonstrate they have tried to create some parameters and strengthen the rule of law in this area, the more acceptable will be their use of this tactic against adversaries who pose serious security threats but are hard to capture and can be eliminated much more easily through armed attack.

As for treatment of captured prisoners, traditionally those persons participating in hostilities who fail to meet the POW criteria contained in the Third Geneva Convention (the need to wear uniforms with fixed insignia, etc.) have been denied "prisoner of war" protections. The United States and other countries have felt pressure to treat all prisoners more humanely, even if it means in some cases rewarding militants who have committed brutal atrocities or resisting the temptation to use "enhanced interrogation" techniques to extract vital intelligence information from them that could save lives. Perhaps a new rule might allow for prisoners to be given something approaching POW status, as long as they can claim to have themselves observed the laws of war even if technically not wearing insignia to distinguish themselves from civilians. Some prisoners might well be labeled "unlawful combatants." However, Common Article 3 entitles them to due process in the form of review by a "competent tribunal" before they are categorized and detained in a jail. Once imprisoned, under the Geneva Conventions and other international law, they must be accorded humane treatment, including the right not to be tortured. "Torture" itself may require more careful definition. Although prisoners should not be held indefinitely – the laws of war traditionally require they be released upon the conclusion of hostilities – the indeterminate nature of the war on terror makes it difficult to say when they should be let go; too often, prisoners have been released from Guantanamo or some other prison only to turn up on the battlefield again. (For example, the aforementioned Abu Bakr al-Baghdad had been released twice from prison before becoming the emir who headed ISIS.) Rules must aim to strike a balance between the rights of the prisoners and the rights of the detaining authorities to minimize the risk of recidivism.

The laws of war should not put the onus for lawful behavior entirely on states. Nonstate actors must be held accountable as well for violations of international humanitarian law.[14] Here we must come to grips with the thorny issue of how to apply rules to "non-international" as opposed to "international" conflicts and, more broadly, when to treat an act of violence as a "crime" subject to law enforcement (with all the trappings of jury trials, Miranda warnings, and the like) or rather as an act of "war" subject to the laws of war (including "targeted killings" and the like). When capture of al Qaeda or other suspected militants is feasible, properly constituted military commissions may often provide a halfway house between regular jury trials for the accused and simply "throwing them in the slammer." The United States under the Obama administration, while expanding the use of drone strikes, has had some success trying and convicting prisoners through the normal channels of the criminal justice system; however, for security and other reasons, it may not be possible to process a large caseload through civilian courts. Whatever rethinking of rules occurs, we should be careful not to make it easier for "asymmetric opponents" to exploit "a nation's compliance with the law of war."

As with rethinking *jus ad bellum* rules, rethinking *jus in bello* rules entails a lot of "should" and "must" entreaties in terms of what *needs* to be done. Again, "will the need forge a way?"

Rethinking Jus Post Bellum

When Winston Churchill pondered in 1942 whether Britain was near "the beginning of the end" or just "the end of the beginning" of World War II, he was working out of a conventional war paradigm. Today, as Jeh Johnson was doing in his speech before the Oxford Union, we struggle during many conflicts to understand what "end" means. For those who urge that international law add *jus post bellum* to the concerns surrounding *jus ad bellum* and *jus in bello*, there is often a real problem in ascertaining when a conflict has shifted to the "post-conflict" phase such that the rules governing the aftermath of a war can take over. It is not just the war on terror that seems chronologically boundless in the contemporary international system but many other conflicts as well.

Even if hostilities largely have ceased, so that the end is in sight, that does not solve the problem of what rules to apply. Max Boot has argued that, aside from the question of whether the United States has engaged in too many wars lately, a big mistake Washington has made in participating in regime change recently in Afghanistan, Iraq, and Libya (in toppling the Taliban in 2001, Saddam Hussein in 2003, and Gaddafi in 2011) has been the lack of a plan for what the military calls "Phase IV" – the postwar reconstruction that is needed following the "kinetic" phase in which the immediate military objectives have been achieved.[15] What complicates such planning is the dilemma of how long one can stay in a country, even with the best of intentions to help repair the country, without being saddled with the label of "occupying power."

We have noted that there are few rules of international law governing "peacebuilding," "nation-building," and the other postwar processes associated with efforts to produce a durable peace based on "just war" theory. Among the rules that need further development are: What are the responsibilities of the international community as a whole, as opposed to "victorious" powers, in rebuilding states and societies decimated by war, whether Afghanistan, Gaza, or other places? What should be the role of the International Criminal Court, as opposed to ad hoc international tribunals or national courts, in trying alleged war crimes that may have occurred during a conflict? If regime change has occurred, how does a new government get formed that can claim legitimacy? Is it enough to engage in "restoration," or is the proper obligation "restoration plus"? Should the UN accept responsibility for "failed states," and, if so, at what point is it appropriate for such states to reclaim their sovereignty?

As difficult as it is to rethink *jus ad bellum* and *jus in bello* rules, *jus post bellum* rules would seem to pose even more daunting challenges.

Toward a More Advanced Anarchy

It has been said that "in relations between nations, the progress of civilization may be seen as movement from force to diplomacy, from diplomacy to law."[16]

Clearly, we are far from the endpoint Louis Henkin refers to here. We cannot hope to eliminate conflict. We probably cannot hope to eliminate violent conflict. But we can hope to reduce the latter or at least manage it better. Law itself can play a key role in this endeavor, if we can find a way to address the need to adapt the laws of war to "the new warfare." In developing rules for an unruly world, we should set our sights high, but not excessively so. A reasonable goal might be to aim for what Barry Buzan has called "a more mature anarchy."[17]

A more advanced anarchy will not be easy. The past dynamics of international institution-building suggests that a major effort at improved global governance in the peace and security field tends to be associated with the existence of a systemwide crisis combined with the existence of a critical mass of actors disposed toward and capable of moving the system forward. These conditions do not seem to exist today. There is no clear systemwide crisis on the scale of World War I or World War II that can serve as a catalyst to jar us into action. Instead, the very thought of the "obsolescence of war," at least among highly developed societies, may be cultivating a sense of complacency rather than any reformist imperative. Moreover, central guidance through global organizations is more problematical than previously, given the diffusion of power along with the multitude of nation-state actors now claiming a seat at the global bargaining table and the increasingly convoluted relationships evolving between their governments and a host of nonstate actors also clamoring to be heard. Compared with 1945, when – in President Harry Truman's words – "there were many who doubted that agreement could ever be reached by these fifty-one countries [the original UN membership] differing so much in race and religion, in language and culture,"[18] the challenge of global governance appears all the more formidable today in a world politic consisting of almost four times as many members representing considerably greater diversity.

Still, although the constraints are formidable, at the same time the contemporary international system may hold out certain fresh opportunities for enhanced global governance – particularly in the area of reformulating the laws of war – that perhaps can be seized. As suggested earlier, while power has become more diffused, there still remains a considerable concentration of power sufficient to constitute a dominant coalition of actors capable of moving the system. What has been lost in power concentration in the waning of the superpower era has been more than offset by the reduced rigidity and polarization of alignments and reduced thinkability of great-power war, allowing more creative possibilities for an enlightened "concert of power" approach to world order. Enough states and people still have a stake in the Westphalian system to want to see it functioning more smoothly.

This book has attempted to identify gaps in the current international regimes governing the use of armed force and to suggest the kind of rethinking that is necessary to adjust the regimes to new realities. One can only hope that leaderships and mass publics will summon the resolve to act, as previous generations have responded to the challenges of their times.

Chapter 8 Discussion Questions

1.   In your judgment, which area of international law is most problematical today and in need of the most rethinking in light of "the new warfare" – *jus ad bellum, jus in bello*, or *jus post bellum*?

2.   In asymmetrical warfare, how does one observe such rules as those relating to "distinction, necessity, and proportionality" when the other side feels no similar obligation and, thus, when your compliance may make you a sucker or martyr?

3.   Can we know anymore when, and where, armed conflicts begin and end?

4.   After reading this book, are you hopeful or skeptical about progress toward "a more mature anarchy," where law can be brought to bear in helping to manage and reduce violence?

Notes

1 Professor Allison made this comment to me at a conference at the University of Missouri-St. Louis on April 7, 2005.

2 See Richard O'Brien, *Global Financial Integration: The End of Geography* (London: Pinter, 1992); and James N. Rosenau, "Declaration of Interdependence," *International Studies Perspectives* 6 (February 2005): inside back cover. On the "new feudalism," see Susan Strange, "The Defective State," *Daedalus*, 124, no. 2 (Spring 1995): 55–74; and John Rapley, "The New Middle Ages," *Foreign Affairs*, 85, no. 3 (May/June 2006): 95–103.

3 Thomas L. Friedman, *The World Is Flat* (New York: Farrar, Straus and Giroux, 2005).

4 See Note 7 in Chapter 1.

5 Kalliopi Chainoglou argues that "cyber attacks and cyber weapons are *sui generis*, and their unique and evolving characteristics do not easily fit within the existing framework of legal norms." See "An Assessment of Cyber Warfare Issues in Light of International Humanitarian Law," in Robert P. Barnidge, ed., *The Liberal Way of War* (London: Ashgate, 2013), 191–192. Also, Heather Dinniss, *Cyber Warfare and the Laws of War* (Cambridge: Cambridge University Press, 2014); and "Cybersecurity's Uncertain Battleground," in Glenn Hastedt et al., eds, *Cases in International Relations* (Thousand Oaks, CA: Sage, 2015), Chapter 7.

6 Max Boot, "More Small Wars," *Foreign Affairs* (November/December 2014): 5–14. For a competing view, which sees conventional great-power conflicts as still a potential reality, see Richard Betts, "Pick Your Battles," *Foreign Affairs*, 93, no. 6 (November/ December 2014): 15–24.

7 "Kerry Condemns Russian 'Incredible Act of Aggression' in Ukraine," *Reuters*, March 2, 2014; accessed August 5, 2014 at www.reuters.com/article/2014/03/02/us-ukraine-crisis. U.S. Vice-President Joseph Biden referred to the action as "nothing more than a land grab." *St. Louis Post-Dispatch*, "Russia Absorbs Crimea," March 19, 2014. See the reference to Kerry's remarks in Chapter 2, when I discussed the "territorial integrity norm."

8 See Jeffrey Mankoff, "Russia's Latest Land Grab," *Foreign Affairs* (May/June 2014): 60–68. For competing views on whether this case represented a return to politics as usual in the Westphalian system, see Walter Russell Mead, "The Return of Geopolitics," *Foreign Affairs*, 93, no. 3 (May/June 2014): 69–79; and John Ikenberry, "The Illusion of Geopolitics," *Foreign Affairs*, 93, no. 3 (May/June 2014): 80–90.

9 See "U.S. Bombs Militants," *St. Louis Post-Dispatch*, August 9, 2014, reporting on the initial U.S. airstrikes against ISIS in Iraq; and "U.S. Bombs ISIL Targets in Syria," *USA Today*, September 23, 2014, reporting on the first American airstrikes against ISIS targets in Syria.

10 Jeh Jonson, "The Conflict Against Al Qaeda and Its Affiliates: How Will It End?," speech to Oxford Union, Oxford University, November 30, 2012.

11 Boot, "More Small Wars," 5.

12 Stanley Hoffmann, *Primacy or World Order* (New York: McGraw-Hill, 1978), 193.

13 William C. Banks, *New Battlefields/ Old Laws: Critical Debates on Asymmetric Warfare* (New York: Columbia University Press, 2011), 1.

14 See Ezequiel Heffes, "The Responsibility of Armed Opposition Groups for Violations of International Humanitarian Law: Challenging the State-Centric System of International Law," *Journal of International Humanitarian Legal Studies*, 4 (2013): 81–107.

15 Boot, "More Small Wars," 6.

16 Louis Henkin, *How Nations Behave*, 2nd edn (New York: Columbia University Press, 1979), 1.

17 Barry Buzan, *People, States, and Fear* (Chapel Hill: University of North Carolina Press, 1983), 97.

18 President Truman's address to the UN Conference on International Organization, cited in *U.S. Department of State Bulletin*, 13 (July 1, 1945), 4.

INDEX

9/11 terrorist attack(s) 3, 48–49, 95–96; reactions to 21–22, 49–50, 90

Abbas, Mahmoud 116
Abu Ghraib prison [Iraq] 73n36, 103
aerial bombardment 58, 59, 63, 100, 101; "shock and awe" campaigns 63, 64, 89
Afghanistan: abandoned by US in 1990s 81, 87, 130; bin Laden in 49, 95–96; drone strikes in 64, 109; ethnicity of population 130–131; US invasion 49, 64, 82, 95, 96, 97, 105n26, 130
aftermath of war 75–78; see also: jus post bellum rules; peacebuilding
al-Awlaki, Anwar 7, 8, 113
al-Baghdadi, Abu Bakr 143, 149
al-Majid, Ali Hassan 91
al Qaeda fighters and affiliates 22, 65–66, 98
al Qaeda terrorist attacks 3, 48–49, 90, 95–96
Albright, Madeleine 77, 87, 101
Allison, Graham 139, 141
Alston, Philip 67–68, 112, 114
American Civil War 55
Annan, Kofi 29, 46, 70, 93, 99
Ansar al-Sharia [Islamist group] 134
"anticipatory self-defense" 6, 32, 48, 50, 93
Aquinas, St. Thomas 31, 55
"Arab Spring" 132
Arend, Anthony Clark 20–21, 29
armed conflict: definition 47, 62, 122, 144; historical efforts to regulate conduct of war 55–58; historical efforts to regulate outbreak of war 31–36; international regime(s) dealing with 20–22; non-international 34, 44–45, 60, 61, 67; rules regulating conduct of war 21, 54–74; rules regulating outbreak of war 21, 39–50; trends 7–19; see also: jus ad bellum rules; jus in bellum rules
assassination-banning executive order 113
asymmetrical warfare 6, 62, 90, 114, 119–120
Augustine, St. 4, 31, 55

Balfour Declaration 115
Banks, William 21, 60, 62, 108, 147
Barnidge, Robert P. 16, 61, 62, 119–120
Bass, Gary 80
Beck, Robert 21, 29
Belgian Congo 121
Bergen, Peter 114, 130
Best, Geoffrey 55
Better Angels of Our Nature, The [Pinker, 2011] 1, 7
bin Laden, Osama: and al Qaeda activities 95–96; background 95–96; killing of 6, 96, 103, 145
Biological Weapons Convention (BWC) 68
Boczek, Boleslaw A. 85
Boot, Max 6, 10, 64, 121, 142, 150
Bosnians–Serbs conflict 15, 46
Boutros-Ghali, Boutros 52n20, 77

Brahimi Report [on UN peace operations] 78
Brennan, John 73n43, 106n30, 110
Bush, George H.W. 3, 43
Bush, George W. 50, 76, 89, 92, 93, 94, 109
Bush Doctrine 32, 50, 93, 94
Buzan, Barry 151
Byman, Daniel 109–110

Caldwell, Dan 77
Camp David Accords [1978] 116
Carnegie Endowment for International Peace 92
Caroline test 50, 93, 98, 145
Carter, Jimmy 116
casualties: drone strikes 70, 74n51; interstate war 11, 35, 57, 63, 72n22
Charlie Wilson's War [film] 81, 87, 130
chemical weapons 57, 68, 71n10; Geneva Protocol on 57, 68
Chemical Weapons Convention (CWC) 68
child soldiers 122, 123–124
Churchill, Winston 145, 150
civil war(s) 14–16; internationalization of 15; rules applying to 44–45 *see also* intrastate violence
civilian casualties 11, 57, 63, 70, 72n22
civilians: protection of 55, 60, 62, 65, 118, 148
Claude, Inis 34
Clausewitz, Karl von 33
Clinton, Bill 14, 92
Clinton Doctrine 45–46
"coercive diplomacy" 13–14, 24n33
Cohen, Michael 8
Cold War 3, 12, 15, 39, 45
"collective security" concept 37, 43, 146; limitations 38–39
Concert of Europe [1815] 34
Congo conflict 120–124
Congress of Vienna peace conference [1815] 10, 34
Convention on the Rights of the Child [1989] 123
Corn, Geoffrey 66, 113
Correlates of War (COW) Project 11
counterinsurgency strategy 72n27, 77
Crimea [Ukraine]: annexation by Russia 9, 102, 143
"crimes against humanity" 58, 87, 101, 103, 122, 123, 134
criminal justice system 66, 149

customary law 39–40
"cyberwarfare" 141

D'Amato, Anthony 85
Declaration of Paris [1856] 55
Democratic Forces for the Liberation of Rwanda (FDLR) 122
Democratic Republic of the Congo (DCR): civil war 120–124; founding of 121
Department of Defense directives 63
deterrence 94
Diaspora 115
Diehl, Paul 79–80
Dirty Wars [Scahill, 2013] 4, 5–6, 141
"distinction" principle 55, 58, 59, 62, 67, 103, 108, 110, 111–112; divergence between principle and practice 62–66; violation of 119, 148
Donnelly, John 10, 76–77
drone strikes 7, 8, 64, 67, 69–70, 108–114; advantages 109, 111; casualties 70, 74n51, 109–110; CIA control 113, 114; legal issues 69, 70, 111–114; moral issues 69, 110–111; strategic considerations 111
drones: international convention on use 114; weapons proliferation 114
Druckman, Daniel 79–80
Dylio, Thomas Lubanga 122, 123

Easterbrook, Gregg 7
Eisenhower, Dwight D. 1
Emerson, Ralph Waldo 9
"enhanced interrogation techniques" 21, 66, 73n35, 103, 149
"ethnic cleansing" 47, 91, 100, 103
ethnopolitical conflicts 15
Etzioni, Amitai 86
extrastate violence 5, 16–19; *see also* terrorism

"failed states" 14, 16, 80, 102, 131, 134, 150; postwar repair of 80–81, 135
Fatah [Palestinian group] 48, 116
Ferguson, Niall 93
First Congo War [1996–1997] 121
First Gulf War [1990] 40, 43, 63, 72n24, 90
"fog of law" 4
"fog of war" 4
"force without war" 5, 13–14, 24n33
Ford, Gerald 113

Foreign Intelligence Surveillance Court 67, 111
Friedman, Thomas 103, 131, 141

Gaddafi, Muammar 13, 46, 80, 131–132
Gates, Robert 9–10, 77
Gaza Strip 115, 116; governing authority 116
Gaza Wars 114–120; *see also* Israeli–Palestinian Gaza War [2008–2009]
General Treaty for the Renunciation of War [1928] 35–36
Geneva Convention(s) 55–56, 58–61; Additional Protocols 61, 65, 123, 144; Common Article [3] 60, 65, 66, 67, 73n31, 149; Fourth Convention [protection of civilians] 60, 62, 118, 148; POW protection under 7, 58, 59–61; violation of Fourth Convention 118
Geneva Protocol [1925] 57; violation of 68, 91
genocide 9, 58, 91, 122
Georgia–Russia conflict [2008] 9, 103
Ghani, Ashraf 80–81, 135
Gleditsch, Nils Petter 8
Glennon, Michael 4, 44, 86, 97
Global Terrorism Database 18
"Global War on Terror" 16, 95, 96, 97, 98, 105n23, 111, 112, 144; *see also* war on terror(ism)
"golden arches theory of conflict prevention" 103
Goldstein, Joshua 7
Goldstone, Richard 118
Goldstone Report [on Gaza Conflict] 118
Gonzalez, Alberto 67
great powers: war(s) between 12
Gross, Leo 32
Grotius, Hugo 32, 145
Guantanamo Bay detention facility 7, 22, 66, 73n36, 103
Gulf War(s): First Gulf War [1990] 40, 43, 63, 72n24, 90; Second Gulf War [2003] 8, 10, 63–64, 76, 85, 89–94, 103
Gurr, Robert 15

Haass, Richard 93
Hague Convention(s) 54, 56, 57, 58
Hamas 48, 114, 116, 117, 118, 119, 120, 147
Hasan, Nidal 113

Henkin, Louis 20, 43, 44, 151
Heyns, Christof 111, 112
Hezbollah 48
Hoffman, Bruce 19
Holder, Eric 73n43, 86, 97, 98–99, 106n30, 111
Holsti, K.J. 14
Human Rights Watch 123
Human Security Report 7–8, 11, 15, 43
humanitarian intervention 6–7; limitations 101–102; rules applying to 45–47
Huntington, Samuel 86
Hussein, Saddam 43, 68, 89, 90, 91, 92

Idris I [King of Libya] 131, 133
Ikle, Fred Charles 81
International Commission on Intervention and State Sovereignty 14, 46, 99
International Committee of the Red Cross: on international humanitarian law 54, 72n12
International Court of Justice [World Court] 37
International Criminal Court (ICC)134 101, 122, 123, 134, 150
international humanitarian law (IHL) 5, 54–55, 108; *see also*: *jus in bello* rules
international regime(s) 19; and "armed conflict" 20–22; examples 19–20
international war: definition 11
internationalization of civil wars 15
interstate war 5, 10–14; decline in 11–13
intrastate violence 5; *see also* civil war
"invisible armies" 6, 121
Iran: chemical weapons used against 68, 90, 91
Iraq: US invasion of 49–50, 63–64, 76–77, 89
Iraq Liberation Act [1998] 92
Iraq War [2003] *see* Second Gulf War
Islamic State of Iraq and Syria (ISIS) 8, 98, 134, 143–144
Israel: self-defense justification for actions 48, 50, 118
Israeli–Palestinian conflict: background 114–116
Israeli–Palestinian Gaza War [2008–2009] 87, 114–120, 147; casualties 117, 118, 119, 147; cease-fire(s) 117; criticism of Hamas 119; criticism of Israel 118–119, 148; reason for strt 116–117, 147; UN report on 118–119

Jensen, Eric 64
Jewish state 115
Johnson, Jeh 144–145, 150
jus ad bellum rules 4, 21, 29, 31–53; applied
  to New Warfare 89–107; inadequacy of
  94; post-1945 evolution 39–50;
  rethinking 142–147
jus in bello rules 4, 21, 30, 54–74; applied to
  New Warfare 108–128; post-1945
  evolution 62–70; rethinking 147–149;
  see also international humanitarian law
jus post bellum rules 4, 30, 75–83; applied to
  New Warfare 81, 129–137;
  development of 78–81; rethinking 150
"just peace" 78–81
"just war" doctrine 4, 31, 35, 39, 50, 150

Kabila, Joseph 122
Kabila, Laurent 121, 122
Kagan, Donald 10
Kahl, Colin 63
Kaldor, Mary 5, 16
Kellogg–Briand Pact [1928] 36
Kennedy, David 34
Kerry, John 43–44, 142
Kissinger, Henry 85
Koh, Harold 111–112
Kony, Joseph 122
Korean War [1950] 40, 41
Kosovo 100
Kosovo civil war: humanitarian
  intervention in 47, 86–87, 100,
  101–102
Kurds: chemical weapons used against
  68, 90, 91
Kuwait: Iraq's invasion of 40, 43, 63, 90

landmines 68
Lauterpacht, Hersch 1
"lawfare" model 38n38, 147; and targeted
  killings 7, 112–113; and warfare model
  66–68, 98–99
"lawful combatants": definition 60, 65
laws of war *see: jus ad bellum* rules; *jus in
  bello* rules; *jus post bellum* rules
League of Nations Covenant 35
Levy, Jack 12
Libya 131–132; General National Congress
  (GNC) 133–134; humanitarian
  intervention in 46, 76, 80, 131–135;
  National Transitional Council (NTC)
  132, 133
Lieber Code 55

Lockhart, Clare 80–81, 135
"long peace" 12–13
"Long War" 16, 95, 105n23; *see also*
  "Global War on Terror"
Lord's Resistance Army 122
Lumumba, Patrice 121
Lusaka Peace Agreement [1999] 122

M23 rebels [Congo] 122, 123
McChrystal, [General] Stanley 72n27
McDonald's restaurant network: effect on
  conflicts 103
Macmillan, Harold 139
Mai-Mai groups 122
Martens Clause 56
Mehsud, Baitullah 110
"militarized disputes" 13–14, 24n33
military contractors 65
Milosevic, Slobodan 47, 91, 100, 101
Minorities at Risk project 15
Mobutu Sese Soko 121
"mootwa" (military operations other than
  war) 76
Mubarak, Hosni 133
Mueller, John 7, 19

Napoleonic Wars 11, 33
nation-state(s) 21, 32
National Congress for the Defense of the
  People (CNDP) 122
National Consortium for the Study of
  Terrorism and Responses to Terrorism
  (START) 18–19
"necessity" principle 59, 62, 67, 108
New Warfare 4–6; *jus ad bellum* rules
  applied to 89–107; *jus in bello* rules
  applied to 108–128; *jus post bellum* rules
  applied to 81, 129–137
"new wars" 5, 10, 16
news bulletins 8–9
Nicaragua v. United States [World Court]
  case 47–48, 62, 144
"non-combatants" 60, 66
non-international armed conflicts 34,
  44–45, 60, 61, 67, 149
non-intervention in affairs of other
  countries 45, 46
Nuclear Nonproliferation Treaty (NPT) 69
nuclear weapons 69
Nye, Joseph 20

Obama, Barack 109, 112, 130
O'Brien, Richard 139

occupation: accusation after humanitarian intervention 81, 130
O'Connell, Mary Ellen 111, 112
oil revenues: Libya 131–132
Orend, Brian 75, 76, 78–79
Ottawa Landmine Treaty [1998] 68
"overseas contingency operations" 9, 24n13

Pakistan: bin Laden raid 96–97, 98; drone strikes in 109; government 96
Palestine: partition of 115
Patriotic Forces for the Liberation of Congo (FPLC) 122
Patton, [General] George S. 54
peace enforcement 42
Peace Research Institute in Oslo (PRIO) 8, 14
Peace of Westphalia 10, 32
peacebuilding 42–43, 77–78, 80, 129, 150
"peaceful engagement" 9, 24n13
peacekeeping missions 42, 77–78, 79–80
Pearl Harbor attack [1941] 13, 36
Peres, Shimon 117
perpetrators of terrorism: identity 18
Petraeus, [General] David 77
Pinker, Steven 1, 7, 14, 19, 103
poisoned weapons 57
political reconstruction, post-conflict 80
politically motivated violence [as characteristic of terrorism] 17–18
Pollack, Kenneth 91
post-conflict reconstruction 129
"Pottery Barn" analogy 87, 130
Powell, Colin 87, 130
pre-emptive use of armed force 21–22, 32, 48, 50, 90, 93; contrasted with preventive force 50, 85, 93–94, 145
Pretoria Accord [2003] 122
preventive use of armed force 94; contrasted with pre-emptive force 50, 85, 93, 145
prisoner of war (POW) protection 7, 56, 58, 60–61, 148–149
"proportionality" principle 59, 62, 67, 108, 112; violation of 117, 119, 148
Putin, Vladimir 102, 142, 143

Rand Corporation study [of UN operations] 43
Ratner, Steven 99
Reagan, Ronald 13
"Reason of State" 33

regime change 76, 79, 129; Afghanistan 130; Iraq 150; Libya 46, 76, 80, 102, 150; Serbia 47, 101
"responsibility to protect" (R2P) doctrine 29, 46, 99; criticisms 46–47, 99–100, 102, 146
Rice, Condoleezza 85
Roberts, Adam 30
Roosevelt, Franklin D. 13, 36
Rose, Gideon 30
Rosenau, James 141
Rousseau, Jean-Jacques 55
Russell, Bertrand 1
Russia: annexation of Crimea 9, 102, 142, 143; invasion of Georgia 9, 103; invasion of Ukraine 9, 102, 142, 143
Rwanda: genocide 9, 102; involvement in Congo wars 15, 121

Scahill, Jeremy 4, 5–6, 16, 67, 86, 97, 141, 147
Scheffer, David 63
Schmitt, Michael 111
Second Congo War [1998–2003] 120–124
Second Gulf War [2003] 8, 10, 63–64, 76, 85, 89–94, 103
"self-defense" 37; rules applying to 47–50, 98, 111, 144
September 11 attacks see 9/11 terrorist attacks
settlement of conflict 78, 79
"shadow warriors" 5, 6
Shiite Muslims 89, 143
"shock and awe" aerial bombing campaigns 63, 64, 89
Six Day War [1967] 13, 48, 116
Skocpol, Theda 86
Slomanson, William 46
Somalia: intervention in 42, 46, 77
sovereignty 32, 46
Stahn, Carsten 129
Starr, Edwin 1
START 18–19
"state responsibility" [for denying safe haven to terrorists] 49, 98, 145
state-centric approach: Hague and Geneva Conventions 56, 60; United Nations Charter 20, 21, 44, 99, 142
Stevens, Christopher 134
Stevens, John Paul 86
Sudan: Darfur region 42, 102; ethnic conflict 15
Sunni Muslims 89, 132, 143
Syrian civil war 8, 47, 102

Taliban 49, 64, 96
"targeted killings" 7, 8, 67, 69, 99, 108–114, 148
targets: of terrorism 18
terrorism 16–19; characteristics 17–18; definitions 17, 18, 25n54, 48, 49, 144, 145; historical examples 10; UN resolution condemning 49
terrorist attacks: examples 3, 17
terrorists: compared with regular soldiers 64–65
Thirty Years War: casualties 11; end of 10, 32
"threat to peace" 37, 45
Tillema, Herbert 44
Tito [Josip Broz] 100
"transnational terrorism" 17; see also extrastate violence
treaty law 40
Treaty of Versailles [1919] 75
Truman, Harry 38, 151

Ukraine: invasion by Russia 9, 102, 142, 143
unconventional violence [as characteristic of terrorism] 17
United Nations: economic sanctions 41; formation of 36; mixed success in peacemaking 40–41, 43; peace enforcement 42; peacebuilding 42–43; peacekeeping operations 42, 122; resolution condemning terrorism 49
United Nations Charter 4, 20–21, 29, 36–39; Article 2(4) 20, 29, 37, 44, 143, 144; Article 2(7) 46–47, 86, 99, 145–146; Chapter VII 37–38, 146; and customary law 44; state-centric approach 20, 21, 44, 99, 142
United Nations Security Council 37, 38–39; expansion of 146–147; Resolution(s) on Afghanistan 96, 97, 105n26, 130; Resolution(s) on Iraq 90, 93; Resolution(s) on Israeli–Palestinian conflict 116; Resolution(s) on Kosovo

civil war 100–101; Resolution(s) on Libya 46, 80, 102, 132, 133
United States: self-defense justification for actions 47, 48–49
"unlawful combatants" 61, 65–66, 67, 149; drone operators as 113–114
"unlawful extrajudicial executions": targeted killings as 112, 148
Uppsala Conflict Data Project (UCDP) 11, 14

Vietnam War: POWs in 60–61

Walzer, Michael 1, 4, 30, 75, 78, 86, 94, 101, 102, 130, 135
war see armed conflict
war crimes 58, 113, 122, 123
"war on terror(ism)" 7, 16, 62, 66, 67, 95, 96, 97, 98, 105n23, 112, 144
"warfare vs. lawfare" debate 66–68, 98–99, 147
"wars of national liberation" 44–45, 61; see also civil wars
weapons of mass destruction (WMDs) 68; in Iraq 90, 91–92
weapons regulation 68–70
West Bank [of Jordan River] 115, 116; governing authority 116
Westphalian state system 32, 43, 46, 56, 99, 151
World Court case 47–48, 62, 144
World War I 34–35; casualties 11, 35, 57
World War II 13, 36; casualties 11
Wouk, Herman 1

Yemen: drone strikes in 7, 8, 113
Yoo, John 21–22, 73n35
Yugoslavia 15, 100; see also Kosovo; Serbia

Zacher, Mark 43
Zaire, Republic of 120, 121
Zakaria, Fareed 7
Zenko, Micah 8
Zionist movement 115

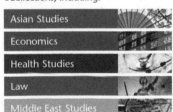